MAJOR GENERAL RAFI

HISTORY OF
THE BALOCH REGIMENT
1820 – 1939

The Colonial Period

The Baloch Regimental Centre
Abbottabad

First Edition 1998

Published by
The Baloch Regimental Centre
Abbottabad, Pakistan

Printed and bound by

Antony Rowe Ltd
Eastbourne

DEDICATED TO

_____ those rugged warriors, who greet every trial and hardship with spirit and resolve; on the marches or in the trenches, wet and shivering with cold or scorched by the burning sun; uncomplaining against thirst and hunger or pains of wounds and injuries; cheerful and chivalrous, always responding to calls of distress; undaunted and fearless, their unwavering lines charging into the smoke and dust of the battlefield, to honour and glory; to victory or death_____

**THE SOLDIERS OF
THE BALOCH REGIMENT**

CONTENTS

ACKNOWLEDGEMENTS

Soon after retirement from service, I was approached by the Baloch Regimental Centre to undertake the compilation and writing of the History of the Baloch Regiment; the first of its kind since its raising. From the nature and dimension of the proposed History, spread over nearly two hundred years of wars and campaigns, in India and overseas, from France, Africa and Middle East to Burma, Malaya and distant China; of a Regiment which had expanded from two battalions to fifty eight was indeed a challenging assignment. Since March 1996, as I proceeded with the work, not without apprehensions, the sheer thrill and delight of rediscovering the Regiment, created the requisite momentum and earnestness and set the pace, which has happily resulted in the completion of the first of the three planned volumes of the History.

There may still be blank areas and some of my views on the events may not be entirely satisfactory. These imperfections are humbly admitted as my own.

The support and encouragement extended to me during the research, compilation and writing of this volume are gratefully acknowledged:

To Brigadier Ghulam Hussain, the Commandant of the Baloch Regimental Centre, for officially sponsoring the project and placing his trust in my ability; for arranging a fruitful visit to London for research in the British libraries and museums; for providing the premises of Kai Kai Guest House in the peaceful and picturesque surrounding of Abbottabad to complete the work and for the staff assistance and reproduction facilities at the Centre.

To Brigadier Gulzar Ahmed, OBE the senior most Balochi officer (having joined the 5/10th now the 12th Baloch Regiment during 1936), despite his old age and poor health, for a professional review of the manuscript.

To the numerous authors and the old Balochi officers whose valuable works provided foundational information and have been quoted; with special reference to Lieut Colonel N W Poulsom for permitting to reproduce his research on the old Baluch regimental buttons from his forthcoming publication: 'Indian Army Buttons 1857-1947'.

To the Director, National Army Museum, London and the Trustees of the Imperial War Museum, London, for the facility of consulting their photographic archives and the permission to reproduce old photographs and paintings pertaining to the Regiment.

To Professor Sayyid Qudratullah Fatimi, my father-in-law, whose life-long dedication and sacrifice in his scholarly pursuit had been a source of great inspiration to me, and to my son Rifat, an army doctor by profession but a spirited son of the Regiment; for their diligent revision and correction of the manuscript and valuable suggestions for its improvement.

To Naik Clerk Sardar Azam of 23 Baloch for patiently typing and retyping the manuscript and Sepoy Muhammad Najaf of 12 Baloch for the excellent administrative care during my long stays at the Kai Kai Guest House.

And finally my most profound gratitude to my wife whose persuasion and continuous care and attention made this undertaking possible.

GLOSSARY

OF INDIAN AND MILITARY TERMS

Angrikha (or Angrakha): Loose, robe-like frock or coat, forming the upper garment of the native dress in Northern and Western India.

Bandobust (or Bundobust): Literally 'arrangement'; a commonly used term in the regiments for logistical or administrative arrangements. Still in use.

Biradari: A close brotherhood of clan or caste relationship with customary mutual rights and obligations, operating at family, village, clan and tribal levels.

Chuna and Gairi: White lime and a special sticky soil used on the mud walls and floors for a cleaner get up. It was a routine practice before an inspection of the regimental lines. Its excessive use was regarded a cheap show off.

Diwani (or Dewani, Dewauny): The collection and administration of land revenues under the Mughul rule, usually entrusted to the governors and carried with it legal powers and authority.

Darbar (or Durbar): Public audience, court or levee of a ruler. An informal assembly in the regiments to hear and settle common complaints of the soldiers, came to be known as the regimental darbar. The term and the practice are still in vogue.

Farman (or Firman): An order, patent or a passport; a Mughul decree, authorization or grant.

Ghazi: Muslim volunteer fighting for a religious cause. Irregular bands of Ghazis actively participated in the Great Rebellion of 1857 and were noted for their unusual tenacity and courage. Irregular Afghan lashkars and bands during the Afghan War, have been recorded as Ghazis in the British annals.

Hindustani Muslims: Settled Muslim communities of Northern India (the upper Gangetic valley and adjoining areas), mainly comprising of the Afghans, Pathans, Turks, Persians and the Arabs and numerous clans from the Punjab, who came with the invading armies from the north-west and formed the martial elite of the ruling dynasties. Those amongst them who moved south with its subjugation were later classified as 'Dakhani Muslims'. Rohilkhand, Oudh and Bihar held an affluent majority of Afghans, Pathans, Turks, Rajputs and Maliks and it was not uncommon to find Yousufzais and Afridis in the Deccan.

Jagirdar: A person holding an assignment of land through a decree or award against payment of its rent as annuity. The Mughuls generally did not award jagirs in perpetuity, but during the period of their decline and collapse, these were appropriated by their holders as hereditary possessions.

Jawan: An Indian soldier or sepoy as called after 1857. The term is still in vogue.

Kammarband (or Cummerbund, Kummarbund): A girdle, 'loin-band' worn by irregular troops of Indian regiments as an article of uniform. Colourful Kammarband was traditionally worn by Mughul troopers as a regular item of dress as recorded by Van Twist in 1648 ('in the middle they have a well adjusted girdle called the commerbant') and by A. Hamiltan in 1727 ('a dagger was stuck into a fine commerbund')

Koi Hai: Literally 'anyone around'? or 'is anyone here'?; It was the typical call by officers for mess/club attendants/servants and is still practiced in the army messes.

Lal Kurti: Shopping centres or bazaars for the army soldiers in the old Indian cantonments. These centres have survived and swelled into big commercial areas and are still called by their older name.

Lashkar: From Arabic, al-askar; an army or a camp. Also an irregular tribal army, contingent or band assembled or organized for battle or armed engagement.

Mansabdar (or Munsubdar): The holder of an office and dignity under the Mughuls, a quasi-feudal assignment with jagir against the obligation of supplying specified horses and soldiers to the imperial army. It was a temporary title.

Mufti: Civil or native walking out dress for the Indian soldiers when off-duty. Every regiment had its own mufti, made distinct through colour combination, peculiar item of dress or style.

Nawab: A Mughul viceroy, deputy or governor of a province with delegated power and authority. A conferred peerage which was not hereditary. There was a mushroom growth of nawabs with hereditary claims and self-styled lineage after the collapse of the Mughuls and was patronized by the British as a part of the colonial order.

Oudh (or Oude, Awadh): The large and rich Mughul province between rivers Gogra and Ganges, with Lukhnow as its capital. After 1857 it merged with the United Provinces (presently Uttar Pradesh).

Pargana (or Pergunneh): A sub-division of a district under the Mughuls.

Pathan: Commonly applied to the tribal people of the Frontier (NWFP), ethnic Pushtun or Pukhtun, including Afghans along the border and those of Afghan descent settled in India.

Pindari (or Pindarry): Belonging to the bands of plundering predators, an outgrowth of anarchy during the decline of the Mughuls and known for his savage atrocities. Pindaris were most active in central and south India in the late nineteenth century but there outrages extended in all directions.

Pugree: A typical upper Indian head-dress with colourful variations in style peculiar to ethnic tradition and practices.

Puttees: Legging wrapped around the ankle, below the knee for ease in marching or riding.

Rajput: Belonging to the warrior clans of Rajputana and the Punjab and known for their martial passion and traditions.

Sanghar (or Sangar): A crude stone breastwork, commonly erected for defence in the hills of the Frontier.

Satyagrah: Non-violent resistance.

Talukdar: The holder of 'taalluk' either of revenue or estate; a landholder of large jagir, belonging to petty aristocracy of the Mughuls.

Wali: A title corresponding to governor, commonly used in Afghanistan.

LIST OF MAPS AND ILLUSTRATIONS

MAPS

ILLUSTRATIONS

Preface

The Baloch Regiment, like most other regiments of the Pakistan Army, was part of the old British Indian army and its origin and nearly 150 years of eventful history are rooted in the British colonial rule in India. During this period, the Indian regiments evolved themselves into remarkable institutions and acquired enviable reputation and mystique as the guardians and the sword of the British empire. However, the role of the Indian soldiers and the regiments during the period of colonial conquest of India and consolidation of the empire came under much criticism and controversy with the rise of nationalism in India and during the period of struggle for independence. During their agitation for political power, the Indian National Congress frequently reviled Indian soldiers as mercenaries and Indian regiments as tools of the imperialists. The Muslim leaders however maintained a mature and pragmatic attitude on the military issues.

The bitter invectives of the Indian National Congress against the Indian army, its regiments and the soldiers were politically motivated, because of the predominance of Muslim and non-Hindu soldiery from the western and north-western India and their failure to subvert its discipline and loyalty in the name of Indian nationalism, whose Hindu flavour could not be easily concealed. It was this peculiar composition of the Indian army which was threatening to the Congress' political ambition and not its colonial antecedents. When it came to exploiting the sacrifices and contributions of this colonial army, during the First Great War, the Indian National Congress did not hesitate in encashing these for political concessions and subsequent grab for power. Their consistent strategy was to force a change in the British recruiting policy to create a favourable leverage in the composition and eventual control of the Indian army. Shadows of many centuries of

India's imperial history, more vividly those of 1857, haunted the minds of the Hindu Congress leaders.

This peculiar composition of the Indian army was not a mere coincidence or a creation of the British by design for colonial purposes. It was a result of long historical processes, becoming explicit in the martial culture of the people of these regions and the military traditions of imperial India. The historical perspective of these processes and the peculiar socio-political developments in India during the eighteenth and nineteenth century is highly relevant in understanding the growth of the Indian regiments, their professional character and performance and the attitude, motivation and responses of its soldiers. It is equally important to sustain the continuity of the distinct ethos and the traditions of the people of these regions, now forming part of Pakistan, particularly against subjective and adhoc implants and patchworks, even emotional contradictions and distortions. Lack of objectivity in interpreting history has led to undermining the colonial part of the regimental history as a distasteful chapter. It cannot be changed by deriding, ignoring or being apologetic about it. It should be faced for the reality it represents and the lessons it offers.

The military institutions that evolved during the late nineteenth century were characterized by their acute professionalism. They were the product of peculiar military requirements and bred and groomed universally common military outlook, behaviour and virtues within their ranks, which supported the essential function of an armed force, to fight a battle successfully and that of a soldier to fight it bravely and skilfully. This professional character of the military institutions, 'set in blood and iron', distinguishes it from other imperial or colonial apparatus which operated under political or vested considerations and expediency. It was this professional permanency in the military institutions that facilitated conversion or 'regularization' of the imperial or colonial armies into standing or national armies, rapidly and without the necessity of psychological reorientation. Military values and traditions are rooted in history and form essential parts of military institutions and their professional efficiency. The regiments without their traditional character would be structures without foundation; colourless military systems devoid of inspiration and stability.

This is the first of the three planned volumes of the History of the Baloch Regiment and recounts the first hundred years of its birth and growth; its military exploits and achievements as a proud regiment of the Bombay Army and later of the British Indian Army. It is set in the turbulent Colonial India but without the colonial trappings, exaggerations or distortions. It provides the requisite historical background and is integrated with the political developments in India to maintain an Indian or national perspective.

The colonial history of the Baloch Regiment is essentially the story of its valiant and chivalrous soldiers; of their martial passion and virtues of honour, discipline and loyalty and their superb response to the call of battle under capable leadership. It reveals their motives, sentiments and aspirations, often complex and mixed up but rarely based on material self interest alone. Pay or 'loyalty to the salt' was only the visible and legal element of the contract; implicit in it was a whole range of duties, rights and obligations, deeply rooted in the traditional culture and martial ethos of the soldiers. The battalions and the regiment symbolized their collective identity as an organized professional body, where soldier's inherent virtues and the ingrained qualities and skills were integrated to fight the battle through victory. It provided a professional environment to the soldiers to live an ordered life, whose orderliness was liberating rather than oppressive. It was a hard and austere life but not without its peculiar elegance.

In substance, it is neither imperial nor colonial. It is simply a professional history of the Regiment, providing roots and continuity to its cherished traditions of valour and chivalry, of honour, discipline and loyalty, which had been its distinction and must remain its ideal.

RAFIUDDIN AHMED

21, Askari Villas
Chaklala Scheme-III
Rawalpindi
10 February, 1998

PART ONE

HISTORICAL PERSPECTIVE

'India's (traditional) soldiery was no common hireling. He gave his loyalty and devotion as long as his employer was honourable and kept faith with him'.

T.A. Heathcote

'He (the Indian soldier) fought for honour, no doubt, and a hereditary love of sword'.

General Sir G. MacMunn

Chapter One

Decline and Fall of the Mughuls

By the beginning of the eighteenth century, the legendary Mughul empire was manifestly in decline. Though still resplendent and apparently expanding in the south, the foundation of its imperial power had begun to crack. As the century wore on, the slow decaying process was overtaken by 'the release of vicious and destructive elemental forces', which shattered the Mughul power and disintegrated the empire beyond recovery. By the turn of the century, the Mughuls,[1] but in name, had ceased to exist as a political force.

The causes for the decline and fall of the Mughuls were manifold, each more complex and compelling than the other, like the web of spreading cancer which slowly eats into the vitals of the body organism. In abject contrast to its past achievements and glories, the empire had lost its forward momentum and was being inexorably drawn backward by the forces of inertia and degeneration. Lack of vision, professional ability and moral commitment in the succeeding Mughul rulers and their aristocracy, continuously weakened the established institutions of power which found itself increasingly incapable of coping with the new dimensions of threat during the eighteenth century. The growing bankruptcy of the empire gradually rendered its military and socio-political structure to despair and collapse, creating favourable conditions for the growth of new political powers.

The key to the success of nearly two hundred years of rule by the early Mughuls lay in their sheer ability as capable administrators and bold and determined military leaders, who asserted imperial authority with cold ruthlessness. They made continuous efforts to understand India's highly complex ethnic and religious diversities and evolved consistent and progressive policies for the governance and consolidation of their sub-continental empire. Although the Great Mughuls could not succeed in really integrating their vast empire and its diverse multi-ethnic population, 'their military power held it together, long enough to make it a part of the accepted order of things'. In the process the Mughul rule acquired an Indian character and mystique and the House of Taimur was revered as a symbol of political unity. Delhi became a focal point and a centre of political power for all India. Even in decline and without the trappings and authority of imperial power, Mughul recognition and patronage were eagerly sought for political legitimacy by breakaway states, rebels and avowed enemies such as the Marathas. 'Indeed the empire had attained such an ascendancy in the minds of the people that the idea of it proved a potent spur to action, nearly a hundred years after it had broken up and ceased to be a political power'.[2]

As pragmatic rulers, early Mughuls won the loyalty and support of the warring clans and tribes of Rajputana and the Punjab and encouraged good governance of their large non-Muslim subjects; but military power remained central to and formed the vital element of their imperial authority. The cold logic of the sword was apparent and explicitly relevant to India's highly complex socio-political conditions and the Mughuls heavily depended on their military supremacy and dominance. The core of this power base lay in their army and the bureaucratic system evolved to support and reinforce it. The great importance given to military power is apparent from the fact that the 15,000 strong Mughul army under Babur had swelled to 440,000 under Shah Jahan, which included 200,000 strong cavalry, 40,000 strong infantry and 7000 elite 'ahadis' of the imperial army and 185,000 strong cavalry and infantry provided by the 'munsubdars', allied princes and chiefs, besides a large arsenal of light and heavy artillery.[3] When Aurangzeb embarked on his fateful Deccan campaign in 1681, his army consisted of 240,000 strong cavalry and 15,000 infantry soldiers besides a large number of militia and camp followers.

The Mughul army had become a permanent institution and employed soldiers in its service on a regular basis. Almost the entire Mughul soldiery came from the north and north western India, which in the course of India's long and chequered history had become highly militarized both by racial and martial disposition as well as occupational necessity. Its soldiers were selectively drawn in almost equal proportion from the Muslims of Persian, Turkish and Afghan descent settled in the 'Doab' (Jamuna-Ganges plains); the Rajputs from Rajputana and the Punjab; and the Afghans and frontier tribesmen west of the Indus.[4] Mughul preference for cavalry made it the dominant component of the army – the most favourite and the priveleged. The infantry and artillery were held in inferior status and generally formed of the non-Muslim volunteers from the plains such as Purbias, Bundelahs, Mewatis and Bilahs.[5] Although Hindu Rajputs formed a strong component, the Mughul army remained Muslim in composition and essentially an army of horsemen. To contemporary observers, even a small portion of this army, a mere ten thousand horsemen galloping across the plains, presented a terrifying spectacle of power and mobility. Mughuls held foot soldiers in low esteem and could not become proficient in the use of artillery. To them 'to fight with artillery was stripling's pastime; the only true weapon was the sword'.[6] Thus service in the Mughul army, particularly the cavalry, was regarded socially an honourable profession and even a common trooper was looked up with respect and where capable amongst them could aspire and frequently rose to the highest ranks in the army.[7]

However, the long period of affluent peace and unchallenged political and military supremacy had begun to sap the Taimurid sense of daring and enterprise into inertia and mental immobility. Vision and objectivity suffered with display of pomp and grandeur and extravagance of wealth and power. Rulers became increasingly fond of ease and luxury. Mughul aristocracy which through generations had so efficiently contributed towards political stability and richness of the empire, had gradually succumbed to the temptation of corruption and abuse. Political and factional intrigues and rivalries for wealth and power crept in and began to dominate the court. As decline set in, Mughul nobility degenerated into 'merely an aristocracy of culture with no moral commitment or public virtue'.

This demonstrative, corrupt and inertly complacent Mughul culture seriously affected the military potential of the imperial army, both in quality and growth. The army had continued to expand without complementary improvements in organization, armament or tactics. Mughuls' growing preference for horse armour reduced the striking power and mobility of the cavalry, which formed the mainstay of the army. For this reason alone, the Mughul commanders frequently found themselves outmanoeuvred by the swift moving light cavalry of the Marathas during the Deccan campaign. Infantry was poorly equipped, was without organization or discipline and not much relied upon. Its growing potentials in the European battlefields were as yet unknown to the Mughuls. Artillery which had acquired a decisive status in the battlefield did not receive the attention it deserved, beyond increasing the size and weight of the pieces, merely to create awe and terror.[8] It was heavy and cumbersome, inaccurate and ill-served and could fire solid shots only, once every 10-15 minutes.[9] In comparison, the Europeans were already employing light guns which could fire 2-3 times a minute and used lately introduced grape-shots with great accuracy and devastating effect on the charging cavalry and the morale of the opposing army [10]. In retreat, the Mughuls invariably abandoned their heavy guns, which seriously reduced their ability for quick re-engagement.

Its leadership, mainly drawn from the Mughul nobility was afflicted with mutual distrust and jealousy which frequently undermined the prospects of battle. It generally lacked professional education and experience in leading the army in battle and often took to corrupting the enemy through bribes for compromise or settlement to avoid battle. The practice was adopted with equal efficiency by their adversaries, exploiting greed and personal rivalries amongst Mughul commanders who were frequently tempted into disloyalty.[11] This factor of unreliability affected the morale of the soldiery and their confidence in their leadership and continuously undermined the staying power of the army as a disciplined and cohesive body. These weaknesses had become apparent during Mughuls' longest military campaign in the Deccan, where despite Aurangzeb's stern measures to arrest the deterioriation in the army's leadership, the rot could not be stemmed and the exasperated emperor lamented in pity and despair that, 'his officers love repose and long for his death to escape the exertion of field'.[12] A Cambridge report titled *Account of War in India* published in 1772, aptly summarized the ills of the Mughul army: 'the cause (of Mughul failures) lies in the inexperience of their leading men who never understood the advantages of discipline and who kept their infantry on too low a footing. Their cavalry is not backward nor it lacks courage, but the most ruinous to their military affairs is their false notion in respect of artillery'.[13]

A permanent virtue and perhaps the only redeeming feature of the decaying Mughul army was its soldiery; renowned for their individual courage and bravery to the extent of recklessness and their ever-readiness to engage the enemy with sabres.[14] For all the glamour created around the fighting prowess of the white British soldiers, it was ungrudgingly admitted that, 'in single combat a European seldom equalled the address of a native horseman'.[15] The Mughul soldiery was largely drawn from particular classes of people, distinguished for their martial ancestry and traditions. They adopted and followed 'sipahgari' (profession of arms) through generations[16] not only as an honourable career for living, but also and perhaps more truly as an extension of caste or tribal culture and religious faith, where daring and valour were held and glorified as the highest virtues. They generally came from peculiarly harsh environment, where subsistence and survival were at premium and struggle for livelihood and tribal and clan strifes were nature's inheritance. They were 'hard men bred of hard countries' and soldiering suited their natural instincts, physical skills and abilities. The sword was an integral part of their culture and a symbol of their professional honour.

Mughul India was too large, highly feudal, deeply divided and chaotic for common patriotic awareness. The latent but ever growing tensions and rivalries generated from the staggering racial and cultural dispersion and diversities in the composition of Indian polity – often mutually hostile and conflicting; prevented social integration and growth of organic sentiments. In the continuing despotic traditions of the empire from the Chakarvartins to the Mughuls, India's political character was essentially one of imperial unification.[17] People were closely bound to their tribes, 'biradaris', castes and ethnic and religious groupings which provided some basis for social unity. But these too suffered with endless internal dissensions and limited the growth of broader social cohesion. The masses seldom took part in wars or political upheavals, leaving the fighting to the professional classes and castes and generally accepted the established political order for its visible military power. The perception of fidelity and patriotic obligation of the soldiery was therefore dominated by their age-old tribal (or caste) traditions and code of honour which demanded allegiance to the 'suzerain' and 'loyalty to the salt'. These bound them with moral obligations whose betrayal under the custom were regarded as shameful or dishonourable. In Mughul India, Muslim soldiers fought as valiantly under able Hindu Rajput generals as did the Hindu Rajputs under Muslim commanders for the same reasons.

In the Indian milieu, victory or prospect of victory was an important factor for honour, riches and survival, and reinforced soldiers' loyalty and professional devotion and for this reason his choice of service with well established political order and better organized and led armies, was a matter of common sense. But there were exceptions as well when soldiery sided with individual and collective causes for and under capable and charismatic leaders, irrespective of consequences.[18] In India, traditional soldiery fought, as General MacMunn observed 150 years later, 'for honour no doubt and a hereditary love of sword'.

Despite the obvious deficiencies and afflictions which beset the Mughul army during the period of its decline and which continuously diminished prospects of honourable survival in the compelling conditions of recurrent conflicts, the soldiers invariably rallied around capable commanders with fortitude and loyalty and frequently led the army to victory. Numerous battles won during Aurangzeb's Deccan campaign, crushing of the Sikh and Jat uprisings in the Punjab (1708-10) after Aurangzeb's death, the only defeat inflicted on Ahmad Shah Abdali in the Punjab in 1748 and the resounding victory at Panipat in 1761 while fighting along side and in the ranks of the Afghan army are a few examples. When the Mughul army had broken up, the soldiers reemployed by the splinter states continued to give a good account of themselves under resolute and capable commanders.

Thus, in the conditions of increasing political turmoil and instability, the weaknesses and deficiencies of the Mughul army became fatally pronounced and despite its excellent manpower, the symbolic instrument of Mughul power succumbed to a chain of fateful events.

In the middle of the seventeenth century, while the Mughul empire stood firmly, two events: the Maratha rebellion in the Deccan and the loss of Kandahar to the Persians in the west, threatened its frontiers and became precursors of the storms that during the course of next hundred years would reduce the empire to utter helplessness.

In 1649, the Mughuls finally lost their strategic fortress of Kandahar to the Safavis, which brought the entire Iranian Balochistan plateau under Persian control, exposed and weakened their grip over the north western provinces and encouraged Sikh and Jat uprisings in the Punjab. No major threat developed from this direction till after the overthrow of the Safavis by Nadir Shah in 1726, but Mughul failure, due mainly to their involvement in the Deccan, opened the gate for the devastating Persian–Afghan invasions and permanent loss of Afghanistan and the Punjab which provided the bulk of Mughul soldiery and 'the steady stream of adventurers from Central Asia which had traditionally supplied the empire with so much of vigour, ability and loyalty'.

The Mughuls had never accepted the legitimacy of the splinter Muslim states of the old Bahmani Kingdom in the Deccan and regarded them as rebels. The military annexation of these states had commenced in 1616 and in the sixteen eighties, these were finally subjugated by Aurangzeb. It was during this period that the smouldering Maratha menace grew into a powerful rebellion posing a serious challenge to the empire for political power in the Deccan. For its long term destructive and predatory consequences, the Marathas hitherto an obscure people became a scourge for the Mughuls, indeed for most of India, for over a hundred years. In 1681 when Aurangzeb entered the Deccan, he could hardly perceive the fateful dimensions of this disastrous campaign – in violence and wastage, which would rage with ruthless intensity for twenty years. Although he extended the empire to its utmost limits and shattered the dream of a Maratha empire, he could not crush the elusive enemy decisively. 'He continually won battles but hidden behind these victories lay the bitter fact that the Mughul power was actually losing the war'. The cost in resources and exhaustion to the empire was enormous; 100,000 men and three times that number of horses, lost every year for almost twenty years![19] It is said that the disappointments of the Deccan campaign broke the heart of the old emperor; it indeed broke the back of the empire.[20] It nearly wiped out the flower of the Mughul soldiery and severely damaged its military prestige. Effective control of the new extensions of the empire were much beyond the resources and the capacity of the weak Mughul successors, which provided opportunity for the revival of the Marathas and exposed the empire to a new dimension of threat from the sea, that of political involvement and territorial encroachment by the rising European mercantile powers.

Within five years of Aurangzeb's death a fierce and exhausting war of succession raged for seven years (1712-19) which divided the army and its loyalty to the throne and brought to surface the moral degeneration of the Mughul aristocracy. It brought young Mohammad Shah to power who ruled for 29 years (1719-48), but lacked vigour to inspire and lead the empire to recovery. During his reign the Deccan separated under Nizam Asif Jah, and the Marathas having revived themselves in a lose confederacy defeated the Nizam in open battle and resumed their predatory attacks which gradually extended towards the north. In 1738 they reached the outskirts of Delhi and forced secession of Malwa to the Confederacy, which effectively divided the empire in two halves and opened the strategic passage for their plundering raids into Orissa, Bihar and Bengal as well as Rajputana in the north. In 1739 came the Persian invasion of Nadir Shah. Despite a 90,000 strong Mughul army, ineptitude and treachery of its leadership led to its military debacle at Karnal, and the occupation of Delhi, massacre and whole-sale plunder. When Nadir Shah left, the Mughul empire lay prostrate in utter humiliation, its army badly mauled, treasury emptied and prestige shattered.

In the following years, as the crippled empire struggled for recovery, an Afghan power arose in Kabul under Ahmad Shah Abdali, who began his career as a Mughul adversary for the possession of the Punjab and upper Indus, but was destined to play a momentous role in India. On the death of Muhammad Shah in 1748, Mughul India again plunged into another vicious struggle for succession which continued for eleven years (1748-59) and sealed the fate of the empire. Intrigues and treachery in the court and violent civil war amongst the contending nobility dominated the scene. The regular imperial army disintegrated and even the semblance of political unity of the empire finally disappeared. Kabul was already lost; now Sind and Gujarat broke away in 1750, Oudh in 1754 and the Punjab was taken by the Afghans in the same year. Bengal sent tribute but was virtually independent. In 1757, Ahmad Shah Abdali marched into India and sacked Delhi to hammer some sense into the quarrelling Mughul princes and the nobility. The same year, the nascent British power asserted itself in Bengal in a military encounter at Plassey, as a serious contender for the spoils of the crumbling empire. Before the end of the decade, a powerful Maratha army was marching towards Delhi on the request of some distracted Mughul nobles, ostensibly to rid them of the Afghan invaders but more likely to seize the throne for themselves.

After Aurangzeb the Marathas found another formidable opponent in Ahmad Shah Abdali. In January 1761 in a fierce battle at Panipat, the Marathas suffered a crushing defeat and their army was destroyed so completely that for the next decade no Maratha chief dared to look towards the north. The battle of Panipat was decisive and the faltering Mughul empire lay within the grasp of the victorious Afghan ruler, who had won the gratitude of the people, Muslims and Hindus alike, for ridding them of the hated Marathas. He had the ability and the military resources to infuse the empire with new vigour and vitality and save it from certain collapse. But under pressure from his army, Ahmad Shah Abdali chose to return to Kabul, leaving India and the Mughuls to their inevitable fate. Thus the decisive value of a brilliant battle was lost. The sceptre of power denied to both the Mughuls and the Marathas, India was left in a power vacuum to suffer at the hands of contending predators, a long and painful spell of despair, turmoil and anarchy.[21]

At this time India lay deeply fragmented and in ruins, its centre of power demolished, its people exhausted, uncertain and without inspiration. The ravages of civil wars and anarchy had nearly destroyed the socio-political order and drained the country of its economic wealth. Bewildered and demoralized soldiery (Europeans referred to them as adventurers from the north) of the once imperial army had dispersed through the maze of splinter states and fiefdoms that had arisen from the ruins of the Mughul empire and were eagerly sought and employed by the British, the European power that had established itself firmly on the Indian soil. Increasing depradations and brutalities of the Marathas and the Sikhs and innumerable feudal and renegade chieftains had created highly oppressive conditions and people earnestly looked for relief. Everywhere the links between the rulers and the people had sapped.[22]

It was a patent situation for a political or military intervention. The British power represented by the East India Company with a trading charter using the traditional reservoir of Indian soldiery; in a ruthless combination of opportunism, military audacity and political pragmatism, nibbled its way to imperial power in Delhi. Following the defeat at Buxar in 1764, Mughul ruler Shah Alam granted 'diwani' of Bengal to the British Company, virtually surrendering Mughul sovereignty over its vast eastern provinces. The Mughul empire practically vanished and was reduced to the Kingdom of Delhi, which in 1805 came directly under the protection of the Company when General Lake decisively defeated the plundering army of the Marathas below the walls of Delhi.

Chapter Two

Rise of the British Power in India

The first direct European contact with India was made in May 1498, when Vasco da Gama discovered the sea route to the 'Indies' around the Cape of Good Hope and landed at Calicut. During the next twenty years, the Portuguese seized Goa and established a chain of trading posts from Sacotra, Colombo, Malacca to Maccao in China to dominate the Arabian Sea and the East Indies, mainly to protect their monopoly of spice trade through sea power. Their control of the Arabian Sea irked the Mughul rulers in Delhi since the Portuguese levied heavy toll on Indian trade from Surat and the pilgrim traffic to Makkah. They were known as good fighters and generally feared and hated for their religious intolerence and perfidy. It was for them that the word 'firingi' (or farangi) was coined whose opprobrium was applied later to all Europeans.[1]

By the end of sixteenth century rise of the British and Dutch sea power overwhelmed Portuguese position in the East and reduced their presence in India to insignificance. In 1580 Portugal was annexed by Spain. In 1588 the Spanish Armada was decisively destroyed by the British fleet and simultaneously the Dutch revolted against the Spaniards bringing an end to their monopoly of sea – trade in the East. In 1595 the first Dutch fleet established itself in Batavia (now Jakarta) and proceeded to oust the Portuguese from the East Indies and established a chain of trading posts through Cape Town, Coromandal coast in India and Ceylon (now Sri Lanka). Their main object remained the protection of the spice trade from the East Indies and regarded India of secondary importance. The British East India Company formed on the last day of the year 1600, with a charter from the Queen and with similar commercial objectives also

13

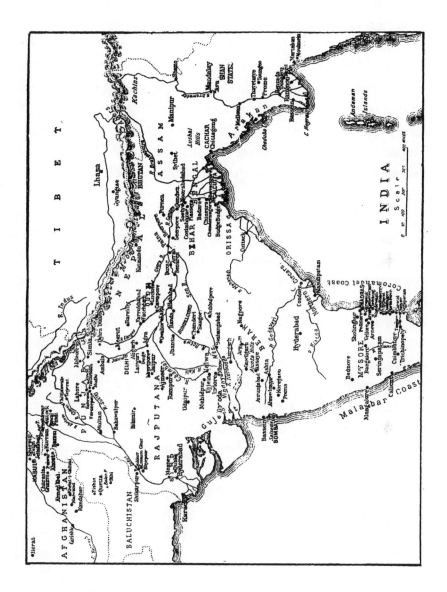

1.   A 19th Century General Map of India

made an attempt to establish itself in the East Indies. The Dutch, unwilling to share their monopoly, stubbornly resisted the British intrusion, which was finally terminated after the massacre of the British trading post at Amboyna in 1623. This ejection from the East Indies became momentous in long term consequences, since the British were now compelled to concentrate on trade with India, hardly knowing that an imperial destiny awaited them here. Wars in Europe weakened the Dutch and in time Britain and France became the chief contenders for power in Europe as well as overseas in India.

In August 1608 the first British ship under Captain William Hawkins anchored at the mouth of River Tapti south of Surat. Hawkins' travel to the Mughul court and stay there for four years, however, could not get him the permission to trade. He was the first British officer to enrol fifty Pathan horsemen as his escort to cover his journey to Agra.[2] But when the Company's fleet defeated the Portuguese off Surat in 1612, proving its naval strength and ability to protect the pilgrim traffic, the Mughuls allowed the embassy of Sir Thomas Roe and a 'farman' granting trading privileges at Surat was given to the Company. In 1622 the Company's fleet ejected the Portuguese from the Persian Gulf acquiring relative domination of the Arabian Sea and tacitly became a maritime auxiliary of the Mughul empire.

From Surat the Company steadily expanded its trade activities. A trading post[3] at Masulipatam in 1633, was followed by a factory at Madras in 1640. Another factory was established at Hugli in Bengal (moved to Calcutta in 1690). In 1674 the Company's headquarters shifted from Surat to Bombay, when it was leased by the British Crown. Relations with the Mughuls and their local officials were generally congenial except for once when an ambitious Company chairman, Sir Josiah Child, on some differences over customs and taxes with the Mughul governor of Bengal thought it opportune and ventured to fight a small war against the Mughuls during 1687-91.

With the formidable Aurangzeb on the throne, the Company was promptly and severely chastised and expelled from Surat and Bengal and was allowed to resume its trade activities only on payment of a heavy fine.[4] Thereafter the Company did not dare to challenge the empire till 1756 when its power had nearly broken up.

By the end of the century, the Company was organized into three independent Presidencies, at Bombay, Madras and Calcutta, each with a number of adjoining trading posts, consisting of factories and settlements, controlled directly by a Board of Directors in London. The Company possessed a strong naval fleet which was frequently reinforced with the royal Men-of-War for the protection of its trade through sea and to provide some military and logistic support to the settlements. The Company's trade prospered steadily and the size of its settlements and the number of its factories expanded with increasing native population and the merchants from Britain. For local security and protection, particularly after the growing instability and lawlessness in India, regular British soldiers were hired into Company's service through royal sanction. The first of these were the remnants of a battalion that landed in 1662 to garrison Bombay and were transferred to the Company in 1674.[5] Besides, a mixed composition of natives were employed at all posts for local security and administrative duties.[6] The total strength of these 'native guards and peons' till 1746 did not exceed 3000, of whom only 900 were issued with muskets.[7] Although in the decades following Aurangzeb's death, opportunities for political adventure had opened up in Mughul India, the English merchants generally confined themselves to trade activities, whose increasing competitiveness brought them to study more closely the local conditions. In the process they acquired knowledge of India's socio-political situation, its people and their character; which prepared them well for their future role on the Indian political stage. It was, however, the growing Anglo – French political rivalry in Europe and its extention to India which led to the British involvement with and intervention into local politics and for discovering the possibilities of acquiring influence, wealth and political power.

The French in competition with the British had set up their East India Company in 1664 and established trading posts at Pondicherry, Chandernager (Bengal) and Masulipatam and also on the Malabar coast. They were the first to perceive the political opportunities offered in India and that the native Indian soldiers could be organized, disciplined and trained on European lines for military and political purposes. They raised the first native company in 1674 at Pondicherry. In 1693, with 36 French soldiers and 3-4 native companies (about 400 men), the French successfully defended Pondicherry for twelve days against a force of 19 Dutch ships carrying 1500 regular Dutch infantrymen. By 1739, they had created an embryonic native army of 4000, mostly Muslim soldiers, well-armed and trained after the European model.

To the French, their opportunity for political influence in the local affairs came in 1740, when a Maratha army swept into Carnatic and the widow and family of the slain Nawab who had taken refuge in Pondicherry were successfully protected from the Marathas through a tactful show of force. The French were handsomely rewarded by the new Nawab and their services were acknowledged by the Nizam and the Mughul emperor. In 1746, a French officer with 230 French and 700 native soldiers attacked across a river at San Thome (South India) and defeated a vastly superior army of a rival contender of Carnatic; demonstrating for the first time the superiority of European organization, training and tactics. The same year as an extension of war in Europe, the French captured the British fort at Madras (later returned after the Peace of Aix-la-Chapelle of 1748 in Europe). The French acquired a military reputation and became an important factor in the politics of South India. Joseph Dupleix, the ambitious French governor, following an aggressive policy in exploiting their growing political influence, succeeded in 1748, in getting his own proteges installed as the new

Nizam and the Nawab of Carnatic, with visible French military presence in their respective capitals. French political motives had become obvious; using sponsored Indian rulers to threaten British trade by encircling and squeezing them out of Madras and South India.

The British suddenly found their commercial interests threatened and seriously began fortifying their settlements, getting military reinforcements from Britain and raising and training native forces. As a result, in 1748, twelve hastily raised independent companies with eight light guns, landed at Madras. The first complete regular British regiment, the 39th Foot, arrived in Madras much later in 1754. The British response to the growing French threat and in the process their discovery of a soldier of fortune proved the first turning point in their rise to power in India.

To counter the French hold on Carnatic, the British supported the rival contender with 600 British and native soldiers at Trichinopoly. In early summer of 1751, it was invested by a strong army of the Nawab, reinforced with a French contingent of 900 regular and 2000 native infantry. Under increasing pressure, saving Trichinopoly from its imminent fall became crucial to British in South India. At this moment an unknown writer (or clerk) of the Company at Madras, Robert Clive, proposed a daring plan of seizing Arcot, the Nawab's capital to relieve pressure from Trichinopoly and offered himself to lead the force. Despite a precarious troop situation in Madras and no British ship in sight, the plan was accepted. Clive with 200 British and 300 native soldiers and three light guns, in a surprise attack, seized Arcot in August 1751 and stubbornly defended it for 53 days and succeeded in drawing a major portion of Nawab's army from Trichinopoly. When reinforcements came from the sea, Clive broke through the siege and defeated the disorganized forces of the Nawab at Arni. Within a year, through clever manipulation of local politics the British forced the ruling Nawab to surrender. The French having been isolated,

Clive with a new force of 380 British and 1800 native soldiers sought out and defeated the French forces at Kaveripak in February and again at Volconda in May 1752, resulting in the French surrender at Trichinopoly.

The march to and the defence of Arcot and the subsequent battles and engagements are described as 'settling the fate of India' which, indeed firmly set the course for deeper political involvement and military assertion of British power in India. The political and military benefits of the French experiment were taken away by the British and from now on the initiative clearly passed into their hands. Arcot gave the British a remarkable leader in Robert Clive and a promising young army of native soldiers with a new-found confidence to seek greater fortune.

The British soon got their opportunity in Bengal, a large and rich Mughul province but virtually independent of the empire. The British trade in Bengal had continuously prospered but differences on taxes and trading privileges had always existed with the Nawab (or Mughul viceroy). When the war broke out in South India, the British and the French began fortifying their settlements in Bengal, contrary to the Mughul decree. The French however, desisted on the Nawab's insistence but the British were evasive, which heightened the existing mistrust and animosity against them. In April 1756, the old Nawab died and was succeeded by his young grandson Siraj-ud-Daula, who in June marched on Calcutta and sacked the garrison.[9] The British governor with most of his Council fled to Fulta, taking refuge in the British ships and called for assistance from Madras. At this time the British situation in Madras was vastly superior and with the recently landed British regiment, the Madras army had expanded to 2000 British and nearly 8000 native soldiers, who were well organized, drilled and experienced. The British council at Madras therefore decided to despatch 900 British and 1200 native soldiers in five British naval vessels under Robert Clive to reinstate British possessions and the trade in Bengal. This force reached Fulta in

December 1756 and managed to recapture Calcutta without major resistance.

Clive sued for peace to gain time, to study the prevailing situation and raise new forces. Although the Company's mandate had been fulfilled, Clive was determined to exploit his advantages to the utmost. He was an opportunist without scruples though with remarkable political insight and diplomatic and military abilities. He was moved by ambition and cupidity[10] and was soon involved in intrigues and conspiracy with the Nawab's vassals and disgruntled Hindu elements, using the meanest trickery and forgery for the success of his treacherous plot. His first move was to eliminate the French presence in Bengal, for which he used a dubious permission from the Nawab and attacked the French settlement at Chandernagar and forced its surrender in March 1757. This angered the Nawab, who moved out with his army consisting of 45,000 infantry and 18,000 cavalry and over 50 pieces of artillery to deal with the British impertinence and camped at Plassey. Clive faced him with 1100 British and 2200 native soldiers (including the newly raised first native infantry battalion) and 10 pieces of light artillery. On 23 June 1757, the battle commenced with a heavy cannonade of artillery, followed by a cavalry charge from the Nawab's centre which was severely mauled by the highly effective British artillery and repulsed. Meanwhile the vastly enveloping wings of the Nawab's army with strong contingents of cavalry, merely watched the destruction of the centre with treacherous indifference and without any reaction. The Nawab fled in panic[11] and Clive captured his camp and declared Mir Jafar, the chief conspirator as the new Nawab.

Though regarded as a decisive battle, Plassey, from the military point of view was hardly a battle,[12] but in political terms its gains were immense. Immediately, the British acquired 24 'parganas', nearly 900 square miles of territory south of Calcutta, incredible wealth from the Nawab's treasury[13] and controlling influence in the affairs of Bengal. With the newly found resources, British forces in

Bengal expanded rapidly into a powerful army, whose unchallenged military superiority threw the country at the mercy of Company's agents. Bengal was systematically plundered and helplessly suffered from British greed, extortion and highly unscrupulous trading practices. The years following Plassey are regarded even by the British historians, as 'the most distasteful' and sadly dominated by intrigues, coercion and blackmail; insurrection and treachery. During his second appointment in 1760, Clive made an effort to check the cruel and often shameful practices of the British agents and officials, but it was essentially from this highly dubious and unpromising start that the Company began its eventful career for political power in India.

During the Seven Years War in Europe (1756-63), the French made a fresh effort for the revival of their power in India and landed new reinforcements, but their attempt to capture Madras in 1758 failed. From the expanded Bengal army, a strong force under Major Eyre Coote was shipped to Madras and the French were decisively defeated in 1760 at Wandiwash (South India). With the surrender of Pondicherry next year, the French chapter in India was finally closed and the British emerged as the sole European power in India.

Continuing political instability in Bengal induced Shah Alam, a contender for the Mughul throne in the ongoing civil war, to march into Bihar with the support of the Nawab of Oudh. This brought the British council in Calcutta in direct confrontation with the Mughuls and involved them in a series of encounters and battles between 1759-64. In 1760 the Mughul army besieged Patna but the effort though distracted by the great event developing around Delhi was finally frustrated by the unexpected arrival of a reinforcing British column under Captain Knox, who had marched 300 miles in 13 days to reach Patna. After the Battle of Panipat and the return of the Afghan army to Kabul, Shah Alam proclaimed himself emperor and again turned to Bihar. Mir Qasim, the beleaguered Nawab of Bengal rebelled against the British council at Calcutta and in June 1763, attacked and routed the British forces in Patna but was soon intercepted by a strong British force under Major John Adams. A fierce battle ensued at Katwa in July in which Mir Qasim was defeated and his army pushed into Oudh. By the beginning of 1764, the combined armies of Shah Alam, Nawab of Oudh and Mir Qasim again entered Bihar and besieged Patna. A spirited but poorly coordinated attack by Oudh forces on 3 May was repulsed and the siege was lifted due to the onset of monsoon.

By early October, a vastly expanded and reorganized British army (eighteen native infantry battalions had since been raised) under Major Hector Munro marched towards the Mughul camp at Buxar. On 23 October 1764, the Mughul army, despite gallant cavalry charges failed to break the solid infantry mass of the British army. Its left wing was repeatedly driven back on its centre and both were broken into fragments during the fierce fighting. The carnage was terrible on both sides but the British victory was complete and the Mughul army retreated into Oudh. The British followed their success through a rapid advance to Allahabad and dictated a peace treaty. Buxar, the last of the series of battles, beginning with Plassey was bloody and the hardest fought and indeed the real foundation battle for the British dominion in India. The Company ceased to be a company of merchants and became a formidable military and political force which could no longer be ignored. The British did not push their advantages beyond Bihar and for accepting the status quo in Oudh and backing the Mughul emperor, were granted by Shah Alam in 1765, the Diwani of Bengal (collection and administration of revenues), through a farman, which provided a legal status and recognition to the Company and made it virtually the ruler of Bengal.

Robert Clive founded the British rule in Bengal in 'rather the style of a robber baron' with the Company's agents behaving more like gangsters, making the European incursions into India highly rapacious. But his successor, Warren Hastings, during his 18 years in office as the Governor of Bengal brought some sanity and order into the state and the process was maintained, though at no stage of the Company's rule, it acquired a semblance of benevolence for the people of India. Reforms were introduced to evolve effective civil and military systems and the three independent Presidencies were brought under the Governor General (new designation of the Governor of Bengal) for concerted effort towards common goals. Three powerful armies of Bengal, Madras and Bombay came into existence. The Company became accountable to the British Parliament and responsive to its government's policies. Thus the structure was laid for the future extension of British dominion over all India. But before this eventual goal could be achieved, over the next hundred years, the Company would face formidable opponents and endure many setbacks. There were the wars against Hyder Ali and his son Tipu Sultan, the Tigers of Mysore, both leaders of exceptional military ability and skill; the remarkable campaigns and hard battles fought against the predatory Marathas and the warring Sikhs; the impulsive war with Afghanistan and the disastrous retreat from Kabul; and the last great challenge, of the Rebellion of 1857. And there were the overseas military expeditions to Malaya and the Dutch East Indies, to Egypt and Abyssinia and to Burma, Persia and China. During the second half of the nineteenth century, the whole of India had come under direct or indirect British rule while most of Asia lay under the influence of this new centre of power.[14]

In less than a hundred years, a mercantile body from a distant land had seized a vast sub-continent which carried long imperial traditions and rich political and military experience. It was a remarkable achievement. Many British writers attributed it to the intrinsic superiority of the West and the Anglo – Saxons, while the more recent Indian arguments confine it to British deceit and wickedness. Both are extreme views. All empire builders have been ruthless in their drive to political power and the British in India, undoubtedly also had their share of deceit and wickedness, which however shameful and oppressive, were only a part of the total

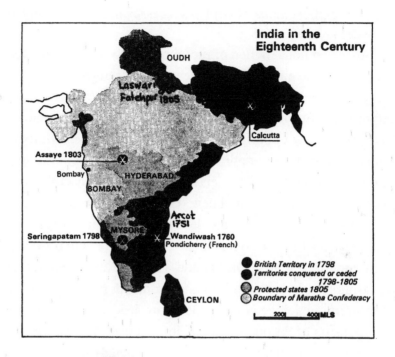

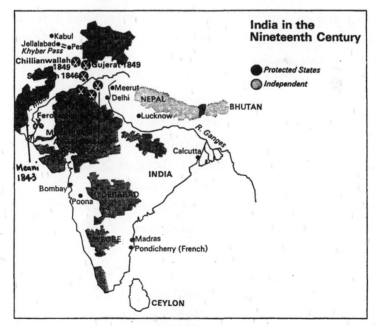

2.   Rise of the British Power in India

reality. The phenomena of British successes in India should be seen in a wider perspective.[15]

An exceptional period of profound changes had been sweeping Europe from the mid-eighteenth century, challenging the old socio-political order and military traditions with new experiments and innovations. European supremacy of the sea had opened up a floodgate of new opportunities of wealth and power. Europe was vibrant with bold ideas, optimism and self confidence, leading to the growth of assertive national sentiments and more disciplined social attitude. The armies acquired new respectability as the defenders of their lands and people and the decisive instrument of state policy. Military values became common and popular. The lure of wealth and power combined with creativity and daring, released peculiar urges and inspirations which infected and groomed generations of gifted adventurers, which provided pioneering leadership to the growth and expansion of Europe's colonial imperialism. In addition to these developments, the British enjoyed the unique advantage of political stability and security at home, which promoted and ensured unity, resolution and continuity to her policy and efforts. Her merchants, civil servants and soldiers around the world symbolized a common outlook and a unified political will.

Against these British assets, the Indian situation was its antithesis. Fragmentation and collapse of the Mughul empire had shattered India's socio-political equilibrium, causing a continuing spell of instability and turmoil. In the absence of a strong central authority, numerous successor states seeking to consolidate their rules created endless opportunities for internal conflict and friction. There was no dearth of military manpower in India, where fighting was a hereditary occupation and warfare a popular and common recurrence. During this chaotic period, India also threw up some exceptionally capable and resolute leaders, but their efforts to resist the expanding British power, frequently succumbed to their mutual suspicion and rivalry as much as to their personal ambitions. They lacked a collective outlook and could not infuse their efforts with the unity of a common purpose. In the prevailing Indian situation, the British had to make little effort to apply their policy of 'divide et empera' (divide and rule). Indeed, willing collaboration from the native rulers and feudals was readily available, making the British success story almost a joint venture. It was also a stroke of their good fortune that the British had appeared on the Indian scene at the weakest moments of its chequered political history. Her political leaders and military commanders were generally conscious of the unusual opportunities offered by the peculiar Indian situation which under different circumstances would not have yielded the same results. The British learnt it better during 1857 when they came dangerously close to losing everything.

In India, the British outlook was peculiarly conditioned by military values, being heavily out-numbered and within its own ranks, the military being predominant. India was regarded a garrison by the British and her government remained military in character.[16] In the realization of her imperial ambition and rise to political power in India, the decisive instrument and key to her success was essentially her military power; the qualitative superiority of the emerging armies of the three Presidencies, with soldiers – in increasing proportion the Indian soldiers – as the cutting edge of this instrument. Undoubtedly, 'every phase of imperial expansion brought its own share of bloodshed and hard fighting; it could never have been acquired by its white soldiers alone'. Indeed it was impossible without the strength and quality of the Indian soldiers. As it often does, history was repeating itself and in the old imperial tradition of India, a new and better organized army was creating a new empire.

Chapter Three

Evolution of the Indian Army

The first of the Company's military forces was formed in the lodgement of the Bombay Presidency in 1674 from the remnants of a royal regiment, whose depleted strength was made up through periodic reinforcements from European mercenaries and volunteers. Beside these, the Company employed native Muslim and Hindu 'sipahis'[1] (or sepoys), 'mestees' (mixed Indo-Portuguese) and 'topasses' (Indian Christians) as armed guards or watchmen in its factories for local protection, whose strength had steadily increased to 3000 in 1746. But strictly in military sense, they were not soldiers. They were not directly recruited, organized in companies, trained or disciplined for military duties. However, the French capture of Madras in 1746, prompted the British to enrol and organize native soldiery into companies for military purposes and thereafter the evolution and growth of the Company's armies was quite rapid. The first of the several native companies were raised in Madras in 1747, some from local Muslims and Hindus but most from 'the adventurers from further north'. With her expanded native forces, the British fought a highly successful military campaign against the French and their native allies in South India and established their early military reputation and political influence. From this campaign, the British learnt that the native soldiers carefully selected and trained were not only amenable to military discipline and possessed natural inclination for fighting bravely, but also when well organized and led, could defeat much larger undisciplined native forces. It was a discovery, nothing less than a gold mine, and from here onward the British were to stake their imperial future on it.

The campaign against the French created the first of the Presidencies' armies: the Madras Army, which in 1754 included the first regular royal regiment, the 39th Foot, eight British (or European)[2] companies and 8,000 well trained native soldiers organized into numerous companies. Bengal followed soon and in 1756, Clive raised the first native battalion at Calcutta, under Captain Robert Knox and distinguished it with the scarlet uniform of the British infantry.[3] Within five years of Plassey, the Company's army in Bengal expanded to 10,000 native soldiers mainly recruited from volunteers from 'up the country' which meant Oudh, Rohilkhand, the Punjab and even Afghanistan; mostly Muslims, being 'proud and possessed of a sense of honour' and being 'habitually in the profession of arms'.[4] By 1765, there were 34 native battalions in Madras and Bengal armies. In Bengal, Clive had formed three 'geographical brigades' each comprising of one European and 6-7 native infantry battalions with an artillery corps (about 6500 strong), creating self-sufficient little armies to operate in the peculiar Indian situation.[5] In time, due to the large territories and vast resources acquired in the province, Bengal became the fulcrum of British rule in India and the Bengal Army grew into the largest and the strongest arm of its military power for nearly a hundred years. The Bombay Presidency was slow in raising its army due to lack of political or military opportunity, being restrained in its small territorial base by the powerful Marathas and for its dependence for recruitment from distant areas in the north. Thus by the closing decades of the eighteenth century, as the decaying military power of the Mughuls collapsed, a new military power was rising on the Indian scene, with new concepts of organization, training and tactics; indeed, a new approach to the very art of war and the profession of arms. The inspiration came from Europe which during the eighteenth century had become a vast experimental battlefield.

Continuous warfare in Europe was bringing changes in the organization, armament and tactics of the contesting armies and constantly affecting the established concepts and practices of war and the art of fighting. Fire arms (muskets and the artillery) had added a new dimension and were challenging the traditional military thinking and its sole dependence on the cavalry to win battles. Infantry had begun to evolve itself as a potential arm with a whole range of new options in organization and its employment. By the beginning of the century, infantry organization was firmly established and now equipped with the new flintlocks with long bayonets, its formations of companies and battalions deployed in depth presented a continuous and moving wall of devastating fire power. Prussian army developed and perfected the fire and movement drills for the infantry formations and combined its superiority in fire power with battlefield manoeuvres to turn or strike the enemy's flank. At the same time it employed the cavalry in close order, with the same precision and speed, charging at the gallop. European wars were generally limited and centred on winning battles through tactical manoeuvres. Prussians made the tactical battle artful and their concept dominated European battlefields for most of the eighteenth century. It however demanded a high standard of skill, precision and discipline from the soldiers which required a long period of hard training, making the military service highly professional. As a result, the emerging armies in Europe, during this period gradually acquired an institutional outlook and structure with increasing stability, almost reviving the concept of professional armies of ancient Rome.

Europe was however soon overwhelmed by the French Revolution and its vast conscripted armies under Napoleon Bonaparte. His military genius gave a strategic dimension to the art of war. Through swift and daring movements, he turned the flanks and rear of the enemy and forced the decisive battle with the advantage of superior concentration of artillery and infantry. The limited scope of set-piece battle dramatically expanded to include the movement as the strategic arm of war and became far more destructive and decisive in its outcome. For a while the strategic domination of the movement and the rise of cavalry, seemed to undermine the role of infantry in the battlefield. Only the British, protected by the sea and her sea power escaped the overwhelming effect of the continental wars and had time to organize and train her infantry to the Prussian standards of drill, precision and discipline, which they finally used to decisive advantage at Waterloo. The superior skill and fire power of the British infantry asserted itself and dominated the outcome of that decisive battle. In the process the concept of professional (or standing) army was re-established.

The evolution and growth of the Company's native armies in India were profoundly influenced by the military developments and British experiences of the European wars as much as their own peculiar military tradition of depending for centuries on the 'foot' soldiers.[6] It is therefore not surprising that when the Company began raising and organizing native armies in India, the British officers placed their faith in the infantry, making it a novel addition to warfare in India, where the native armies, traditionally fought from horseback. In the highly fragmented India, the main operational concern of the British commanders was to win battles in a restricted sense, frequently a single battle against divided adversaries and the superiority of their artillery and infantry provided them the most effective and perhaps the most economical means. As the Company's armies evolved in the sixties from the 'rabble of peons and watchmen', through Arcot, Plassey, Buxar and numerous other battles, the fighting potential of the well organized and trained native soldiers was fully established. Thereafter, the raising and organization of native infantry regiments accelerated rapidly. The raisings of native cavalry regiments were prompted by Hyder Ali's successful campaign in the eighties and as the British rule crept closer to the Indus where horse reconnaissance and mobility over an increasingly vast area and expeditions against hostile nomadic tribes, made cavalry an operational necessity.

Major Stringer Lawrence, appointed in 1748 as the first commander of the Company's armies in India, is regarded as the founder of the British Indian Army. During the continuing crises with the French, he organized the native volunteers into companies of 100 sepoys with regular pay and establishment and created the basic military structure which remained unchanged for over a hundred years. As the army and scope of war expanded, the company appeared too small a unit for operational purposes. Clive had already set the precedence by raising the first native infantry battalion in Bengal and employing it successfully at Plassey. In 1758 two new battalions were raised and the process of integrating the companies into battalions was initiated, which provided two European and three native reconstituted battalions. By 1765 the Company's armies included 34 fully organized and trained native infantry battalions with distinctive uniforms and regimental colours. The earliest of these battalions to survive till 1947 was originally the 3rd Battalion Coast Sepoys which after many redesignations became the Ist Battalion of the Ist Punjab Regiment. Each battalion consisted of nine companies, the last named as the grenadier company;[7] had two British officers as the Commandant and his deputy (or adjutant) and three Non-Commissioned Officers (NCOs) for training. The command of the companies remained with the native officers (called as Indian officers, equivalent of present Junior Commissioned Officers but with far greater responsibilities, privileges and expectations) of certain ability and experience. The senior most amongst them was designated as the 'Black Commandant', a kind of semi-feudal or tribal chieftain who either contracted to supply men or wielded tribal influence.[8] In 1763, the Indian officers were recognized as commissioned officers of the Company against payment of a fee and given a place of great respect and responsibility. As early as 1762, families of sepoys killed or disabled during service were compensated; a provision which was quite a new idea for the Indian soldiers.[9] Similarly, arrangements for substantial advance of pay and regular disbursement to the families, before and during operations or service overseas, were made.

A major reorganization of the armies in 1766 provided the first formal army rules and a form of oath to be taken by all Indian officers and sepoys. It covered for the first time a code of military discipline: offences and punishments, court martial procedures[10] and promotions besides many administrative and welfare matters. This reorganization laid down the foundational framework on which the Indian army would grow into a 'professional army' and despite the shattering effects of the 'Great Rebellion' of 1857, would survive for nearly another hundred years. More reorganizations will follow and new rules will be added, but the basic professional structure of the army would not change. A peculiar aspect of this reorganization, certainly an extension of the British military tradition, was the highly sanctified ceremony of the sepoy's oath-taking on the Colours of the regiment.[11] The oath and the ceremony made the regiment and its Colour sacred and inviolable and were artfully integrated with the soldier's sense of loyalty and personal honour. With this was implanted the British regimental concept which during the evolution and growth of the native regiments, formed and moulded the professional outlook of the soldiers and their officers and deeply influenced the character and the performance of their regiments. As the system matured with the growth of the Indian army, Indian regiments became synonymous with the glories of the empire and acquired an enduring mystique, evoking both admiration as well as curiosity.

The regiment was and remains an exclusive British concept and a part of her long military experience and tradition. It dates back to 1661, when Cromwell's republican army was disbanded except for one regiment; the Coldstream Guards, which provided the continuity as well as a new beginning to the system. Thereafter, the British army grew by the regiment, both infantry and cavalry; the former being more numerous, each with its own Colour, uniform, character and traditions. It became 'the core, the heart, the very essence of the British army'[12] and developed into a remarkable institution during the Victorian-Edwardian period. It became a clean, hierarchical extended family, offering to officers and men, a meaningful place in life with pride and self-respect; and in the age of chivalry, an opportunity to glorify themselves with the regiment. It was more than a community where camaraderie and the espirit de corps were nourished out of hardships and sufferings endured and the achievements won together; where the pledge and commitment for the honour and glory of the regiment and its Colour were collectively borne and shared and where sentiments flourished on old traditions and bloomed into resolve and tenacity on the battlefield. It extended much beyond, as Lord Wolseley during his address to a British regiment, declared the soldier's devotion to his regiment as an act of patriotism and that 'for a soldier, his regiment was his country'[13]. This was the ideal of the British regimental model which sustained itself against diverse pressures and many changes and was a product as much of evolution as of design. The history of the British empire is essentially the history of the achievements of its regiments, as J.W. Fortesque in his book the 'Empire and the Army' aptly summed up: 'the British empire, but without the soldiers would never have been'. It must, however, be remembered that the British contribution to its expanding armies never exceeded beyond thirty five percent even at the height of the gravest crises, such as the Great Rebellion of 1857, which threatened the very existence of the British dominion in India.

This was the concept and the ideal on which the native regiments of the growing armies of the three Presidencies were evolved. It admirably suited the fragmented socio-political conditions and economic deprivations prevailing in India at that time and was highly complimentary to the martial culture and traditional psyche and attitude of the Indian soldiery, whose trust and loyalty could be groomed and professionally institutionalized around the regiments. The British officers right from the beginning insistently followed the British regimental pattern as a model and diligently developed it to a remarkable level of distinction, not only as an essential and expedient instrument of military power but also, and perhaps more truly, for the love of profession and devotion to the regiment they raised and served and shared the pangs and hardships of its growth. The system gradually evolved itself and native regiments flowered in their respective compositions; distinguished by their gorgeous and sparkling uniforms, resplendent Colours emblazoned with battle honours, silver and war trophies, even riches created from the management of its funds and war booties. Events and actions gave birth to traditions and pride, generating the regimental spirit which meant devotion to the glory and honour of the regiment.[14] As traditions took root, it struck the soldier deeply who felt the regiment solid about him. It became like a family and sons followed fathers as was true of the British officers. In a better groomed regiment, the soldiers invariably identified their personal honour with that of the regiment. In due course the fighting ability and discipline of the native regiments frequently excelled their British counterparts. As the colonial riches poured in and affluence increased, the glorified quality of British manpower deteriorated to an extent that 'only the scum of the society' and 'the riff raff of the streets'[15] joined the much celebrated British regiments. While in India, the native regiments flourished into remarkable institutions, with the continuous flow of traditional soldiery, which despite many political upheavals and organizational reforms and changes in the sub-continent, survived and maintained its professional distinction.

The British constituted the earlier native regiments on pure caste or ethnic compositions, each identified by its peculiar social or racial 'tone', providing distinction for the integrity and pride of the regiment.[16] But this also made the regiments vulnerable to collective resentment and even mutiny. Religion, caste and cultural bonds; all asserted themselves in different contexts, working powerfully on the peculiar psyche and motivation of the Indian soldiers. Growth of the Indian regiments was not smooth sailing and the British had their share of problems, trivial as well as serious, frequently compounded by the strong religious and social inclinations of the Indian soldiers and incompetent handling by the British officers. There were atleast three regimental mutinies before the Great Rebellion of 1857 and disbandment of at least fourteen regiments for reasons of disaffection and mutinous behaviour and quite a few even after. But, most British officers agreed that 'invariably all (of these mutinies) were caused by some injustice or breach of faith on the part of the Company's Government.' After the upheaval of 1857, the British diligently sought to improve the quality of native manpower of their regiments and in their obsessive quest for the best, there was an unmistakable drift to the north and north-west into the traditional ground of the Indian soldiery.[17] Evidently it was not a mere coincidence or discovery that they eventually settled for the same manpower which constituted the imperial armies before them except for the new addition of the Gurkhas and the Sikhs. In fact it was the recognition of something already implicit in the social traditions of the people in specific areas.[18]

During the closing decade of the eighteenth century, a regimental system on a two battalion basis was introduced; one as parent and the other as an 'extra battalion' under one commandant with twelve British officers in each battalion, which obviously reduced the authority and importance of the Indian officers. This system did not work satisfactorily for its many defects and the old system of single battalion regiments was reverted to in 1824.[19] Till now the British officers came from the royal regiments on secondments or were directly contracted by the Company and the custom of purchasing commission or a position in the regiment was strongly in vogue, making it a preserve of the upper class. In 1812, the Company established its own academy at Addiscombe in Surrey for the training and education of talented middle-class volunteers as officers, that between 1812-1861, produced 2000 infantry, 1100 artillery and 500 engineer officers, out of which a substantial number distinguished themselves in the service of the Company's armies and rose to higher ranks.[20]

As a result of the Company's involvement in wars with Mysore and the Marathas, its armies had grown much larger and included a sizeable component of cavalry regiments and artillery companies and batteries. The bulk of the cavalry regiments was raised as irregular forces on the basis of Mughuls' 'silladari' system, under which the troopers provided their own horses, weapons and uniforms. Similar irregular infantry battalions were also raised but their numbers would increase after the annexation of Sindh and the Punjab and would include the first two 'Belooch' battalions. By the first quarter of the nineteenth century, the Bengal Army expanded to thirteen cavalry (including five irregular) and 68 infantry regiments, organized into six brigades; the Madras Army comprised of eight cavalry and 52 infantry regiments in four brigades and the Bombay Army fielded three irregular cavalry and 24 infantry regiments including a marine battalion, besides independent corps of sappers and miners.[21] The artillery had more than doubled and was divided into brigades and batteries of horse and foot artillery. During the short period since 1748, the Company's armies had travelled a long way, evolving themselves into an increasingly professional and highly responsive war machine; one of the world's largest European-style standing armies, and certainly the only one to have been raised and managed by a mercantile company! The structure of the armies, composed of diverse native soldiery, their integration with a demanding military system and above all the quality of discipline and professional integrity infused into the regiments, which varied considerably in texture of command, language, cultural inclination and tradition, are the amazing part of its evolution and growth and a credit to the professional ability and devotion of its builders.

This was also the period of vast territorial expansion and direct confrontation with the remaining centres of power in India: the two great rulers of Mysore and the Marathas; a period of continuous conflict and warfare, which put to test, the new-born Indian army, its organization, training and tactical doctrine, its formations and regiments, the ability of its commanders and the skill and discipline of its soldiers. It witnessed battles fought on classical pattern and style; artful movement of infantry regiments to turn the Maratha flanks at Assaye and its destruction by the spirited cavalry charge; annihilation of the fierce Maratha cavalry charges by the devastating fire of the rock-like infantry formations at Kirkee; destruction of the Maratha armies at Laswaree and Fatehpur through daring cavalry attacks and siege and destruction of Tipu's army at Seringapatam. It also witnessed military setbacks; Campbell's defeat at Mangalore and the humiliating withdrawal of the British army opposing Hyder Ali, during the second Mysore War; disastrous retreat of Monson's forces from Agra; and the most costly battle of Bhartpur. In the Indian context, these were great and decisive battles where every element of the newly formed armies came into play against opponents who were fierce and no less capable and who had time and a model to organize and train their armies and invariably fought with courage and professional skill. No doubt, the British exploited the rivalries between native states and the endemic divisions within the Indian polity, through inducement, coercion and even perfidy; it was the superiority of their military arm which frequently dominated the battlefield. This superiority sprang from the skill and discipline of their regiments, highly professional leadership and the tactical doctrine which rapidly adjusted to and sought to dominate the battle situation.

Chapter Four

Afghan War and the Annexation of Sindh

During the closing decades of the eighteenth century, Europe was swept by the French Revolution. It seriously challenged the legality of the traditional continental powers and moral basis of their imperial possessions and colonization. Napoleon's campaigns in Egypt and Syria for their implied threat to the east caused a frantic stir in Britain as well as in India. To the classically educated British officers, there was nothing improbable in the idea. If Alexander had reached the Indus, why not Napoleon? It however proved short lived and Napoleon's romantic ambitions were firmly contained through Nelson's decisive naval victories in the battles of Nile and Trafalgar, which also gave Britain complete supremacy of the sea. In India, the indomitable Tipu Sultan became the victim of the failed French revolutionary zeal.[1] So great was the threat from him, that despite severe limitations imposed by war in Europe, it was decided to deal with him immediately and decisively. In May 1799, Lord Wellesley defeated Tipu in the desperately contested battle of Seringapatam, in which he fell, fighting bravely in the breach of his fortress capital. This was the real beginning of British territorial dominion in South India, which had remained blocked for thirty years due to the stubborn resistance of Tipu Sultan and his brilliant father. Now the rest of India lay open to the British military power.

Wellesley evolved an ingenious device to bring Indian states under British domination through the Subsidiary Treaty that guaranteed autonomy and security to a threatened state in return for control of its external relations through British residents and by stationing Company's forces in the state, whose cost of maintenance was to be borne by the respective rulers themselves! Nizam and the

Peshwa fell to the temptation peacefully; other Maratha chiefs, refusing to submit, were defeated in separate battles (1803-5) by Wellesley and Lake, which also finally drove the Marathas out of northern India and the territories from the Ganges to the Sutlej came under the Company's firm control. In 1815 Napoleon was finally defeated at Waterloo, which released the restrained British energies for the consolidation of her territorial gains in India. The growing menace of the 'Pindaris', a product of prolonged period of anarchy in central India, provided the aggressive Governor General Lord Hastings (1814-23), a powerful and most opportune pretext for intervention. The British plan for the annihilation of the Pindaris demanded cooperation of the Maratha chiefs (known for patronizing the Pindaris) on pain of war. They were too proud to submit and too divided to unite. The result was that during the next two years, while the Pindari gangs were relentlessly hunted down and scattered, the dissenting Maratha chiefs were defeated in three separate battles (1817-18) and forced to accept the British terms which finally terminated over a hundred year of Maratha depradation and military ascendancy in India, with no one to mourn for their demise. The Rajput states freed from the Maratha oppression hastened to conclude the Subsidiary Treaty with the Company as the traditional feudatories of the Paramount Power. By 1820, the British had established themselves as the sole political and military power in India and their hegemony upto the banks of the Sutlej was complete.

The defeat of Napoleon changed not only the political map of Europe but also the British strategic position in India. Any threat to her paramount position within the sub-continent would now come from beyond its frontiers. From henceforth the British policy in India focussed on the security of its north western and north eastern frontiers. While its concern against encroachments by the Burmese rulers led to a series of expeditions, resulting in the eventual annexation of Burma to the British dominion, the situation on its north western frontiers was highly complex. Across the Sutlej was the Sikh Kingdom of the Punjab with a strong and well organized army, but on friendly terms with the Company's government. Beyond the Punjab lay the turbulent Afghan Kingdom, frequently distracted by tribal wars, though presently in the capable hands of Dost Mohammad Khan. While in the south along the lower Indus and the Sulaiman ranges lay the divided realm of the Sindh Amirs and the warring Baloch chieftains, a splinter first of the Mughul empire and then of the Afghan Kingdom. To the north of Persia and Afghanistan was now the extending shadow of the Russian empire, which after Napoleon, had emerged as the strongest European power and was steadily expanding itself towards the Mediterranean and the Oxus, generating a potential threat to the British interests in the Near East and India.

Russian expansion had really commenced in 1774, when it acquired from Persia territories stretching to the foot-hills of the Caucasus and had continued inexorably across the great steppes of Central Asia. In 1800 Georgia was absorbed, and in 1828, through a treaty, Persia conceded Central Asia to Russian political influence. In 1833 the Turks came under Russian pressure and agreed to close the Dardanelles to all foreign ships. In 1837 the Persians on inducement and backing from Russia, attacked and besieged Herat. The Russian threat to India suddenly seemed uncomfortably close and Afghanistan acquired strategic importance and became a focus of direct British attention.

The fortunes of north western India and Afghanistan had traditionally been closely inter-linked. Of the nearly twenty five major invasions of India from the north-west over the past milleniums, no more than three had been Afghan; but one and all had passed through Afghanistan, first conquering it and then using it as a base for their eastward march. In the historical perspective, therefore, Russian influence in Afghanistan and its possible use for further expansion, constituted a threat highly dangerous to the British interest in India. Its denial to the Russians became a paramount concern, which brought Afghanistan into the ambit of British politics both of coercive diplomacy as well as military intervention. To gain the desired political influence, the Company's government in India despatched a 'commercial mission' to Kabul under Alexander Burnes in 1837. However, the mission's refusal to side with the Afghans in their territorial dispute with the Sikh ruler over Peshawar valley[2] resulted in its failure and return to India. When in early 1838, a Russian emissary was welcomed in Kabul, the Company's government in connivance with the exiled Afghan ruler Shah Shuja (residing at Ludhiana) and the Sikh ruler, declared war against Afghanistan in October 1838.

British forces for the invasion of Afghanistan, called the 'Army of the Indus' under General John Keane, were assembled in Sindh and entered Afghanistan from the South through Bolan and Khojak passes and after securing Kandahar in May 1839, marched on to Ghazni and Kabul. The army achieved the initial surprise by choosing the Kandahar route, causing confusion in the Afghan dispositions and when Ghazni fell, Dost Muhammad fled away to the north and the British stooge, Shah Shuja, was installed as the Amir in August.

British soon learnt that the new Amir could not be maintained without an army of occupation, whose presence itself was becoming an affront to Afghan pride. The attitude of the Afghans towards the new rulers became clear from the ruthless slaughter of any stragglers from the line of march. The whole situation deteriorated abruptly and started that fateful sequence of events which pushed the fortunes of the expedition to singular disaster. The simmering hostility and indignation erupted into a violent uprising in November 1841 and the British garrison in Kabul, leaving women and children behind as hostages, was forced into an ignominious retreat towards Jalalabad, on 6 January 1842. During the next seven days the retreating columns comprising 4500 soldiers and 12,000 followers were mercilessly attacked and cut down by the Afghan rebels, leaving a solitary survivor to tell the story.[3] The humiliation was shocking and the British government in India tried to salvage its prestige through swift retaliation. A strong column each from Kandahar and Peshawar marched to and recaptured Kabul in September and having recovered the hostages and after some punitive actions, hastily retreated into the Punjab. It was during this march to Kabul that the British for the first time were confronted with the hostile Frontier tribesmen. The Afridis blocked the Khyber pass, and forced the British columns to secure the heights, dominating the line of march through 'piquets'; which subsequently became a regular routine of the frontier operation.[4] In January 1843, Amir Dost Mohammad returned to Kabul and was duly recognized by the British.

Thus ended the First Afghan War,[5] which for the rising British power in India was the first major military disaster and a setback to its political prestige. It led to serious debates in Great Britain and fresh evaluation in India, over its frontier policy, with respect to the obsessive fear of the Russian design as well as the status of Sindh and the Punjab as independent states, between Afghanistan and British India. These states were regarded detrimental to its defensive strategy and the control of the Indus plain and unhindered access to the passes into Afghanistan were considered essential against the Russian threat. The reluctant and un-cooperative attitude of the Amirs of Sindh during the Afghan War and later, the chaotic conditions prevailing in the Punjab after the death of Ranjit Singh were therefore used as pretexts for the annexation of Sindh in 1843 and of the Punjab in 1849. This extended the frontiers of the British Indian dominion to the eastern foothills of the Hindu Kush in the north and the great rampart formed by the Sulaiman ranges in the south; keeping Afghanistan as the only buffer state between the two great empires.

It would be nearly forty years before the British would enter Afghanistan again to test their strategic policy but during the intervening period much would happen. One of these would be, 'the constant concern and involvement for the integrity of a frontier belt stretching from Chitral to Nushki, and inhabited by fierce marauding tribes; which geographically and ethnically would be the most tangled and turbulent in the world'. It would involve formulation of political and military policies, development of specialized skills and tactics and the birth and growth of irregular frontier militias into formidable frontier forces in the Punjab and Sindh with regiments, which in due course would acquire a name and reputation for their military exploits, not only on the frontiers but throughout the British empire.

During the First Afghan War, the British army for the first time had marched through Sindh and the inhospitable barren tracts of Balochistan and came across and was confronted by the ferocious Balochi tribes,[6] whose incessant marauding attacks had caused heavy losses and sufferings to the marching columns and baggage trains. It prompted the British, besides taking punitive actions, to raising local militias and irregular forces to provide security to its operational base and the line of communication. British annexation of Sindh, for its highly unjust and hypocritical basis would remain an imperial perversity,[7] but it was essentially as a consequence of their involvement in Sindh and the decisive battles fought with the Baloch Confederacy under the Amirs of Sindh, that the British saw and were deeply impressed by the raw courage and ferocity of the Baloch warriors, which led to their recruitment in the ranks of the Indian army and the raising of the first two battalions of the Baloch Regiment.

Since the establishment of the Company no significant contact was maintained with Sindh beyond enrolling on almost regular basis wandering natives, possibly Numrias and Jokias from south-western hills of lower Sindh and the Sindhi Rajputs of Kutch, as early as 1758 as 'Scindees' and contrary to general belief prevalent

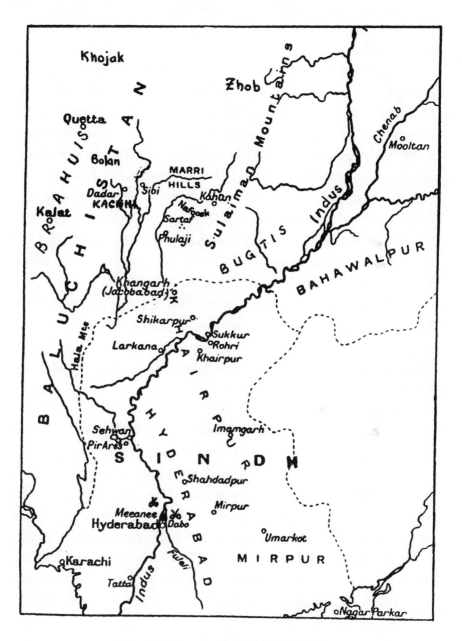

3. Sindh – Balochistan 1838-43

later, carried a good reputation as soldiers.[8] But by the beginning of the nineteenth century, as the British power consolidated itself and established its hegemony in northern India, strategic importance of Sindh grew along with the Russian scare from the north west. Navigability of the Indus for military purposes as well as its defensive potential as a formidable barrier against invasion from the direction of Kandahar had been projected by a French adventurer, Rene Madec as early as 1774 and by later British travellers, Moorcraft and Mason, who had left detailed accounts of the country and the people of Sindh and Balochistan. The Company had generally avoided confrontation with the Amirs but its troops lately were more active on the borders of Kathiawar and Kutch. In 1819 an expedition under Colonel Milnes and later under Colonel Grant Keirs successfully crushed the rebellion of the Rao of Kutch. Again in the same year, a punitive expedition against the marauding Khosas, a Balochi clan from Lower Sindh, resulted in the occupation of Runn of Kutch and the raising of the mounted 'Cutch Levy' as an irregular component of Poona Horse for local protection which later provided the nucleus for the raising of Scinde Horse. During the period 1820-25, Kutch border witnessed continuous engagements with the Balochi raiders from across the Indus and an increasing risk of war with the Amirs of Sindh.

In 1831 Alexander Burnes, a young Captain of Bombay Native Infantry, on the pretext of escorting the royal gift of horses to the Sikh Durbar, travelled through the Indus and carried out a detailed survey of the river. Burnes' comprehensive report (later published as 'A Voyage on the Indus') contained valuable information on the river and a perceptive description of the country, its rulers and the people. Burnes observed that the Talpur Amirs of Sindh did not maintain a regular army but being of the Baloch race, ruled on the support of the numerous Baloch clans who over the years had continuously encroached into Sindh and seized large tracts of land west of the Indus. Although the Amirs boasted of a large following,[9] they were only a sept of the great Rind clan with a glorious past but now decrepit due to internecine tribal warfare, whose bigger components: Lasharis, Marris, Legharis, Chandias and many others, were hostile and mutually jealous. He found the 'Beloochees' (Balochis) a particularly savage race but peculiarly brave whose children used swords as toys to play with[10]. The 'Sindian' (Sindhi) population, no less martial was generally despised and oppressed by the Balochis, though Burnes remained overwhelmed by the Balochis' barbaric virtues.[11] It was during this voyage that Burnes reported having heard the prophetic lament of a 'Sayyid' near Thatta; 'Alas! Scinde (Sindh) has now gone, since the English has seen the river'.[12]

British travellers Moorcraft and Mason and now Burnes had observed the Baloch race at the lower scale of social and cultural advancement, almost in a savage state, yet they did not fail in observing the sterling qualities and those natural virtues which glowed with brighter lustre and strength under the tents of the Baloch warriors. Hardened by the severities of their physical environment and moulded by the traditions of their ancestors, these 'wanderers of the deserts and mountains' displayed exceptional qualities of courage, chivalry and a code of honour far superior to that of their Afghan neighbours. These 'noble savages,' as Sir Richard Temple observed 'were not without virtue and generosity; reckless of the lives of others, not sparing of their own; brave and revengeful to a fault, who lived by the sword and fire'.[13] The traditional Baloch folk lore and ballads ('dastanaghs') sung around camp fires and tribal festivals to the accompaniment of 'nar' pipe and 'alghozha' (traditional musical instruments of Sindh–Balochistan), contain an astounding treasure of romanticized Baloch history. These present a lyrical account of their chivalrous exploits beginning from antiquity but more profusely those of the great Baloch ruler, Mir Chakar Rind of the sixteenth century, who united the wandering clans into a powerful confederacy and extended his domain from the

Mekran coast to Multan and Bhera in the Punjab.[14] Babur acknowledged the valuable support of Baloch 'lashkar' (an irregular army of tribes) during the First Battle of Panipat in his memoirs; and in grateful recognition of the spirited stand of the Baloch 'lashkar' against the Marathas in the last Battle of Panipat, Ahmad Shah Abdali had restored the sovereignty of Balochistan to their chieftains.[15] The chivalrous Baloch tradition of responding to a distress call for help runs deep into their character and survives to this day. As the British involvement deepened in Sindh and Balochistan, they were to discover these and more.

Burnes' voyage was immediately followed by another mission under Colonel Henry Pottinger, who extracted a treaty from the Amirs in April 1832, which opened the Indus and Sindh for commercial purposes. When war was declared against Afghanistan in 1839, yet another treaty was forced under threat, to allow the passage along the Indus and assembly at Shikarpur, of the British forces for their intended march to Kandahar. Thus the Amirs, scions of the great Talpurs who only a few decades ago had defeated the Afghan hordes, the Rajputs of Jodhpur and the Brahui chieftains of Kalat in open battles;[16] now divided and weak, were overwhelmed. But not the Baloch spirit. The assembly and march of the British army through Baloch territory inflamed the tribes and resulted in continuous engagements throughout the Afghan War. The British base in upper Sindh was regularly attacked by the border Balochi tribes; Dumbkis and Jakdranis in the 'Cutchie' (Kachi) foothills and Bugtis from 'Kushmoor' (Kashmore). The Marris from their mountain strongholds continuously attacked and harassed the tortuous line of communications through the Bolan pass. Soon the Brahuis from Sarawan joined the fray and became active in Quetta valley.[17] These tribes had never been subjugated by any invader before and now with unlimited opportunities for plunder, posed a serious security challenge to the British lines of communication.

In November 1839, a strong expedition under General Willshire entered into Sarawan and captured Kalat fort. In the ensuing fight the Khan was killed and a pretender was installed which caused more resentment and Nasir Khan the son of the slain Khan took to the hills and became a scourge of the British garrison in the Quetta valley. This necessitated another expedition in 1841 under General Nott, and the situation was brought under control only after Nasir Khan was restored as the Khan of Kalat. In December 1839, a small force of six companies under Major Billamore with a detachment of Poona Horse and three guns under Captain John Jacob of Bombay Artillery (later Commandant of Scinde Irregular Horse and two battalions of Belooch Rifles), conducted a successful campaign for three months and defeated a Bugti 'lashkar' in their own stronghold.

In April 1840, another force consisting of three companies (300 bayonets) under Captain Lewis Brown with one gun and escorted by a detachment of Scinde Irregular Horse (80 sabres) was sent to capture and occupy the small fort of 'Kahun' (Kahan), located in the midst of the hostile Marri country. After much suffering Kahan was reached and occupied on 11 May. The returning baggage train and the cavalry escort, reinforced with a company by Captain Brown, were attacked by the Marris and almost completely annihilated, with one officer and a few troops barely having escaped. Kahan was cut off but Brown stoutly defended the fort for five months. A strong relief column was despatched, but was blocked at 'Nuffoosk' pass, barely six miles from Kahan. A fierce encounter ensued in which the relief column suffered heavily (180 killed and 90 wounded) and was forced to retreat abandoning its guns and wounded soldiers. Soon thereafter Brown surrendered the fort to the Marri chief against assurance of safe passage[18]. The recklessness of the Baloch assailants against the relieving force was noted with amazement when a Marri chief thrust his shield to block the mouth of a British gun as it was about to fire and was blown away with it[19]. The story of Kahan can still be heard around the camp fires of the wandering Marris.

In October 1840, Brahui attack on Dhadar was repulsed after two days of heavy fighting and after a hot pursuit, Colonel Marshall defeated their 'lashkar' at Kotra. In February 1841, an expedition under Colonel Wilson against the Khojak tribes was badly mauled and returned unsuccessfully. After the fall of Kabul, a strong support column (two infantry and two cavalry regiments and a detachment of horse artillery) was moved from Sindh to Kandahar during March 1842, but was blocked at Haikalzai on 28 March and suffered an ignominious repulse and made its way through only after considerable delay and losses.[20] Such events portraying the fiery and unyielding character of the Baloch warriors abound in the period of British occupation of their territories. The severe strains imposed by the tribes in Balochistan and Sindh during the Afghan War may be judged from the fact that in 1841, the British had deployed fourteen infantry and two cavalry regiments (approximately two division strength of present time) for the protection of their line of communications.[21]

The crowning episodes of Baloch valour were the last two major battles fought by the confederacy of the Baloch tribes under the Amirs of Sindh, on the Banks of Fuleli River at Miani and Hyderabad on 17 January and 23 March 1843. Though lost to the British; in his much romanticized book, *'Conquest of Scinde'* (Sindh), Sir William Napier (brother of the British commander in Sindh) has provided a graphic account of the battles. Describing the Battle at Miani, he writes;[22]

'the dead level of the plain was swept by the 'Beloochi' (Baloch) cannons, answered from time to time by Lloyd's battery, as the 22nd (British) Regiment pressed towards the 'Fullailee' (Fuleli river), where the 'Beloochs' (Balochis) waited until the assailants were within fifteen yards when the volleys were delivered. The execution was great; the next moment, the 22nd staggered back in amazement at the forest of swords in front of them. Thick as standing corns and gorgeous as field flowers, stood the 'Beloochs' in their many colourful garments and turbans. Shaking their sharp swords beaming in the sun, with frantic gestures and shouts like the peal of thunder, they rushed forward and dashed against the 22nd with demoniac strength and ferocity. Forever those wild warriors closed up with sword, striving in all the fierceness of their valour to break into their opponents; no fire of the arms, no push of bayonets, no sweeping discharge of grapes could drive the gallant fellows back. They were killed in twenties; in hundreds, but their front were continually filled with eager warriors from the rear. And how fiercely the brave barbarians still fought may be gathered from this; a soldier of the 22nd bounding forward drove his bayonet into the breast of a 'Belooch'; instead of falling, the rugged warrior cast away his shield and seizing the musket with his left hand, writhed his body forward on the bayonet, until he could with one sweep of his sword – for the 'Belooch' needs no second blow, avenged himself; both fell dead. Thus they fought in their fearful struggle and several times the different regiments, aye, even the Europeans were violently forced backwards pushed from the line, overborne and staggering under the might of the barbarian swordsmen. Nearly all European officers were now slain or wounded and several times the sepoys wanting leaders slowly receded. For three and a half hours this storm of war continued without abatement and still the 'Beloochs' undismayed by their heavy losses pressed on with furious force'.

Having failed to make a dent frontally, General Napier launched his cavalry in a wide sweeping movement and struck on the Balochi flank and the rear whose dangerous impact began to break the Balochi front. The closing part of the Battle is thus described by the same author:

> 'Then at last the 'Belooch' swordsmen whose fury was scarcely to be resisted before, somewhat abated their fighting and began to waver, looking behind them. Slowly the 'Beloochs' began to retreat, yet not in dispersion, nor with marks of fear; in heavy masses they moved keeping together, their heads half turned and their eyes still glaring with fury. These stern, implacable warriors would not quicken their habitual stride to a run, though death was at their heels. So heavy were the retreating masses, so doggedly did they move, so disposed did they seem to renew the conflict';

that General Napier, having suffered heavy losses and struck with the raw courage of 'these savage warriors' did not think it prudent to provoke them any further and called off the pursuit.

In the battle of Miani, Napier's army consisted of 5000 men including two cavalry and four infantry regiments and 12 guns, against 18,000 – 20,000 Balochi swordsmen with 18 old vintage guns and a handful of cavalry. British losses were 2000 men while Balochis lost 6000 men and all the guns (the British estimate of their own casualties is much less). The battle was decisive and decided the fate of Sindh.

As the Balochis melted away into the gloom of the approaching night, leaving behind the flower of their braves on the violently contested battlefield, the stories of the terrifying valour of the Balochi swordsmen spread and became proverbial throughout India.[23] A.I. Shand, a great admirer of the Balochis, in his book on General John Jacob, after extolling the courage and tenacity of the Baloch soldiery in the Battle of Miani, finds it, 'strange that those hardy and savage warriors should have succumbed in close fight to a comparative handful'. It was no surprise. The Balochis, the bravest and the finest swordsmen, but for their deep rooted clanism, lacked the discipline and cohesion and a strong leadership and were poorly organized and niggardly equipped. As the Britishers themselves admitted that had there been a combined rush, an organized attack, it was doubtful if the staggering British forces could have stood their ground. Only a sharp and shining sword even as good as that of Salahuddin and sheer hot bravery could not win a battle. It was the same story which had been repeated throughout India.

Following the annexation of Sindh, the British with a stern military policy against the hill tribes and a progressive civil administration in the settled areas, brought Sindh under their firm control. Although the warring Baloch tribes were left to themselves, the British, however, made efforts to revive the hereditary influence of the chiefs in the decadent tribal system of the Balochis and used it as an instrument to maintain peace and stability in the free tribal belt. One of the significant developments during this early period was the raising of the irregular infantry and cavalry regiments and local militias from the Balochi tribesmen, out of which the 'Belooch Regiment' and the 'Belooch Horse' achieved great prominence as the pride of the Bombay Army. By giving it the Baloch designation, the Regiment symbolized the Baloch spirit of valour and tenacity and his code of honour and chivalry. It became the hallmark of the Regiment and the spirit continued to flourish despite the declining number of Balochi recruits; for those who took their place moulded to and aspired for their chivalrous ideals.

Chapter Five

Birth and Growth of the Baloch Regiment

The earliest raising in Sindh was that of Cutch Levy, an irregular component of Poona Horse, which was built on local recruitment from the Rajputs of Kutch, Sindhis and Balochis of lower Indus.[1] It was deployed between the borders of Kutch and Sindh. As the clouds of the Afghan War gathered, this force was transferred to Sindh to provide the nucleus for the raising of Scinde Irregular Horse in early 1842 under Captain John Jacob, which retained a strong component from Poona Horse. Jacob, a brilliant military leader, who will in time leave a deep impression on Sindh and Balochistan, however, did not favour Balochis and Afghans as reliable soldiers and recruited his horsemen mainly from amongst the 'Hindustani' Muslims from northern India and the Deccan. One reason for his disfavour was the growing hostility of Balochi tribes during the Afghan War and after the annexation of Sindh which kept him engaged in a continuous state of war with them. It will be after fifteen years, when the whole northern India would erupt into a massive rebellion against the British rule that Jacob would turn to the Balochis and the Baloch–Sindhis to raise an infantry regiment which will leave his name and give him a place of honour in the annals of the Baloch Regiment. Jacob's Scinde Irregular Horse participated in the two decisive battles against the Amirs of Sindh in 1843 and it was his bold turning movement in the Battle of Miani, which gave the British their victory. In 1846 Jacob raised another regiment, the 2nd Scinde Irregular Horse, and with these two, in a series of bold frontier operations, checked and ended the Balochi raids into the settled areas of Sindh and within five years brought the entire frontier under control. These two regiments were later amalgamated as the 14th (PWO) Scinde Horse and transferred to Central India.

In 1839 another irregular body of cavalry called the 'Belooch Levy' was raised by Captain Ameils, an officer of the Ist Grenadiers, which unlike the Scinde Irregular Horse was composed entirely of Balochis, but during its very first encounter with the hostile Baloch lashkar under Beja Khan, it was severely mauled and dispersed.[2] Another famous regiment, the Scinde Camel Corps, mainly drawn from the Rajputs and Sindhis was raised by Captain Fitzgerald of the Scinde Irregular Horse, but being very expensive in maintenance was transferred to the Punjab Irregulars in 1853 retaining its title as the 59th Scinde Rifles (later 6th Royal Battalion (Scinde) of the 13th Frontier Force Rifles and presently the Ist Battalion of the Frontier Force Regiment).

Following the annexation of Sindh, to meet the expanding requirements of the Army (a war was imminent in the Punjab) and to reduce dependence on the Bengal Army whose regiments disliked service in Sindh and on the western frontiers, it was decided 'to take up the loose soldiery of the country' to form an irregular corps of two regiments of the 'Belooch and Sindee' soldiers for service in Sindh. A proclamation was accordingly issued by the Governor in May 1844 and the 'Ist Belooch Regiment' was raised in the same month at Karachi by Major J. Jackson of the 25th Native Infantry. The soldiers of the regiment were to be armed and paid (Rupees seven per month) like the sepoys of the other native infantry regiments and were allowed 'to wear their hair, beard and mustachios as they pleased'. The first authorised uniform of the regiment was the usual 'Baloch 'angrikha' or coat, the loose trousers (shalwar) and a Sindee (Sindhi) cap'. It was required to undergo some training but not as strict as that of the regular battalions. Although it was not obliged to serve outside Sindh, the battalion soon got organized and voluntarily joined General Napier's army in its forward assembly in Bahawalpur for war in the Punjab. The

'Scinde Force' however returned without participation due to an early defeat of the Sikhs at Sobraon. In June 1846, the '2nd Belooch Regiment' was raised at Karachi. Thereafter the two battalions alternatively rotated between Karachi and Hyderabad for the next fifty years and developed great affection and close association with each other.[3]

The original purpose of enlisting both Balochis and Sindhis in the two battalions on an irregular basis was achieved to a great extent particularly in the second battalion as the initial difficulties in recruitment had decreased during the following two years. Sindhis were not a new element as they were known to be getting enrolled amongst the independent companies of the Bombay Army since 1758 and the Balochis were earnestly sought for and given preference. However, there was from the beginning a good proportion of Pathans of the border tribes in both the battalions, which element afterwards became predominant. Both battalions were organized in eight companies (over 700 bayonets) in distinct tribal composition and were authorized three British officers. The strength of the companies was progressively increased, particularly after the battalions became regular and by the turn of the century, the battalion carried over 800 bayonets. During the following years, the two battalions were frequently inspected by senior officers and were highly commended for their state of training and morale. It was probably during one of these training visits that General Napier is reported to have observed that 'these 'Beloochees' are as quick as their own Chikor' (an alert and mobile bird and highly adaptable to natural camouflage against the barren background abundantly found in Sindh and Balochistan). The flattering remark prompted the officers to wear proudly thereafter, a chikor hackle on the left side of the service head-dress.[4] The battalions were in such good shape that by the end of the contracted period of five years, almost all soldiers opted for the extension of colour service and in 1853, despite the facility of local employment, they volunteered for a distant overseas campaign in Burma.

Unlike the generally unpopular stiff and tight western uniform imposed on the regular native infantry regiments, the two battalions of the 'Belooch Regiment' being 'local' irregular corps, were allowed their comfortable loose native dress. However, to enforce uniformity and to give it a military look, 'the attractive combination of green and red in the uniform was adopted', presumably in line with the preference of red by the British officers and popularity of green amongst the soldiers. Also the high 'Sindee cap' not being popular with the Balochi and Pathan soldiers was replaced with a 'kilmarnock bonnet'.[5] In 1851, General Manson of the Bombay Army Headquarters inspected the Ist Belooch Regiment in Upper Sindh and recorded in his report; 'I saw this regiment for the first time and like the second (Belooch Regiment) it is composed of a fine body of men, well set up and from the peculiarity of the dress forming an imposing spectacle. They wear a red Kilmarnock bonnet, dark green tunic with red collar and cuffs, the rest of the coat being quite plain and scarlet pantaloons'.[6] It seems that during the very short period from their raising, the two battalions had already acquired the colourful uniform, which with minor variation has since stayed with the Regiment. After 1857 kilmarnock bonnet was replaced with the universally worn Indian 'pugree' of the same colour as that of the tunic or coat, with the 'shamla', the ornamental flare of the pugree, worn as distinction by the regiments who earned battle honours during the Great Rebellion.[7] It was however a tradition without official sanction.

During the Persian War of 1856, Captain E. Maude of the Bombay Native Infantry was delightfully struck with the gorgeousness of the '2nd Beloochis' and remarked; 'the Beloochis too have come in; such strange wild looking fellows, in bright dark green laced with red, red caps with green turbans. I hope, they are plucky and ferocious'. Later he commanded a company of these

'Beloochis' as part of his force and recorded his observations in his book, complimenting; 'these men (Beloochis) are fine, martial, wild looking fellows and might be aptly styled the 'Zouaves' of our Indian army'.[8] Now the 'Zouaves', related to a particular Algerian tribe, were a highly distinguished infantry component of the French Army at that time, who went into battle in highly resplendent and stylish oriental uniform (reportedly a profusion of beautiful bright colours) and had earned a name for their exploits in North Africa and the Crimea. Zouaves' colourful style and gorgeousness were proverbial, as it is even today and Maude's complimentary remarks gave the style of the Balochi uniform, a special mark of distinction and was so recorded in the Army Order in 1904. From the Regimental records, it appears that 'the dark green (more appropriately rifle green) tunic and the loose cherry (a darker shade of scarlet) pantaloons of 'the Zouave pattern' with white gaiters (or puttees) and dark green 'pugree' had firmly become the distinctive Balochi uniform by the seventies.[9] To these were added leather belts and bandoliers for field service and a cherry 'kammarband' and 'sash' for ceremonial purposes; the last two being imitation of the practices followed in older native regiments.

In 1856 the two 'Belooch Battalions' were threatened with disbandment. Colonel John Jacob, Commandant of the Scinde Irregular Horse, became acting Commissioner of Sindh and based on his old convictions (and prejudices), recommended disbandment of these regiments to the Bombay Government, being unnecessary and a public danger.[10] His recommendation however was not accepted by the Bombay Army and indeed the 2nd Battalion of the Regiment was ordered the same year for overseas service in the Persian War. It is an ironical episode that Jacob whose name was to be so honourably associated with the Regiment in subsequent years, should have advocated its abolition! But Jacob with his brilliant military dispositions and unusual record of service was also a man of 'fiery and impulsive temperament' with 'strong opinions and prejudices' and could not shake off the harsh and bitter experiences of his campaigns against the Baloch and Brahui hill tribes. He was himself shortly despatched to Persia, where commanding his Scinde Irregular Horse and later the Expeditionary Force during the campaign, saw the 2nd Battalion of the Regiment in action, which not only dispelled his doubts and prejudices, but created a place for the Balochis in his heart. The last two years of his life were totally dedicated to the battalions he raised and trained and for which his name lives with the Regiment.

In May 1857, India was swept with the convulsions of the Great Rebellion (called the Great Indian Mutiny). To meet the desperate situation during the next two years, a number of new raisings were undertaken in Sindh. The 3rd Regiment of Scinde Irregular Horse was raised by Captain Macaulay in 1857 (initially called the Belooch Horse), purely from the Baloch tribes. This regiment was soon associated with the Jacob's Rifles and participated in the campaigns in central India during 1858-59 and later in Abyssinia and the Second Afghan War. It was disbanded in 1882 but from its manpower, 7th Bombay Cavalry was raised in 1885 (later to be amalgamated with 37 Lancers and to become the present 15 Lancers). In June 1858, John Jacob (now Brigadier General) raised two battalions of 'Belooch Rifles' (also called Jacob's Rifles) at Khangarh (later Jacobabad). These were raised as 'silladar' rifles, the only of its kind in the entire Indian army, on the same principles as silladar cavalry. Here the men received higher pay than those in the regular battalions, but had to pay for their uniform and accoutrements, including the rifle invented by Jacob (a double barrelled, muzzle loading rifle, sighted upto 800 yards with a sword bayonet) and bear the cost of an establishment of transport camels. The second battalion of the Belooch Rifles was however disbanded in 1860.[11] A third Belooch battalion was raised at Hyderabad in 1859, briefly employed on operations but disbanded in 1860.[12] In, 1858, Jacob also raised an artillery component called Jacobabad

Mountain Train, which initially was entirely manned by the Jacob's Rifles. It survived various reorganizations in the army, changing its designations to 6th (Bombay) Mountain Battery, 26th (Jacob's) Mountain Battery and again 6th (Jacob's) Mountain Battery (presently the 1st SP Regiment Artillery).

Commenting on the raising and training of Belooch Horse and the Belooch Rifles, A.I. Shand writes:

'if the drill left something to desire from the martinet's point of view, the discipline and order were excellent. Macaulay was granted absolute powers and he got his savage (Balochi) troopers under such perfect control that they actually respected private property and in the midst of flocks and overflowing granaries contented themselves with their own rations. Our soldiers trained in Jacob's school did credit to his rare instinct of selection, for to a man they were born leaders of men'.

Jacob was renowned as a strict disciplinarian and hard trainer but his concepts of training and leadership were based on a philosophy of honour and self respect. He once wrote, 'I do not propose to command them by force or fear. I will have sober, God-fearing men in my troops, as old Cromwell said and command them by appealing to their higher not to their baser attributes. The object of all our training shall be to develop mental power. The more we can raise our subordinates in the scale of rational beings, the more we can command them'. And advising his officers, 'you should show all the men that you respect them as men; you should get them to respect and feel proud of themselves. Then you too will be respected, even adored'.[13] His wisdom holds good for all times.

After the suppression of the Great Rebellion, some major organizational changes were affected in the army which had now come directly under the Crown. Native regiments were redesignated and the strength of British officers was increased to seven in the irregular corps, at par with the regulars. In 1861, the two Belooch battalions and the Belooch Rifles were 'taken into the lines' as regular battalions with the benefits of unlimited service and pension and redesignated:[14]

1st Belooch Battalion as 27th Regiment (1st Belooch Battalion)

2nd Belooch Battalion as 29th Regiment (2nd Belooch Battalion)

1st Belooch Rifles as 30th Regiment (Jacob's Rifles)

The earliest record of the 'New Colours' presented to the two 'Belooch' battalions dates back to 1860 and 1862. Obviously both battalions were already in possession of the 'Colours', possibly given soon after the raising as was the practice, and a change was necessitated after their conversion to the lines and having been distinguished with battle honours. The striking peculiarity of the 'new Colours' was the silver crescent mounted on the standard which through a coincidence or design, well represented the Muslim composition of the battalions. The old Colours of the Regiment were transferred to the United Kingdom before the Partition and most are preserved in the Windsor Castle Museum.

After the Abyssinian War in 1868 the 27th Regiment was redesignated as the 27th Light Infantry (1st Belooch Battalion).[15] In 1881 the 30th Regiment was redesignated as the 30th Regiment (3rd Belooch Battalion).[16] In 1886 a system of linking the infantry battalions was introduced on the basis of common historical origin, experiences and traditions and the three Belooch Battalions were linked together and were also referred to as the 27th, 29th and the 30th Beloochis. On the same basis 7th (Bombay) Cavalry/Lancers (the Belooch Horse) and 6th (Bombay) Mountain Battery were affiliated with the Regiment.

In 1891 the 24th and 26th Regiments of Bombay Native Infantry were converted into frontier battalions and redesignated as the 24th and 26th Baluchistan Regiment and linked with the 'Baluchis' (the old spelling had been reformed in accordance with more accurate orthography during 1891)[17]. These were old battalions of the Bombay Army and were raised at Bombay from the dissolved manpower of the Poona Auxiliary Force (which included the two marine battalions of the line; the 1st and 2nd Battalions of 11th Regiment), as the 2nd Battalion of the 12th Regiment in 1820 and the second Extra Battalion of the 12th Regiment in 1825, respectively. These battalions were re-designated as the 24th and 26th Regiments of Bombay Native Infantry in 1824 and 1826 respectively, which remained unchanged till 1891. The 24th Regiment was raised as a marine battalion, for amphibious operations and to keep order in ships of war; a singular distinction at that time. The Company had periodically raised several marine battalions to support its commercial and military needs on the islands and coasts of the Arabian Sea, but the 24th Regiment was the only survivor, having seen much service particularly in the Persian Gulf and had earned the nick-name of 'Bombay Toughs'.[18]

These battalions had a rich history of major campaign honours, such as Aden, Persia, Central India and Afghanistan and carried high professional reputation. Both had long association of service in Sindh and Balochistan, during the two Afghan Wars. After their conversion into frontier battalions, these were permanently relocated in Sindh–Balochistan, which became the area of their future manpower recruitment and which finally severed their 65-70 years old links with the Bombay Presidency.[19] On relocation, the 24th received as their first commanding officer, the celebrated Colonel M.H. Nicholson and Captain (later Field Marshal) Claud Jacob as adjutant, both of 30th (Jacob's) Baluchis, which initiated the process of that long and eventful association of these frontier battalions with the Baluchis, spread over the next 30 years and which in 1922, happily climaxed in their absorption into the family of the Baloch Regiment as its proud senior battalions. On conversion to

Baluchistan Regiment, the uniform adopted by the two battalions consisted of khaki coat or tunic, scarlet or cherry pantaloons, with khaki pugree and gaiters and cherry kammarband.[20]

Caste composition of the Bengal Army, which was considered as one of the many reasons of the Great Rebellion, had since disappeared and was replaced with class composition (General Mixture) particularly for the regiments of the Northern Army as a measure of greater safety. Also, as the centre of gravity of military operations shifted from Madras to Bengal and from there to central India and the north-western borders, sources of recruitment of the regiments from various Presidencies stretched out and even got severed under straining circumstances, seriously affecting the quality and flow of reinforcements. This necessitated some versatility in the manpower composition of the regiments. In 1892, 'General Mixture' was replaced with 'Class company composition'; a refined variation in which mixed composition of the battalion was maintained through varied class companies, each composed of only one class of manpower. In Sindh, the cavalry regiments except the Baluch Horse had always been recruited from outside the Province, but the local Baluch regiments had maintained their recruitment from the Balochis, Sindhis and border Pathans. However the number of Balochis and Sindhis had gradually declined for various reasons and were filled with fine material from Rajputana, the Punjab and the North-West Frontier and even from beyond. But despite the changes in the composition, the old customs and traditions of the regiment were carefully maintained. The three Baluch battalions had from the outset been completely Muslim battalions, a rare distinction shared with very few others in the Indian army and the two recently converted Baluchistan frontier battalions also became completely Muslim battalions.

In 1895, the class composition of these regiments was as under;[21]

24th Baluchistan Regiment	– One company each of Hazaras, Waziris, Kakars and northern Pathans and two companies each of Ghilzais and Punjabi Muslims.
26th Baluchistan Regiment	– One company each of Kakars, Waziris, Ghilzais and northern Pathans and two companies each of Brahuis/Balochis and Hazaras.
27th and 29th Baluchis	– Two companies each of Brahuis and Punjabi Muslims and four companies of Pathans.
30th Baluchis	– Three companies each of Pathans and Punjabi Muslims and two companies of Brahuis.

In 1895 Presidency armies were abolished and all regiments became part of the Indian Army under a central command. In 1903 Lord Kitchner carried out a major reorganization of the Army into Divisions and Commands and the battalions were grouped and redeployed into brigades at different cantonments throughout India, which dislocated the battalions from their traditional stations and recruiting areas. However a small depot was allowed for recruitment purposes. Quetta was designated as the depot, for the 24th and 26th Baluchistan Regiments, and Karachi for the three battalions of the

Baluch Regiment. The basic structure and the composition of the battalions were not changed, except that in renumbering the old Bombay units, a figure of one was added to their existing numbers and the designations were slightly modified as under;[22]

24th Baluchistan Regiment	–	as 124th Baluchistan Infantry
26th Baluchistan Regiment	–	as 126th Baluchistan Infantry
27th Light Infantry (1st Baluch Battalion)	–	as 127th Baluch Light Infantry
29th Regiment (2nd Baluch Battalion)	–	as 129th Baluchis
30th Regiment (3rd Baluch Battalion)	–	as 130th Baluchis[23]

During the Great War (1914-18), all five Baluch battalions were employed and fought on all major fronts with great distinction. During 1914-15, 124th Baluchistan Infantry had the distinction of providing its original manpower as reinforcement drafts to battalions fighting in France. It sent its 1st and 2nd double companies with full complements to 129th Baluchis and 4th Double company to 47th Sikh and a hundred men of the newly recruited 2nd Double company to 125th Napier Rifles. In fact, except for the Battalion Headquarters, almost the whole battalion actually fought in France under different battalions. At one time, having suffered heavy casualties, 129th Baluchis consisted largely of manpower provided by 124th Baluchistan Infantry. In 1916, when the reinforcement system was improved, remnants of the original manpower provided to 129th Baluchis and 47 Sikh reverted to the parent battalion except the Mahsud companies which were permanently transferred to 129th Baluchis. During 1916-18, 124th Baluchistan Infantry while fighting in Persia raised two additional battalions 2/124th and

3/124th and had the singular distinction of fighting on three major fronts, i.e, Persia, Mesopotamia and Palestine. The 127th, 129th and 130th also raised one additional battalion each. Except for the 130th, the others fought on two fronts, i.e., the 127th in East Africa and Palestine (for a brief period in Persia as well) and the 129th in France, East Africa and briefly in Iraq. After the war all additional battalions except the 2/124th Baluchistan Infantry were disbanded in 1920-21.

The termination of the Great War saw many changes in the Indian Army and those in the Infantry were far reaching. The weakness of the loosely linked system of single battalions particularly with respect to the recruitment for reinforcement or additional manpower had become manifest and therefore a new system of regiments with several battalions and specified depot or centre for uniform recruitment and training was introduced in 1922. This inevitably changed the old numbers and designations, which had been maintained in some old form with minor changes since the raisings. Thus the three Baluchistan Infantry and the three Baluchi battalions were grouped as the 10th Baluch Regiment and the battalions numbered as 1st to 5th and 10th (2/124th Baluchistan Infantry was to be the training and depot battalion). The Regiment received new badges and insignias. Double company system was replaced with single company with additional manpower for the Headquarters and separate heavy weapons component. These changes also affected the class composition of the Regiment which was freshly articulated to ensure uniform supply of recruits to all the integrated battalions. For the 10th Baluch Regiment, equal proportion of Punjabi Muslims and Pathans (Yusufzais and Khattaks) was laid down, which regretfully almost eliminated the Balochi, Brahui, Hazara, Sindhi and the Balochi – Pathan elements. In 1926, for the first time, Dogra Hindu (Brahmin) element was introduced in the Regiment (a company in each battalion). The new reconstitution of the Regiment was as under :–

124th Baluchistan Infantry	– Ist Battalion (DCO),	10th Baluch Regiment
126th Baluchistan Infantry	– 2nd Battalion,	”
127th Baluch Light Infantry	– 3rd Battalion (QMO),	”
129 Baluchis	– 4th Battalion (DCO),	”
130 Baluchis	– 5th Battalion (KGO) (Jacob's)	”
2/124th Baluchistan Infantry	– 10th Battalion	”

During the Great War (1914-18), for the first time, Indian medical graduates were inducted as temporary/short service commissioned officers (KCOs) in the Army Medical Corps and were deputed to Indian regiments in the field as Regimental Medical Officers (RMOs). Soon after the war, under increasing pressure from the nationalists, the British government agreed to a phased induction of Indians into the officers corps (called as the 'Indianization' of the army). The process allowed selection and training of suitable Indians at the Royal Military Academy, Sandhurst (later at Indian Military Academy, Dehra Dun) and induction into selected Indian regiments. In 1932, the 5th Battalion was selected for the 'Indianization' and on posting to the Battalion on 18 July 1932, 2nd Lieutenant Syed Ibne Hasan became the first Indian officer to join the Regiment.[24] He was followed by eighteen Indian officers (KCOs and ICOs) between 1932 and 1939. The process accelerated during the Second World War and by its termination, the whole Indian army had been 'Indianized'.

During the period between the two Great Wars, the Regiment maintained its strength and composition as constituted during 1923-25. Although there was a dramatic expansion in the Regiment during the Second World War, the present narrative covers the detailed history of the times and exploits of the old Balochi battalions upto 1939 only.

PART TWO

THE MARCH OF THE BALOCHIS

Espirit de Corps is the cement which binds together all qualities, which gives the military its value.

Von Clausewitz

Chapter Six

Early Campaigns and War with Persia

Although the first two battalions of the Baloch Regiment were raised in 1844-46, the march of the Balochis into the full glare of history really began with the raisings of the 24th and 26th Regiments of the Bombay Native Infantry, who were in due course linked with the 'old Beloochis' as redesignated Baluchistan Infantry and eventually amalgamated with, and became the senior battalions of the (10th) Baluch Regiment. Their early and subsequent military exploits and battle honours now form a colourful part of its annals and a proud heritage of the Regiment. The historical journey of the Regiment therefore commences with their earliest achievements and throughout the narrative, these and other battalions have been identified with their designations current at that time. But for ease of reference, their redesignation as part of the 'Baluch Group' or the Regiment have been indicated in brackets at the beginning of each historical episode.

From its inception the Bombay Army and its troops had been involved in the Persian Gulf region, for which reason it had raised the marine battalions, the earliest of its kind in the annals of military organization, of which the 24th Regiment, Bombay Native Infantry (later the 124th Baluchistan Infantry and 1/10th Baluch Regiment) was a proud survivor. Although the British naval power had dominated the Arabian Sea for nearly two hundred years, hostile corsair raids from the Arabian peninsula and the Persian (also Arabian) Gulf had been quite common and frequently caused disruption of the British commercial shipping and consequently drew punitive retaliation. In 1809 the stronghold of the 'Joasmi' (Qasimi) Arabs at Ras el Khaima had been reduced through naval action. Later in 1819, a strong force under Colonel W.G.Keir consisting of two British and one native regiments and one company of the Ist/11th (Marine) Regiment with complements of artillery and sappers was landed at Ras el Khaima. Its fort was captured after spirited resistance by the defenders for one week. Simultaneously, the adjoining hostile nests were reduced. The native component of the force was left to garrison the fort, but in July 1820, was relocated to the Island of Kishm. In October the officer in command, Captain Thompson, on his own initiative undertook an expedition from Zohar (Sohar) against a powerful tribe, Beni Boo Ali, and captured their fort. During his further advance towards the tribe's main stronghold, his forces were violently attacked and overwhelmed, resulting in heavy casualties (six British officers and 270 men killed) and a hasty retreat.

It was a serious setback and necessitated an immediate response. The newly raised 2nd/12th (later 24th) Regiment was at once despatched to reinforce Thompson's force, which stoutly defended the island and remained in garrison till 1823. Simultaneously an expedition under General Sir Lionel Smith, in February 1821, in a major encounter defeated the tribe and reduced their coastal stronghold. During this expedition a company of the ubiquitous Marine Battalion participated in the siege and reduction of another hostile fort of Mocha on the Red Sea. On return to Bombay, the 2nd/12th was redesignated as the 24th Regiment, with two of its companies garrisoned at Kharak in the Persian Gulf, where the whole regiment moved in 1838 for impending operations.

In 1839 increasing raids on the British shipping again prompted a retaliation. Following an unsuccessful raid by European detachments on Sirah Island in January 1839, a stronger force consisting of Bombay European and the 24th Regiments with British Navy in support, was used to seize the fort and harbour of Aden. Aden was captured without major fighting, but subsequently was repeatedly attacked by the Arabs and was gallantly defended by the 24th Regiment, for which it earned its first battle honour.

During the same period, its sister battalion, the 26th Regiment (later the 126th Baluchistan Infantry and the 2/10th Baluch Regiment) was moved to Sindh as part of the Army of the Indus for the intended invasion of Afghanistan. However during its stay at Thatta, the regiment suffered so heavily due to sickness that it had to be evacuated back to Bombay. On return from Aden, the 24th Regiment spent a tenure in Sindh from 1848-51.

Since 1855, relations with Persia had been deteriorating. The situation was further complicated when on Russian instigation, the Persian army attacked and seized the city of Herat, directly impinging upon the British policy on Afghanistan. When negotiations during early 1856 failed, the Company's government in India declared war against Persia. The Persian War of 1856-57 has been overshadowed by the Great Rebellion of 1857 which shook the British dominion in India and erupted almost immediately after its termination. The Persian War, however remains memorable for the quality of fighting characterized by boldness and determination in a highly demanding physical environment and against the vastly superior Persian army which had been trained by Europeans. Two of the Baloch battalions: the 26th Regiment and the 2nd Belooch Battalion (later 129th Baluchis and 4/10th Baluch Regiment), participated for the first time in a major campaign overseas and earned three battle honours for the Regiment: Reshire, Bushire and Khooshab. Remarkably, the operational area of this campaign was to be the same during the Great War (1914-18), in which the Baluchis were to distinguish themselves again, sixty years later.

On declaration of war, a force was organized under General Stalker consisting of two cavalry and five infantry regiments including the 2nd Belooch Battalion from Sindh with three battalions of artillery and two companies of sappers. It landed on the Persian coast in Halilah Bay on 7 December 1856. Detaching a company for the defence of Kharak Island, the 2nd Beloochis formed the left

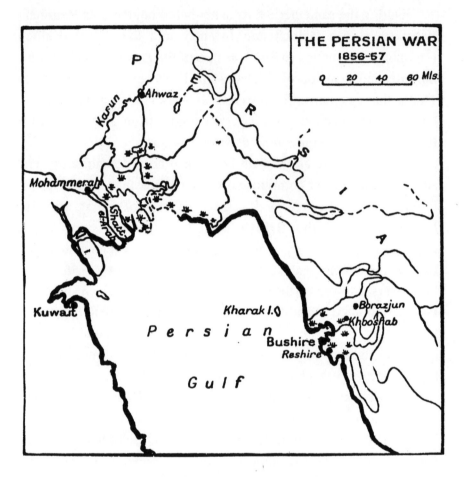

4.   The Persian War 1856-57

wing of the assaulting line, which on 9 December stormed and captured the old Dutch fort of Reshire and earned its first battle honour. Though the fort was courageously defended by the stubborn Tangistanis, it fell without major losses and with the singular distinction of the first Victoria Cross being awarded to Captain J.A. Wood of 20th Regiment of the Company's Army. An Indian officer and a sepoy of the same regiment were also recommended for the same award, but were denied on the ground of rules not permitting.[2] On 10 December, Bushire was captured after heavy artillery bombardment but without major fighting and the 2nd Beloochis for their participation, were awarded the second battle honour.

Despite these developments, the Persians refused to vacate Herat and moved a strong army to face the British forces. This necessitated the despatch of an additional force under General Henry Havelock comprising of four infantry regiments including the 26th Regiment, a regiment of the Scinde Irregular Horse (800 sabres) under Colonel John Jacob and two companies of artillery. The overall command of the entire British expedition in Persia was given to General James Outram. On hearing about the assembly of a 9000 strong Persian army at Borazjun, Outram marched at the head of a 4600 strong force on 3 February 1857, covering the distance of 46 miles in 40 hours, but the Persians had already withdrawn in a hurry. The British force was without proper logistic support, since the earlier march was a bold venture and therefore began to retreat to Bushire on 7 February. During the following night the British column was attacked by the Persian cavalry and emboldened by the disorganization and casualties caused, drew up its army of 8000 infantry and 3000 cavalry in battle order next morning at a place near Khooshab. Outram took the initiative and attacked the Persian army, whose infantry could not withstand the British artillery shelling and the spirited charges of the Indian cavalry and broke up leaving 700 dead. Although both the Balochi battalions were present, the battle was practically won by the cavalry and the artillery, whose performance was rated as one of the best in the annals of Indian army. Again two Indian sowars were recommended for the highest award for gallantry, but the honour was again denied on the same ground.[3] Both the Balochi battalions earned their battle honour for Khooshab; the first of the 26th Regiment. After the battle the British force withdrew to Bushire.

Using the British ships bringing reinforcements and logistics, a 5000 strong composite force was transported across the Gulf to deal with another Persian army assembled at Mohammerah, a fortress south of Basra, up the Shatt-el-Arab. On 24 March the force disembarked and on the 26th, attacked the Persian positions, supported by the naval guns as well as a company of artillery which was rafted to close up with the Persian defences. Another force was landed above Mohammerah, which caused panic in Persian ranks and despite their superior numbers, the Persian army quickly dispersed and was persued by the troopers of Scinde Irregular Horse. The battle ended more abruptly than anticipated with the fall of the fortress. During this period the two Balochi battalions had formed part of the force under Colonel John Jacob, for the defence of Bushire. It was here that Captain Maude of the Bombay Native Infantry, while in command of a company of the 2nd Beloochis, was singularly impressed by the wild gorgeousness of the 'Beloochis' and flatteringly compared them with the 'Zouaves' of the French Army. For his complimentary remarks in his book, the Baluchi uniform became known and was later classified as of 'Zouave pattern'.

The remnants of the Persian army from Khooshab and Mohammerah fell back to Ahwaz, about 100 miles up the Karun River. Taking advantage of the successes and their demoralizing effects on the Persians, Outram boldly despatched a small force of 300 men on naval gun boats for harassment. The Persian army, though still sizeable, panicked under exaggerated strength of the approaching British forces and retreated further into the interior. Soon after, the Persian King agreed to vacate Herat and not to interfere in the affairs of Afghanistan and a peace treaty was concluded. The entire British expedition assembled at Bushire and leaving a contingent of 4000 troops which included the 2nd Belooch Battalion under Brigadier John Jacob, returned to Bombay, just in time for the great event which was about to erupt in India.

Chapter Seven

The Great Rebellion 1857-58

With the annexation of the Punjab in 1849, the territorial expansion of the British dominion in India had almost reached its farthest frontiers. The Company's government in India had been quite sensitive to and had carefully groomed and propagated the myth of British invincibility as part of their political strategy. The recent victories had more than re-established the shaken myth after the humiliating disaster in Kabul during the First Afghan War. Now, many of these children of the Age of Reason, mostly upstarts amongst the new arrivals, deluded themselves with the arrogance of 'superior beings' and used power and dominance as legitimate ground to assert racial superiority. Already a negative change was overtaking the earlier pragmatic and friendly English attitude, which made them acceptable to millions of exhausted Indians, with over-bearance, insensitivity and worse – with contempt. Increasing number of Christian missionaries and zealots amongst the Company's employees with self-assumed civilizing mission were highly indiscrete in criticising the native creeds and culture and expressing their resolve of reforming 'the dark skinned heathens and bigots' and of 'making India a Christian country'.[1] This display of racial arrogance and contempt of the local people was, however, not universal and there were saner voices of caution[2]. But those were not strong enough to check the indecent onslaught of the missionaries or the 'progressive' drive of the self-righteous reformers of the School of Jeremy Bentham, for quick economic benefits. A feeling of deep hurt and insecurity gradually spread amongst the people. The fear continued to grow with every westernizing effort and the new reforms, earnestly launched by the young and energetic Governor General, Lord Dalhousie (1848-56). The rapid development of roads, railways, telegraph, introduction of English as the official language, codification of law, changes in the educational system and the proposal to establish new universities appeared highly threatening and subversive to the socio-religious fabric of India's highly traditional and conservative society[3].

To this simmering state of anxiety more tangible and materially more serious grievances were added. The controversial land settlements in northern India displaced a large number of hereditary 'talukdars' or the native aristocracy. Amongst the southern Maratha country, titles of 35,000 estates were examined by a commission, of which three-fifth not being 'good' were confiscated. These were sold to speculators who were total strangers to the tenants who had served the old landowners through generations and had deep affiliation to them. Similarly large land endowments ('waqf') granted by the Mughuls to shrines, mosques and temples were challenged and reduced. This was followed by a massive land grab through the 'Doctrine of Lapse' and annexation of larger states on grounds of misrule. Eight states including two Maratha and the Muslim state of Oudh in central and northern India fell victim to this arbitrary policy which 'seemed one of pure greed and injustice'.[4] The entire proceeding was unsettling to all men of dignity and caused serious dislocations and social disturbances in the affected areas where hereditary land-holders exerted strong influence on the people and the soldiery recruited from amongst them. The land reforms, however justified on economic grounds,[5] became a threat to the old order and 'the anger of the dispossessed combined with the fear of the orthodoxy', to accentuate the growing tension.

Then came the General Service Enlistment Act of July 1856, which made refusal by native soldiers to serve overseas a cognizable offence. It directly undermined the religious beliefs of the Hindu soldiers, particularly of the largest and highly caste ridden, Bengal Army, with bulk of its recruitment from Oudh and Bihar, the provinces most affected by other hostile developments. Already there had been complaints and reports on the continuing deterioration within the pretentious and pampered Bengal Army which having shouldered the burden of successive major campaigns during the last twenty years had become demanding and believed itself indispensable. Besides, the expansion in territories had placed extra demands for their administration, draining the regiments of their best officers, and encouraging a rush for easy civil and staff appointments. These negative trends were considered as 'dangerously unsettling' by General Charles Napier, the British Commander-in-Chief, who following the annexation of the Punjab, predicting serious consequences, had resigned in protest against the government's attitude in handling the affairs of the native army.[6] The fanatical attitude of the sepoys towards attack on their religious beliefs was explicit in the violent mutinies at Vellore (1806) and Barrackpur (1824). Now with numerous 'clumsy and provocative' incidents of similar nature combined with the spreading fear and resentment amongst the people, 'an unusual agitation began to pervade the ranks of the native regiments', throughout the army. The mysterious calls of the 'chupatis and the lotus' became the menacing whispers of the impending upheaval.

By the end of 1856 when Lord Dalhousie left after his 'monumental public works and progressive reforms', India seemed calm and apparently at peace, but actually concealed a sultry situation filled with simmering tension and discontentment awaiting the flash in a tinder to explode. It was provided by the army – specifically the restless Bengal Army. The cause: greased cartridges of the newly introduced Enfield rifles in the army widely believed to be smeared with cow and pig fat. It inflamed the deep religious sensitivities of the soldiers and in the wake of slow and poor handling by the British officers doubts and anxieties gathered strength of a wild fire spreading to most cantonments in Bihar and Oudh and other parts of India. Fear and anger mounted with every passing day, beginning

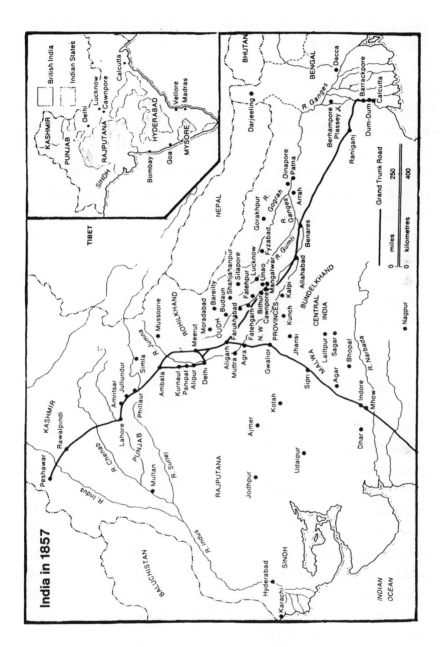

5.   Northern and Central India 1857

January 1857, as disturbed native regiments were disarmed and disbanded under the British guns and defiant soldiers were summarily shot, hanged or sentenced to hard labour. It reached a climax when 85 sowars and Indian officers of the 3rd Cavalry Regiment at Meerut were court martialled for refusing to touch the cartridges of old flintlocks, and were severely punished and publicly humiliated on 9 May. Next day the Regiment rose against the British authority, freed their colleagues from the jail, and were soon joined by two other native infantry regiments. Together, they put a part of the cantonment to fire followed by shooting and some arson, and by evening the rebel regiments were marching to Delhi which lay only 36 miles away.

On 11 May as the sowars of the rebel cavalry from Meerut galloped in, six native infantry regiments in the Mughul capital also rebelled and after bloody encounters with the British detachments, seized the cantonment except the powder magazine which was blown up by the British guards after a brief defence. Delhi was now in the hands of the rebel soldiers which created an electrifying effect. It spurred revolts of the native regiments at Cawnpur, Lukhnow, Allahabad, Agra, Indore, and many smaller and even far flung cantonments in rapid succession, and evoked sympathy and open support from the people, particularly town folks and the aggrieved leaders such as Nana Saheb, the Maratha Peshwa, the Rani of Jhansi and numerous local rajahs, talukdars and strong sections of Muslim ulema. Complementary to these risings were also the terrible news of treacherous attack on and bayoneting of sleeping sepoys in the barracks in Bihar and shooting down of apparently loyal native regiments on parade grounds at Benaras and Allahabad by the British regiments and their guns.[7] Within a month almost the entire Bengal Army had revolted in northern and central India and was joined by the people seething with fear and discontent. Delhi and Lukhnow became the rallying points for the rebels in Oudh and the Great Rebellion had begun.

Despite four months of growing unrest and disturbing incidents amongst the native regiments the British were taken by surprise with the suddenness of the uprising, the intensity of violence, and the rapidity of its expansion to vast areas of Oudh and the Maratha country. They were faced with an acute shortage of British troops in India due to wars in Persia and the Crimea. They had only two British regiments and a few Gurkha and Sikh battalions between Calcutta and the Punjab[8] for immediate reaction before reinforcements could be shipped from overseas or moved from other areas in India so far unaffected by the Rebellion. Armies of the other two Presidencies though generally unaffected (in the Bombay Army, out of 32 native regiments six gave ground for anxiety, only two partially mutinied, while in Madras Army no untoward incident took place)[9], a large number of Bengal Army units were located in the Punjab, Sindh and the Frontier, who were restless and quite a few of these actually rebelled. But swift action by the British Commissioners in these provinces, their dispersed and isolated locations in the various cantonments and a generally unfriendly attitude of the people against the Bengal Army, helped in disarming the restless regiments and capturing or annihilating those who rebelled. The spreading disbelief in the vitality of the British power which could have led to serious disaffection amongst the people of these provinces was thus timely checked. Indeed, within a short time it became obvious that the most favourable factors in the restoration of nearly shattered confidence of the British power were the solid support from the Punjab, particularly of the Sikhs[10], and the complete indifference of the Deccan and South India to the Rebellion in Oudh and the Maratha country, which became the foci and the main theatres of operations. Beyond the borders of these territories there were only sporadic and isolated incidents. However in Bihar the simmering discontent converted itself into a guerilla war under an able Rajput rajah Kanwar Singh, who with a small rebel force kept a number of strong British columns engaged in costly and exhausting operations between the Gogra and Son rivers from August 1857 till the end of next year.[11]

Despite all the initial advantages of surprise, growing popular support, and weak and hesitant reaction from the British whose morale and confidence were visibly shaken, the Rebellion from the very outset remained fragmented, dispersed, and poorly coordinated without organizational unity or operational plan. It desperately lacked a charismatic leader of experience and vision to unify and direct its unbounded passion and energy. By rallying around the decrepit Mughul King in Delhi, surrounded by an intriguing and self-serving court and two Maratha leaders in the south with personal dynastic ambitions, the Rebellion in fact allied itself with the hopelessly exhausted forces which could neither inspire nor sustain it. The powerful patriotic impulses released by the Rebellion got dissipated in India's chronic schism, ethnic rivalries and prejudices and social inertia and failed to create the unifying sentiments for a common cause and soon degenerated into petty and divided vested interests. It was only the desperate situation of the rebel soldiers and the strong infusion of religious fervour in the Rebellion[12] that provided it vitality and kept it going despite lack of professional leadership for higher direction in the continuously diminishing fortunes of war.

'The epic of the Great Rebellion' has been variously portrayed, as a purely military mutiny, a sepoy's war, a conspiracy of the feudals and the clergy, a popular movement of protest against westernization and as the First Indian War of Independence.[13] 'Certainly,' as Hibbert asserts, 'the Rebellion was more momentous than the familiar English term 'Indian Mutiny' implies'. There were agrarian grievances which touched the people besides a common feeling of resentment against the Englishmen, which was shared with the soldiers by both the elite and the masses in the greater sections of Northern India. Despite confusion and hesitation and many operational deficiencies, the rebels at least had identified a common enemy. More likely, 'there were elements of all those factors to be found in the great upheaval', whose enormity shook the edifice of the British rule to its very foundations, and became a major socio-political watershed in the Indian history. Although forming part of a bigger historical perspective, the story of this great epic is highly instructive even in the restricted professional context and needs to be studied to dispel misgivings and to harmonize the conflicting emotional feelings created by colonial distortions and nationalistic prejudices.

From the time it erupted with the uprising of the 3rd Cavalry in Meerut on 10 May 1857, it raged through thirteen months of long and bitter war, of violent encounters, and fiercely fought battles frequently dominated by appalling brutalities and reprisals till the fall of Gwaliar on 20 June 1858. The smouldering fire of the Rebellion however continued to burn beyond 1859. The main campaign centred around Delhi and with its fate was bound not only the future of the Rebellion but also of the British power. The British gathered the largest number of their own regiments and the best available native troops for this operation which included the 1st Belooch Battalion (later the 127th and 3/10th Baluch Regiment). Another Baloch battalion, the 24th Regiment (later the 124th Baluchistan Infantry and the 1/10th Baluch Regiment), formed part of the force assembled for operations in central India. Though separated, their participation for nearly two years covered the entire war and most of its campaigns and major battles in Delhi, Rohilkhand, Oudh and central India; a rare experience for a regiment. In the recounting of their story we can see the military profile of the Great Rebellion which also forms a part of our history and offers many valuable lessons which are relevant even today. We shall begin from the decisive point in the war, the storming and recapture of Delhi.

The Fall of Delhi

The British had correctly evaluated the symbolic political significance of Delhi and its complementary military value. While the relief measures for the other beleaguered cities were initiated immediate recapture of the old Mughul capital assumed the highest priority. All available British troops in the neighbourhood were directed to reach Delhi. The remnants of British troops at Meerut moved to Bhagput (Baghput), 35 miles north west of Delhi, to junction with another column formed at, and moved from Ambala. The combined British forces under General Henry Bernard comprising of 800 British cavalry, 3000 British infantry, and 500 Gurkhas with a light field battery, and three troops of horse artillery marched towards Delhi and met the first rebel force well entrenched at the village of Badli ki Sarae, a few miles north west of Delhi. On 8 June 1857, a fierce battle took place in which the rebel soldiers fought with desperate courage. But they were commanded by junior Indian officers lacking in professional experience of bigger command and battle strategy and suffered with immobility. Despite the advantages of numbers, strong defences and individual skill and bravery the rebels were out-manoeuvred by superior generalship and forced to retreat within the walls of Delhi leaving 26 guns behind. Their failure to use cavalry ahead of defences and against British flanks lost them the day but their failure to occupy 'the Ridge' immediately to their rear, as the second line of defence proved fatal. The British thus captured 'the strategic Ridge' (later became known as the Delhi Ridge), and succeeded in establishing a base, which not only overlooked Delhi but provided some protection to their vital communication with the Punjab, which was to become the main source of reinforcement for the British army. On 9 June, the first reinforcement arrived – the Corps of Guides, after marching 600 miles in 22 days!

Before the Rebellion this ridge was hardly significant. Rising up to sixty feet above the plain, little over two miles in length and varying between two to eight hundred yards in depth with relative observation over the city, it provided a natural defensive position across the road to the Punjab. Its left flank was protected by the wide Jamuna River, unfordable at this time of the year and the northern half was beyond gun range from Delhi. Only the right flank or the southern end was vulnerable being in close proximity of Sabzi Mandi, a suburb outside of the fortress of Delhi. The main old city of Delhi lay within the high fortress perimeter wall, of roughly seven miles, with strong loop-holed parapet and 16-30 feet wide sloping earth work outside the wall, beyond which lay 25 feet wide dry ditch. The fortress wall was broken by strong bastions at varying intervals which also provided gates for entry into Delhi. The eastern side was washed by the Jamuna River, with free movement over a boat bridge.[14] Although British historians frequently talk of the siege of Delhi, in actual fact Delhi was never besieged nor the British could ever muster the resources for it. Indeed the small British position on 'the Ridge' throughout was under threat of getting besieged itself and overwhelmed.

The British understood their dangerous situation and the threat to their right flank and as the reinforcements began to flow in they extended themselves to the south by seizing a number of dominating houses in Sabzi Mandi to secure their threatened flank. The rebels soon realized their mistake and began to attack the British positions in Sabzi Mandi and on 'the Ridge' and the pressure was kept on incessantly for two months. But these attacks lacked unity and coordination and beyond being fiercely fought could not succeed in dislodging the British positions. On quite a few occasions, the rebels came within hair-breadth of capturing British guns on the Ridge, but lost the advantage in the confusion caused by poor coordination and lack of unified command. Having gained tactical advantage, their inability to exploit it for decisive gains was to plague their desperate battles throughout the Rebellion. Strangely, the rebels did not make deliberate efforts to outflank British position from the south to threaten their rear (the British were so panicky that they had soon destroyed all bridges over the canal which lay on their rear) or to intercept and destroy the flow of reinforcements along the road from the Punjab. Although the reinforcements were pouring in, the British morale was at its lowest ebb during these months (the command had changed three times; the last being General Archdale Wilson), under the continuous pressure of rebel attacks, whose strength within Delhi had continuously increased and had been estimated at 40,000. The situation had become so grim that John Lawrence, the Commissioner of the Punjab, contemplated handing over the Peshawar Valley in perpetuity to the Afghan rulers to release troops from the frontier for Delhi.[15]

The British had organized an extensive intelligence network within Delhi with energetic Hindu informers, some Muslim renegades, and quite a few from amongst the Mughul court, notable amongst them being Hakim Ahsanullah and Mirza Elahi Buksh, close confidants of the King and one eyed Rajab Ali, who was busy not only in espoinage but also in sowing dissension in the rebels' ranks. Zinat Mahal, in her obsession to secure a position for her son, was ever-ready to sacrifice the cause of the Rebellion. The rebels had no such advantage and often operated blindly. During these crucial months, rebels' failure to dislodge the small British force from 'the Ridge' or to block or disrupt the vital line of communication to the Punjab proved fatal for the defence of Delhi, indeed, for the whole war. It was 'only the lack of a directing mind amongst the rebels who would have concentrated on the decisive point, instead of wasting strength on dispersed actions that prevented the British getting overwhelmed'.[16] When Brigadier Nicholson (holding the rank of a Captain in the British Army) arrived with a brigade of moveable column on 14 August, the situation dramatically changed. A belated action by the rebel cavalry under Bakht Khan to seize or destroy the siege column, following

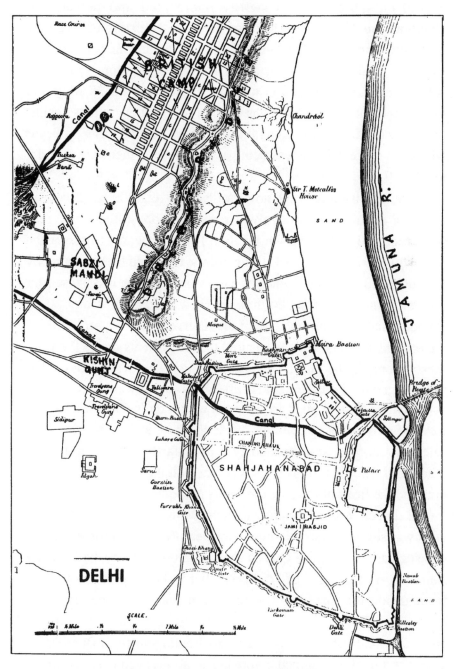

6.   Delhi and Surrounding Area 1857

Nicholson's brigade was swiftly intercepted and defeated at Najafgarh on 25 August. The siege column, consisting of 32 pieces of heavy guns and 42 pieces of light guns and heavy mortars, escorted by the Right Wing of 1st Belooch Battalion, arrived on 4 September. The Battalion had left Hyderabad on 28 May and having detached its Left Wing at Multan for local operations against disaffected units of the Bengal Army, had marched to Ferozepur where the siege column was being assembled and thence escorted it to Delhi.[17]

The British forces had now swelled to over 12000 and the plan to storm Delhi began to evolve. In the first phase the siege guns were required to be 'thrown up' (deployed forward) to target the powerful bastions and rebel strong points, followed by breaching by the engineers at selected gates or entry points. In the last phase four columns and a reserve column, each a thousand strong – 1st Belooch Battalion forming part of the reserve, were to storm through the breached points. Having secured the lodgements inside the wall, these were to be held and continuously enlarged to enable redeployment of all available artillery, as far forward as possible, and carriage of light guns and mortars within the wall to support the forward movement of columns inside the city, and, to bombard the selected targets. Simultaneously a feint farther to the right was planned.[18] The final objectives were the Mughul palace in the Red Fort and the heart of the city, the Jamia Mosque.

Between 7 and 13 September, forward deployment of heavy guns was strongly resisted through artillery fire and physical attacks; one such attack south of Qudsia Bagh was repulsed by 1st Belooch Battalion on the night of 7/8 September.[19] The reported situation from inside the city was favourable. It was a picture of tragic confusion. The respected rebel leader Bakht Khan,[20] who had arrived in Delhi at the head of a strong contingent from Bareilly on 2 July and having assumed command of all rebel forces, had made

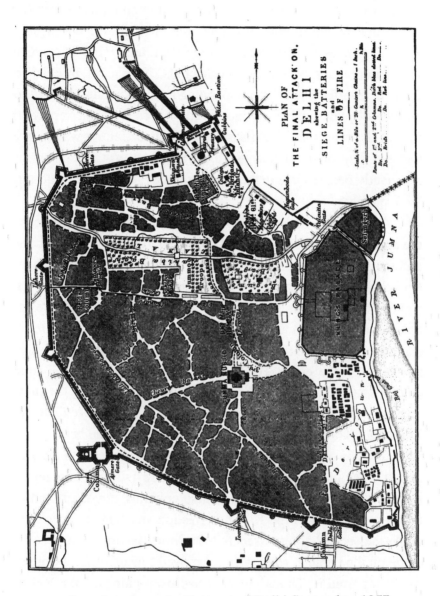

7.   Attack on the Fortress of Delhi September 1857

efforts to bring about some organization and unity, had fallen from grace due to continuous intrigues and wranglings amongst the Mughul princes and notables and reported rivalry with Ghaus Khan, the Commander of the Nimach rebels. The rebel forces were divided, disaffected and were operating in small contingents without an overall plan, control or coordination. Despite these reports the fear of the rebels and the disastrous effects of failure was so great that the date of the actual assault after three postponements was reluctantly decided late in the evening to be the dawn next morning: 14 September.

As the dawn broke and the pounding of the heavy guns ceased, the assault commenced. The first column under Brigadier Nicholson and the second column under Brigadier Jones with a little space in between, moved up to storm the Kashmir Gate. Behind them to the right, the third column under Colonel Campbell and the reserve column under Brigadier Longfield further behind, waited for the capture of the rampart by the leading columns and the breaching of the Gate by the engineers, to follow up the assault. The fourth column under Major Reid, far on the right, after clearing the suburb of Kishinganj was to enter the city through the Lahore Gate. The first two assaulting columns soon discovered that the breaches had been filled by the rebels during the night and their ascent to the glacis and the escalade met with the fiercest resistance, and terrible slaughter. Slowly however the British columns gained ground and the first column secured Kashmir Bastion and fanned to the right, while the second column secured the Mori Bastion, after a savage battle on the parapet, from where it moved towards Kabul Gate and easily captured it. Though ground had been gained, John William Kaye, the historian of the Sepoy War, aptly summarizes the battle: 'the rebels had fought well to the last; their gallantry worthy of the instructions taught were to plague the instructors ever. Alas! for the shattered British columns'.[21]

The first column was still under fire from Lahore Gate and Brigadier Nicholson, with a small British contingent moved through a lane to secure it. The lane was covered by strong rebel positions in the adjoining houses and under observed artillery fire. As Nicholson moved forward, his small column came under intense rebel fire and suffered heavy casualties. Despite his urgings, his men shrank back and soon Nicholson himself was struck down and mortally wounded, forcing the entire column to retreat in fear and chaos.[22] Meanwhile a partial breach had been made opposite Kashmir Gate and the third column followed by the reserve moved through the Gate and streamed into the city towards the Jamia Masjid on whose capture, the first two columns were to recommence their advance. As this column reached Chandni Chowk it came under such heavy fire from the rebels that it was forced to fall back to a Church in the rear, which had just been secured by the 1st Beloochis of the reserve column.

The fourth column was still struggling to clear Kishinganj and was checked by extensive breastworks erected across the two parallel roads to the city. The positions were strongly and judiciously defended and repeated attacks by the column were repulsed with heavy casualties including the commander himself. The rebel pressure was so intense that the Jammu contingent of this column fled in panic, stopping only after reaching the camp on 'the Ridge'. The right flank thus became seriously exposed and the column began to fall back in great confusion. Had the rebels pressed their advantage with speed and resolution, there was nothing to stop them in Sabzi Mandi and reaching the British base at 'the Ridge', which would have seriously jeopardized the entire British plan. While their reaction was hesitant, the British commander sensing the critical situation, swiftly mustered two hundred cavalry troops to block the surging rebels and to cover the retreat of the fourth column and called for immediate reinforcement from the reserve. The 1st Beloochis responded[23] and rushing into Sabzi Mandi area took up a defensive line, behind which the remnants of the fourth column began to fall back. At this time a retreating company of the Guides was surrounded by the rebels and was gallantly rescued by the Beloochis, who helped in their extrication back to the lines.[24] A British officer who watched the grim battle from a vantage point 'could not but admire the dashing manner in which the rebel officer rode in among his ranks, urging and leading them on to the battle'. Here 'the rebels fought well; never better than on this occasion and in truth proved worthy opponents'.[25]

By the evening, except for the lodgements across Kashmir and Mori Gates, the British assault had been effectively checked with forbidding casualties; sixty British officers and nearly eleven hundred men.[26] Exhaustion and demoralization was visible and under the pressure of growing uncertainty the British commander seriously thought of withdrawing his columns to save them from utter destruction.[27] The night and the next day passed without major activity except for the British guns which continued to pound the city.

The day passed in severe tension as the rebels still held Kishinganj and the Lahore Bastion and through a stroke of genius, could strike through Sabzi Mandi in strength to seize 'the Ridge' with hardly any troops to defend it. The British fortunes helplessly trembled in the balance.[28] No counter attack came against the British lodgements on the 15th or even the 16th. 'By all accounts (if the rebels had), they would have won a crushing victory'.[29] In fact, on the morning of 16 September, to their great surprise, the British found Kishinganj vacated by the rebels. Immediately the old Magazine was stormed by the 1st Beloochis and the 61st Regiment and large quantities of ordnance including heavy guns fell into their hands.[30] While the British artillery remained in action, rebel activities had considerably decreased and there were reports of massive exodus of rebels as well as civil population from the city through the Jamuna bridge, which continued the next day. But there were still strong pockets held by the rebels and the renewed efforts by the British on the 17th to advance towards the Palace and across Lahore Bastion were effectively checked. On the 18th the Lahore Bastion had been vacated by the rebels but the Lahore Gate still held out. So great was the fear of slaughter that the British troops designated to assault it refused and the assault was called off. The advance towards Chandni Chowk again met with strong resistance and the casualties inflicted were so severe that the British troops fled in great confusion.[31] On 19 September, there was further thinning out of the rebels and Lahore Gate which had so gallantly defied all British attempts had been vacated. Indeed there was hardly any rebel soldier left in Delhi. Still the British hesitated and only after the assurances of their agents, the advance was resumed against an almost empty city, with no defenders and by 20 September it was in their hands.

The fall of Delhi is a tragic story of lost opportunities, for the victory was so near the grasp of the rebels which could have changed the course of history in India. The British had assembled their best British and European regiments almost equal in strength if not more of the native components for the decisive battle and have since built stories of the valour and tenacity of their soldiers during 'the great assault and storming of Delhi' whose accounts by British historians of repute have been narrated and by whose own admission, 'it was the desertion (more appropriately vacation) of the rebels that made us victors at all'.[32] But what followed this victory was and will remain the most shameful chapter of British history in India. Merciless lynching and murder of thousands of unarmed innocent civilians, wholesale plunder, looting and burning of the 'blood stained city', willful desecration of holy places and abusive and humiliating treatment to everything native, as retribution for white blood and by supposedly disciplined soldiers with exulting approval of their commanders and officers.[33]

Campaigns in Oudh and Rohilkhand

While the decisive battle of the Great Rebellion was being fought around the ancient imperial city, the fire of the Rebellion had continued to spread in Oudh and beyond its boundaries; to Rohilkhand in the north and the Maratha country south of the Jamuna. It was here that the Rebellion acquired a popular agrarian and religious character, but generally remained confined to bigger cities and spread to the countryside only after it was ejected from there. Its major deficiencies and weaknesses were the same; divided and isolated efforts devoid of organization and unity of purpose, a general immobility in the initial stages, and lack of strong leadership or ability for higher direction. The chaos unleashed by the Rebellion gripped the people but it was beyond the capacity of its leaders to restore order even in the short term and proved detrimental to its cause. None could grasp the totality of the situation; all fought bravely and stubbornly in their respective areas and were destroyed or dispersed piecemeal by well coordinated attacks of the British forces under a unified command and strategy.

Initial reactions by the British were weak and desperate. Colonel Neill with two regiments, having successfully overcome the rebelling soldiers at Benaras, moved rapidly to Allahabad and rescued the small beleaguered garrison and secured the fort. During June, General Havelock assembled a force at Allahabad and marched to relieve Cawnpur, but the rampaging Maratha army of Nana Saheb had already carried out the massacre of the white captives. The Maratha army was defeated and Cawnpur was secured but Havelock was too weak to push towards Lukhnow and while conducting small operations in the surrounding country, waited for reinforcements. Meanwhile at Lukhnow the British contingent was defeated in an open battle at Chinhat in early July and forced to hole up in the Residency, which despite increasing rebel pressure, stoutly defended itself. Havelock's two attempts during July and August to reach Lukhnow failed. It was only by mid-September that fresh reinforcements under General Outram enabled a renewal of attempt for the relief of Lukhnow and through sheer hard fighting and suffering heavily, the British relief column succeeded in reaching the Residency on 25 September and joined the besieged. During this period rebel failure to seize Allahabad fort or to eliminate the British defiance at the Residency, despite overwhelming strength at Lukhnow and to come out of the cities to block and threaten British reinforcements, was to prove disastrous for them. To say the least, there was no mutual support or coordination in the Maratha rebel army operating south of the Jamuna, which could have dangerously threatened or disrupted the British flank and rear. Indeed, while their army was plundering Cawnpur Cantonment, the Maratha leaders were sending messages to the British officials for peace against settlement of their dynastic claims. These provided the British a respite, security of operating bases, freedom of movement, hope and a beginning.

On 20 September, Delhi fell and released large British troops for operations in Oudh and Agra. The Right Wing of the 1st Belooch Battalion was moved from Delhi to Bulandshehr and was employed for bringing order in the district where it stayed from October till December. In October, General Colin Campbell, the new British Commander-in-Chief had arrived at Cawnpur. A second relief of Lukhnow in November succeeded partially,[34] since General Campbell had to rush back to Cawnpur, which was under threat of Maratha army under Tantya Topi who was again defeated and pushed back. At this stage it was decided to regain full control of the Doab, before operations against Rohikhand and Oudh could be earnestly initiated. With three nodal points of the Doab: Delhi, Agra and Allahabad, already held; three converging clumns were moved to take the fourth: Fatehgarh on the Ganges, which was secured by the end of December and drove the dispersed rebel forces into Rohilkhand.[35] It was during this operation, that the falling back rebel forces, dangerously surrounded the Belooch Battalion in

Bulandshehr and only the timely arrival of Colonel Seaton's column on 14 December, saved it from severe losses.[36] Meanwhile the Left Wing of the 1st Belooch Battalion left at Multan was attached to a Moveable Column at Amritsar and marched to Delhi in November and later moved to Meerut where in early January 1858, it joined Colonel Penny's column being formed for operations in Rohilkhand which however was delayed in preference to Lukhnow.[37]

Lukhnow fell on 21 March 1858 but bulk of the rebel forces managed to escape to Rohilkhand and other parts of Oudh. By now, the British army had swelled to 25,000 strong from fresh reinforcements and new recruitments. Campaigns for regaining control of Rohilkhand and Oudh were now undertaken through a series of strong converging columns, operating on interior lines methodically clearing the rebel strongholds in the river corridors and dispersing and driving them toward the Lower Himalayan ranges of Nepal. It took almost the whole year and numerous small and large operations in which the dispersed bands and contingents of rebels fought with desperate courage, but for their serious deficiencies were doomed to defeat and annihilation. 1st Belooch Battalion participated in most of these smaller battles and encounters in whose narration would be found a profile of the campaign.

Colonel Penny's column which included the Left Wing of the 1st Belooch Battalion, as a part of the overall army's plan of converging manoeuvre, first moved to Fatehgarh and crossing the Ganges at Nadaoli, marched towards Badaon and Miranpur, where it was expected to join General Walpole's division marching from Lukhnow. During a night march on 30 April, near village Kakraoli,[38] Penny's column was ambushed by the rebels. In the ensuing confusion the British commander was captured by the rebels and killed, and the leading section of the column extricated itself only after suffering heavy casualties. Next day the column found itself confronted with an entrenched rebel position, which was subjected to severe bombardment from two batteries of heavy and field guns and attacked by two assault lines formed by the columns. The position had been vacated by the rebels with small losses and the column, now under command of Colonel Jones, resumed its march reaching Miranpur Katra on 3 May, where it joined General Campbell's force. Meanwhile General Walpole's column had suffered a severe repulse at Ruiya, but Colonel Coke's column had swept the area with great success and reached Moradabad, where on tips and guidance from Hindu informers, rebel leaders were captured after which the column marched to Bareilly.

On hearing of assembly of a large rebel army under the Rohailla leader Khan Bahadur Khan at Bareilly, General Campbell marched with his force (including the late Penny's columns now under Colonel Jones) to Faridkot, arriving on 4 May; a day's march from Bareilly. Although Bareilly did not offer a strong defensible position and the rebel leader knew of the two converging columns, he decided to give battle by deploying his forces in two lines of defence along the direction taken by the main British force, while protecting his flanks with strong cavalry detachments. General Campbell had under him a strong force of two cavalry and two infantry brigades with a siege train of heavy and field batteries. On 5 May, the British force marched to Bareilly reaching there by evening and deployed itself in battle order in two lines; the first assaulting line consisting of the 1st Beloochis and the 4th Punjab Rifles with a heavy field battery in the centre and cavalry on both flanks. Next morning with the opening of the rebel guns, the first British assault line commenced its advance and steadily maintained it. The rebels' first line of defence fell back behind the second line without major resistance. There was a small rivulet, Natia Nadi, in between and while the Beloochis secured a bridge on it, the 4th Punjabis continued their advance across, when a strong contingent of the 'Ghazis' forming part of the rebel army suddenly attacked its right flank, overrunning it with great ferocity and speed, crossed the rivulet and struck the right flank of the second line; a portion penetrating almost to the rear of the British position. The suddenness, speed and the boldness of the rush took the British by surprise but soon their strength absorbed the attack with a large number of Ghazis getting killed. Combined with the Ghazis' rush, rebel cavalry in a sweeping movement made an effort to strike at the British left flank and the rear but was checked by the British cavalry.[39] For the first time the rebels had displayed a tactical design to fight the battle. Only if they had used their infantry in the first line more resolutely in repulsing and causing attrition on the British assault line to draw and involve the British reserves, the Ghazis' rush and the cavalry manoeuvre might have yielded better results. Nonetheless it imposed great caution on the British commander who became very reluctant to enter the built up area of the cantonment which was the hub of the rebel defence. During the night the rebel army quietly withdrew towards Pilibhit, 33 miles north-east of Bareilly, leaving extensive nests of snipers and spoilers to maintain a show of resistance.

During this period another rebel leader Ahmadullah Shah referred in the annals as the Moulvi of Faizabad[40] 'the ablest and the noblest of the rebel leaders', having escaped from the earlier pincers of the British columns at Shahjahanpur, had mustered a small army at Mohmadi. Correctly appreciating the British intentions of marching to Bareilly and their likely involvement for sometime, he decided to attack the weak garrison at Shahjahanpur and capture the town. He marched rapidly and seized the town and the fort on 3 May. But the alerted British garrison holed up in the District Jail which was immediately invested and subjected to incessant artillery bombardment till 11 May, but the British post held out. On hearing the news on 7 May, the day Bareilly fell to the British, General Campbell despatched Colonel Jones with a brigade for the relief of the besieged post. As the relief column approached Shahjahanpur on 11 May, with a show of force, the rebels allowed it to proceed to the Jail while still holding the fort and the bridges on the river and the

Nadi. Jones pushed on to the Jail, when he suddenly realized that he too had been besieged by the rebels.

During the next three days, the enlarged British garrison prepared to defend itself while the rebel camp swelled with new reinforcements. On 15 May, the rebels struck with full force but the British defences held out. General Campbell having despatched a strong column after the retreating rebel army to Pilibhit had left for Fatehgarh on 15 May with a column which included the Left Wing of 1st Beloochis. Next day at Faridkot he learnt of Jones' predicament and that the bulk of rebel army had fallen towards Mohmadi. On 18 May he marched towards Shahjahanpur and skirting the town, joined Jones' brigade at the Jail. Rebel strength and superiority in cavalry forced him to go into defence with the Beloochis covering his left flank. The rebels maintained their pressure but the British artillery prevented them from closing in for the assault. The British commander sent for the column moving towards Pilibhit which quickly turned back reaching Shahjahanpur on 22 May. On 24 May the British attacked the rebel army which fighting a rearguard action skilfully withdrew into Oudh unmolested.[41] General Campbell along with his column marched to Fatehgarh from where the Beloochis were moved to the Fort of Jalalabad which they defended till beginning of July, before marching again to Badaon. Here the Right Wing of the Battalion joined from Bulandshahr on 7 September and the complete Battalion formed part of Brigadier Wetherall's column for the reduction of Oudh.[42]

Again a plan of converging columns was evolved to sweep and clear the areas between the Ghagra and the Ganges and the Ghagra and the Rapti rivers. On 21 October, the Wetherall column captured the Fort of Badri, and commencing its march on 4 November reached the strong fortress of Rampur Kessia held by a Khanpuria Rajput rebel, Ram Ghulam Singh. Here Wetherall was required to wait for another column under General Hope Grant, but decided to attack the fort which fell after strong resistance. Four companies of the 1st Beloochis formed part of the leading assault line and suffered casualties during the attack including its commanding officer, Colonel Furqohart.[43] When Hope Grant joined the column the combined force marched towards the heavily defended Fort of Amethi which however fell when the Rajah surrendered. On 18 November the Wetherall column in conjunction with three others invested Beni Madho's stronghold of Shankarpur. Due to late arrival of one column the rebel leader along with his strong contingent escaped but was intercepted on 24 November and defeated in an open battle at Dundia Khera.[44] The columns had by now formed a complete cordon around Oudh. They now marched on to a central point sweeping and clearing the areas enroute. By end November all major resistance in Oudh had been overcome except for dispersed pockets for which smaller forces were employed. The fate of the Rebellion in Oudh and Rohilkhand has been aptly summarized by Forrest in his History of the Mutiny: 'the rebels proved by their heavy losses that it was not courage in which they were lacking, but as at Delhi, military leadership. If they had been led by men acquainted with the operations of war, the British commander would have found it impossible to hold his extended position and keep open the communications.'

The Belooch Battalion was moved to Lukhnow, where it formed part of General Horsford's first brigade. During December the Battalion was employed in smaller operations at Bahraich (17 December), Nanpara (23 December) and Barjidia (26 December). On 27 December, the Battalion was employed in the capture of the strong fort of Masjidia. Left Wing of the Battalion stayed to destroy the fort, while the Right Wing marched with the column through the forest and surprised the rebel camp at Banki and pushed them across the Rapti river. Right Wing of the Battalion returned to Lukhnow, but the Left Wing remained with Horsford's brigade at Siden Ki Ghat to watch the Nepal border and later participated in dispersing small rebel groups at Sakla Ghat and Sooner valley.[45] By the beginning of next year, 1859, the Rebellion in northern India had almost died down. The Right Wing of the Battalion forming escort of the army Headquarters marched from Lukhnow to Delhi, where it was joined by its Left Wing and the complete Battalion was allowed to return to its home base, Hyderabad, where it reached by 30 May, exactly after two years of active field service. During the entire campaign it had suffered nearly two hundred casualties but maintained its strength at 1000 plus.

Campaigns in Central India

In the Maratha country of central India, the Rebellion against the British had been led chiefly by the two aggrieved leaders, the Nana Saheb and the Rani of Jhansi, with a horde of smaller rajahs and chieftains and the Hindu elements of the rebelling native regiments. But the other two powerful Maratha rulers, the Scindia of Gwaliar and the Holkar of Indore had remained loyal to the British. Their state armies however were restless and those of the latter actually rebelled and joined the rebels in Bundelkhand and Malwa country. Since the outbreak of the Rebellion, the entire central India had slipped out of the British control and three times, the rebel army under Nana Saheb and Tantya Topi, had crossed the Jamuna into Oudh and fought battles for the control of Cawnpur which though constantly pricked the British, never became a serious threat. Here also the leadership of the Maratha rebels, suffered with the lack of military education and experience; the most notable amongst them, Tantya Topi had none. During the period the British efforts however prevented the Rebellion from spreading into Rajputana and southern territories.

As the British steadily regained control in the north, the main theatre of war, a Central India Field Force was formed in December 1857, under Sir Hugh Rose. It consisted of two brigades, the 1st at Mhow under Brigadier Stuart and the 2nd at Sihore under Brigadier

Steuart. The Field Force consisted of five cavalry and six infantry regiments with four field batteries and four troops of horse artillery and complements of siege train and engineers. The 24th Regiment of Bombay Native Infantry (later 124th Baluchistan Infantry and 1/10th Baluch Regiment) formed part of the 2nd Brigade.[46] The main object was to restore order in central India and protect the flank of the British army in Oudh. The plan was to advance by way of Jhansi to Kalpi, restoring order and driving the rebels across the Jamuna into the arms of the main British army north of the river. Two smaller flanking columns on either side, advancing from Jubbalpur and from Rajputana, were to assist the Field Force.

On 10 January 1858, the 1st Brigade marched from Mhow along the road to Chandiari, while the 2nd under Sir Hugh Rose started from Sihore on 16 January along a parallel road for Rathgarh (also referred as Rahatgarh), a formidable fort, strongly held by a rebel rajah. Rose arrived before the fort on 24 January and securing the adjoining town invested it. By 28th a sizeable breach in the fort was made and while attack preparations were underway a strong rebel force under rajah of Banpur appeared in the rear of the British camp. A strong cavalry force however dispersed it. The next day the fort was assaulted through the breach, the 24th Regiment forming the right flank of the attack and it fell without major resistance since the bulk of the rebels had evacuated it during the night. The rajah of Banpur having been repulsed from Rathgarh had fallen behind River Bina, 15 miles across the road near the village of Barodia, and was reinforced by the rebels from Rathgarh. On 30 January, Rose marched to Barodia and in a strongly contested encounter defeated the rebels and dispersed them. At Barodia, a strong contingent of Afghan and Pathan soldiers fought alongside the Maratha rebels and were forced to retreat only after the Muslim leader was killed. At this stage an uprising in Saugar forced Rose to march for the relief of the beleaguered garrison reaching there on 3 February. The fort of Garhakot, 25 miles east of Saugar, was the rebels' stronghold which was invested, and through relentless artillery bombardment, a number of rebels' guns were destroyed forcing them to evacuate the fort on the 12th.

On 27 February, Rose left Saugar for Jhansi, 125 miles to the north through the mountainous region forming part of the Arravalli extensions, and reached the pass of Maltun (also referred as Narut after a fort across the pass) which was strongly defended by the rajah of Banpur. Rose decided to stage a feint before Maltun, while attempt the crossing from another pass at Madanpur, threatening the rebels' flank at the same time. The 24th Regiment was left to stage the front of this strong feint,[47] while the Brigade under its cover moved on 4 March to Madanpur. This pass too was strongly defended and was captured after a determined infantry assault with heavy casualties. The cavalry in hot pursuit threatened the flank and rear of Maltun pass, which too was soon vacated by the rebels. Thereafter a series of strong forts at Narut, Maraora, Banpur and Talbahat fell to the British force almost unopposed. Meanwhile the 1st Brigade advancing along the parallel road had, after ten days of siege and strong rebel resistance, captured the famous and formidable fort of Chandiari on 17 March. Now the road to Jhansi, regarded as 'the stronghold of rebel power in central India',[48] was open.

Rose resumed advance and reached the outskirts of Jhansi on 21 March where he was joined by the 1st Brigade the same day. The fortress of Jhansi, located on an elevated rocky spur, was known for its massive strength. It was surrounded by the walled city of Jhansi, itself heavily fortified and reportedly being defended by over 10,000 rebel soldiers. The city was invested and immediately the process of throwing up the guns for breaching the walls was initiated with a company of the 24th Regiment. As the guns were deployed forward an intense artillery duel continued till 29th when some breaches were affected and preparations for the attack were ordered.

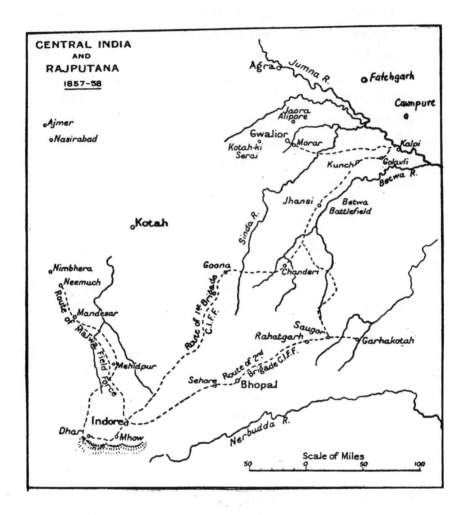

8. Campaign in Central India 1857-58

At this juncture, on 31 March, a powerful Maratha army under Tantya Topi, crossed Betwa river and appeared on the rear of the British forces, creating a dangerous situation. The British commander however decided to face the new threat, without relenting on the siege of Jhansi. While leaving the 2nd Brigade in position, Rose led the 1st Brigade, with all available cavalry deployed on his flanks. As the Maratha army approached the British encampment, deployed in depth with its flanks almost enveloping the small British force; the British cavalry struck both the Maratha flanks with great speed and so surprised the rebels that the first line of the advancing army turned back and soon broke up when the British infantry began their charge on the centre. The bulk of the rebel army however escaped across the Betwa to Kalpi. The siege of Jhansi was resumed and on the morning of 3 April it was attacked and after a fierce battle at every point and suffering heavy casualties, the city was captured. The fortress still loomed above but was spared the assault since it had been vacated and the Rani had escaped to Kalpi. While the captured city and the fortress were being occupied, it was learnt that an escaping contingent of the rebels had taken up position on an adjoining hill. A Wing of the 24th Regiment was ordered to clear the hill, which was instantly attacked and captured, with the loss of an officer and several men.[49] The battle at Jhansi was well fought by the rebels and though lost, made the British pay a heavy price.

Rose resumed his march to Kalpi on 25 April with the 1st Brigade; the 2nd following after two days. A Wing of the 24th Regiment was left behind as a part of the Jhansi garrison. Kalpi was the rebels' arsenal and the last stronghold on the Jamuna, 46 miles south-west of Cawnpur and threatening the British army in Oudh. Learning of the advance of the British army, Tantya Topi moved out of Kalpi and took up a strong position at Kunch. On 5 May, as Rose approached Kunch, he was joined by the 2nd Brigade reinforced with an additional British regiment. On the 6th, Rose made a flank march, bringing his entire force to the unfortified side of Kunch, threatening seriously the rebels' line of retreat to Kalpi and attacked rebels' right with the 1st Brigade. 'The rebels contested their position with great valour', but as soon as it was evident how gravely their flank was threatened, they gave in. But they withdrew to Kalpi fighting a well organized rearguard action. Here on the

15th, on the Jamuna, Rose affected a junction with the detachment sent by General Campbell from Oudh.

Kalpi was an unusually strong position due to natural protection provided by the numerous ravines and the heavily dissected surroundings. Here the rebels had fortified their entrenchments and had been recently reinforced. For five days the two forces faced each other without major action. On 20 May, a strong British reinforcement crossed over the Jamuna to support Rose, who now planned to attack on the 22nd. But on the same day, the rebels attacked on the British left, possibly as a strong feint to draw troops from the British centre and right, which luckily for the British did not materialize. As the engagement became heavy, suddenly the rebels' left batteries opened up and from the concealed positions of the ravines, mass of rebel infantry climbed up and attacked the British right and pressed on fiercely, over-running their first line and reaching the British guns. At this critical moment the reinforcements received from Oudh came handy and were used to counter-attack the rebels' penetration. Not only the rebels' attack was repulsed but their retreat turned into a rout. A Wing of the 24th Regiment formed part of the 1st Brigade and participated in the heaviest fighting on the left flank.[50] The next day Rose entered Kalpi.

Major rebel resistance had been broken and their armies dispersed, although smaller operations against small pockets continued. In one such operation the wing of 24th Regiment as part of the 1st Brigade participated in a fierce encounter on 20 June at Govali against a strong rebel force.[51] However, one last great stand of the Maratha rebels was to materialize at Gwaliar on 19 June in which the Rani met a soldier's death and the rebels were completely defeated. In this battle the recently raised Belooch Horse (later 3rd Scinde Horse and 37 Lancers) greatly distinguished itself as part of a reinforcing column under Brigadier Roberts, and was used in the pursuit and dispersion of Tantya Topi's army and its final defeat at

Banas river[52]. From 10 July to 14 December, the 24th Regiment was employed in small detachments in constant skirmishes with the scattered rebels and was reassembled in Jhansi on the 15th where it stayed in garrison till April 1860. During the entire campaign the Regiment suffered 52 casualties.[53]

Smaller Operations

In the Bombay Presidency, the only uprising by native troops became abortive due to lack of coordination and the fear of having been reported by the small number of Indian Jews serving in the regiments. However on 10 July 1857, a partial rebellion by a regiment at Kolhapur was 'crushed by a striking exploit of Lieutenant W.A. Kerr with fifty men of the Southern Maratha Horse, who travelled over eighty miles through several flooded rivers in twenty six hours to reach the troubled spot.' The officer belonged to the 24th Regiment and at that time was on extra-regimental duties. For his gallant action, he won the first Victoria Cross for the Regiment.[54]

Early in 1858, a major uprising of the Bhils caused considerble disturbance in the Khandesh area. It was however brought under control by defeating the rebels in two separate engagements at Amba Pani and Daba Bavli on 11 April.To meet such situations a corps of Deccan Kolis was raised and the 26th Regiment (later the 126th Baluchistan Infantry and 2/10th Baluch Regiment), recently repatriated from Persia, was deployed in its support. It remained engaged in small skirmishes against the dispersed rebels throughout the year and fought a major action at Mandway in Nasik.[55]

A small uprising by the Rajputs of Nagar Parkar in eastern Sindh during 1858 was successfully suppressed by the newly raised 3rd Belooch Battalion (disbanded in 1860).

After the Rebellion

The Great Rebellion was suppressed by brute force and was marked by fierce and indiscriminate violence, appalling atrocities and reprisals. Perhaps the acute desperation of the situation, sharpness of emotional conflicts, and the shattered trust and confidence had much to do with it. The British suffered nearly 12,000 casualties, one third of them at Delhi, and half of their officers.[56] The losses of the rebels were much more and could not be easily computed. Although the victory was complete and the empire was regained, the thinness of the British power, built on the slopes of the rumbling Indian volcano, became manifest. The magnitude and intensity of the upheaval prompted evaluation and debate leading to changes in policy and attitude and extensive reorganization, and reorientation, which would profoundly affect the Indians as well as their soldiers during the course of next sixty years (called the heyday of the Raj). But it would also leave deep scars on their psyche, and despite the process of reconciliation the dark shadows of the Rebellion will continue to haunt both and would exacerbate with the growth of nationalism in India. Perhaps, with many other reasons, it was also the deep seated trauma of the horrors of the Great Rebellion that prompted the British to back down and part with the brightest jewel of their Crown and much against their wishes accept the Partition of India in 1947.[57] But for now they had found out the weaknesses both in their rule and the Indian situation; the former could be rectified and the latter exploited to rebuild the empire.

'Public works rather than public morals or western values' would become the guiding principle of the British rule. Interference in the domestic affairs, native customs and beliefs and proselytization would completely cease. Discussion on 'politics, religion (and women)' was banned in the clubs and army messes. The first and the immediate change was the demise of the East India Company, the notorious 'Company Bahadur', which was abolished through a Royal Proclamation on 1 November 1858, which brought

India, its people, administration and the army directly under the Crown, with commitment to justice for all.

On the political and administrative side, the British had realized their failure to maintain a closer liaison with the people, and to treat the influential classes still holding sway over them with greater consideration. Of the 500 or more princely states in India, only a handful had sided with the Rebellion. Indeed, 'the prospects of the British would have been desperate if these princes, particularly of Patiala, Jhind and Nabha had not given valuable aid'.[58] For their loyalty and support they were rewarded with new titles and privileges. Amongst the talukdars, and the feudals, who had joined the rebels, most had personal reasons and were ever ready to compromise for self interest. Lord Dalhousie's controversial land settlements and reforms were reviewed and a large number of talukdars of Oudh and rajahs and jagirdars of central India were restored to their lands and granted old privileges and financial and judicial powers. Some rebels amongst them were given amnesty and rehabilitated. The new policy, in complete reversal of Dalhousie's progressive drive against India's decadent and oppressive feudal system, sought to patronize it vigorously 'as a valuable bulwark against future *emeutes*'[59] and to serve the British interests in India as an integral part of the new colonial order. Consequently, 'a class of new influentials' or feudal jagirdars was also created in the Punjab and other sensitive regions for the same purpose.

Clearly the British had reconciled with the imperial traditions of India and compromised with its decadent feudal values and attitude, which soon manifested in the pomp and grandeur of the Raj and permeated into all facets of its activities. One of these would be the 'darbar' a semi-formal council or assembly held regularly in the Indian regiments, where the commanders would allow the men to vent out their complaints and seek remedies outside the channels of military law, as had been in vogue in the days of the Mughuls.[60] The main victims of this 'imaginative' reversal would be the common

Indians, the peasants and the tenants. The new British attitude was firm and sympathetic, aimed at gaining people's confidence and at the same time convincing them of the requisite resolve, ability and resources to maintain their supremacy. They would however remain contemptuous of the native Indians, particularly the people from the crowded Northern India and would get detached from India's chronic domestic chaos, inevitably leading to racial segregation and their confinement to exclusive clubs and military cantonments. But the liberal surge of the western ideas and enterprise could not be completely checked and its movement in time would create a fast growing middle class, where the first fissure would develop between the British and the 'new Indians'.

The British pragmatism however did not allow the new attitude to undermine the importance of, or stifle the special relationship with, the native soldiers of the army, who had gallantly saved them from total destruction. They had seen the common professional virtues of the Indian soldiery, in the fierceness with which the rebelling soldiers had fought their desperate battles till the bitter end without losing their sense of dignity, honour and chivalry. Amongst the many is the story of an Indian officer of the 20th Native Infantry, recounted by Lieutenant Gough (son of General Hugh Gough as recorded in his book 'Old Memories') who was rescued from the rebellious 3rd Cavalry on 10 May 1857 at Meerut. Having delivered to the safety of the British lines, to the earnest entreaties and persuasions of the British officer to the escort to stay with him, the proud Indian officer replied that he had paid back the debt of a soldier but his duty was with his comrades and for life or death they must return to the regiment and face the consequences.[61] Most of the early allegations of atrocities attributed to the rebelling soldiers were later disproved and the hasty and often excessive British retribution against them were found highly unjust. As the emotional bitterness subsided the special position of the Indian soldiers got reinstated as the sword and the shield of the Raj. They were now to be called 'the

Jawans' and not sepoys and the Indian officers 'the Sardars' (the leaders) and the derogatory word 'native' was soon discontinued for them and their regiments.[62] Indian army became the main concern of the British and was subjected to major reorganization following the Rebellion between 1859-63. Indeed the process of reorganizing the army to meet the challenges of the empire would continue throughout the British stay in India.

The three armies were retained as effective safeguard against one another. European regiments of the Company were absorbed in the British army. The ratio of the Indian (native) and British troops was to be maintained at 2 to 1 and two Indian regiments were to be always brigaded with one British regiment. Corps of artillery and engineers of the three armies were amalgamated with the Royal Artillery and Engineers and the native component of the artillery was abolished except for a few batteries of mountain and horse artillery, which included Jacob's 6th Mountain Battery, originally the Jacobabad Mountain Train, which was manned by the Jacob's Rifles. Before the Rebellion the three armies had followed different and irregular patterns for their regiments; these were rationalized to bring uniformity in organization, equipment, and standard. Henceforth, an Indian infantry regiment or a battalion, irrespective of its status of being of the line or otherwise would consist of eight companies, and that of cavalry of six troops each to be commanded by the Indian officer or the Viceroy's Commissioned Officer (VCO). The strength of the British officers in each regiment was fixed at seven, who would command cavalry squadron, or infantry wing, or half battalion.[63] Officers ceased to be borne on the regiment and became part of the Indian Staff Corps. Promotion in the regiment was made strictly on merit. The Bengal portion of the army had practically disappeared and was made up from the new raisings. To fill the vacant numbers of the old regiments struck off from the list due to rebellion or disbandment, a number of newly raised battalions and those from the irregular corps were brought up to the lines and renumbered. This created some problems of seniority and symmetry but in the peculiar evolution of the Indian army this had been chronic.

One of the significant changes was related to the new manpower composition of the regiments, which was now based on mixed varieties of different nationalities, and racial groups in India. These were identified as 'class' and the new system was called 'Mixed Class Composition' or 'General Mixture'. While the desire was to develop 'clan emulation and martial characteristics' to the full, it also sought to impose safeguards against mutiny on a large scale. It posed problems but eventually it was settled by 'Class Company' regiments in which each company was kept homogeneous with one class composition. Caste basis was abolished and enrolment of Brahmins was discouraged. Despite this emphasis on 'general mixture', many regiments retained one class composition, and the latter gained popularity in the army.[64] It was this system of dividing regiments into class companies which led the army to study closely the many diverse people in India and to classify them according to their assumed martial characteristics.

Enlistment was made universal but the British preference for tall and stolid peasants and rugged hillmen from specific racial classes and areas, gradually became an obsession, which for all practical purposes would greatly restrict the future recruitment of the army to Rajputana, the Punjab and the Frontier. The initial impetus behind the drift towards the north and north-west came from the growing Russian threat. After the Rebellion with the bulk of the soldiery from Oudh declared unreliable, shift to the west and north-west became permanent. It manifested into the theory and policy of the 'martial races' of India with clear regional dimension, which in time would dramatically change the composition of the army. The Punjab became 'the nursery of our best soldiers' and led Yeats Brown to comment, 'weaklings die in North India; the survivors are a fine stock'.[65] Although India was a country with a staggering diversity of people, the British with good reason maintained their policy and by 1930, thirty percent of the Indian population formed the pool from which eighty seven percent of its soldiers were drawn.[66] Amongst the Muslims; Balochis, Rajputs, Punjabi Mussalmans (later to include Muslim Rajputs as well) commonly referred to as the PMs and Pathans were part of martial classes. The largest Muslim groups were taken from the Punjab, who were considered all-round soldiers, 'the backbone of the army'. Accordingly, the number of infantry battalions from the Punjab increased from 28 in 1862 to 31 in 1885 and to 57 in 1914.[67]

The uniform of the regular Indian regiments also underwent modification. The shako and kilmarnock cap were discarded in favour of the 'turban' or 'pugree' and long, closely fitting trousers in favour of wide breaches or 'knickerbockers' and 'puttees', approaching the Indian rather than the European style of dress.[68] Although a khaki field uniform, believed to have been developed by Harry Lumsden of the Corps of Guides, was principally approved for the army, the regiments for the time being were allowed the distinction of their uniforms with such additions as were adopted through tradition.

As a result of the reorganization, the two Belooch battalions and the Jacob's Rifles, were taken into the lines as regular battalions and redesignated as 27th, 29th and 30th Regiments, with additional distinction of remaining 1st and 2nd Belooch Battalions and Jacob's Rifles. The 24th Regiment and 27th Regiment (1st Belooch Battalion) were awarded the battle honours of 'Central India' and 'Delhi' respectively; the latter adding a 'Shamla' to their turban as distinction for the battle honour of 'Delhi', as was adopted by other regiments. The Belooch Horse, now 3rd Scinde Horse was also given the battle honour of 'Central India'.[69] The first two Belooch battalions (the 27th and the 29th Regiments) received their new colours in 1862 and 1860 at Karachi and Hyderabad, respectively.

As the flame of the Rebellion died down, any threat of its recurrence or of internal disorder had almost disappeared. With normalcy returning to India the British growth and expansion in India had reached its limits and its borders were fairly well defined. The British government now looked beyond its borders and to far away places such as China, Malaya, Abyssinia, and Egypt, where its armies from India will fight for the extension of its colonial empire. But nearer home the Russian threat would continue to exert its pressures, and will keep it deeply involved with the turbulent tribesmen of the North West Frontier and yet another war with the Afghans. As time will pass, the old charisma of the regiment will revive itself, in the sensational successes gained on the battlefield and the new adventures in distant lands.

War in China[70]

In August 1862, 29th Regiment (2nd Belooch Battalion) was earmarked to travel to China to participate as part of an expeditionary force in the Third China War also known as the Arrow War. It was a continuation of the series of Opium Wars provoked by differing opinions between the British and the Chinese on matters of free trade, national sovereignty, public health, and the proverbial principle; 'might is right'. Ironically, the British and other European powers were fighting to protect their highly profitable opium trade! Earlier in 1858-60, the British had seized the cities of Canton and Tientsin, but suffered a setback in attempting to capture Taku fort on the mouth of the Peiho river. Additional forces were being assembled near Shanghai when the Chinese Emperor agreed to the British terms. The Chinese attempt to enforce anti-drug laws during 1861 again resulted in a British protest and soon after the march of an Anglo–French Expeditionary Force to Peking (now Beijing). An unexpected withdrawal of the Chinese army required to meet this advance, resulted in a people's rebellion in Taiping which spread rapidly, and devastated a large area upto the walls of Shanghai. The advance of the Anglo-French force was temporarily checked to protect their settlements in Shanghai. It was at this juncture that the 29th Beloochis landed at Shanghai on 24 October 1862 and joined the force in expelling the rebels from the declared international zone, and remained employed in its defence.

The Third China War 'is perhaps more confusing than most because it is difficult to sort out the players', particularly, amongst the Chinese. While the Anglo-French stand was clearly anti-Chinese, a good number of Chinese warlords and merchants sided with them and in one instance the British themselves helped the Chinese Governor of Shanghai in crushing a mutiny against him. The rebellion itself degenerated into a confused internal war with the Imperial Chinese Army. As the rebellion subsided in 1864, the Anglo-French forces resumed their march to Peking, and just as the British guns were poised to open fire on the capital the Chinese surrendered, and acceded to the Anglo-French demands including the lease of Kowloon opposite Hongkong and the port of Tientsin. Sadly, the capitulation could not save the wanton plunder and burning of the Summer Palace by the British and French troops in a most outrageous act of vandalism.

During the same year an Anglo-French naval fleet destroyed the Japanese defences at the entrance of her Inland Sea, as a retaliation to Japanese harassment of their commercial shipping and representatives at Yokohama. As a precautionary measure two companies of 29th Beloochis were shipped to Yokohama in August 1864 for the protection of its legation, where it remained on garrison duties for nearly one year. Perhaps, 29th Beloochis are the only British troops to have ever set foot on the Japanese Islands till the Second World War. In June 1865, the Regiment returned to Karachi.

Chapter Eight

Abyssinian Campaign - 1868

The Abyssinian Campaign of 1868[1] is peculiar for the extreme harshness of the physical environment of the country demanding a very high standard of determination and endurance from the troops, and an elaborate logistic support. The cause which led to war was equally peculiar, even comical; imprisonment of British envoys along with some European representatives and traders, and of a few families, by the highly temperamental Abyssinian King Theodore for not receiving in time a suitable reply to his letter to Queen Victoria. It was a serious violation of diplomatic norms and international ethics, and to the rising British imperial power, an affront from an apparently thoughtless 'savage' King. When negotiations failed to get the release of the prisoners a military expedition became unavoidable.

Abyssinia in the 1860's was a wild African country at the lowest level of its cultural and economic growth. It had lost all its lustre of antiquity. A vast and peculiarly rugged country of sprawling highland plateaux, made almost impregnable by nature, and long stretches of arid and trackless valleys and deserts, was divided and torn by internecine tribal wars which had left it barren and desolate. From this continuing turmoil Theodore had risen to prominence by asserting his authority over the warring princes and tribal chiefs, and proclaimed himself King of Abyssinia. He had gathered a large army, was reputedly impulsive and cruel, and ruled through terror. His adversaries; Kassai, Prince of Tigre, Wagshum Gobaze of Lasta, Menelek of Shoa, and many smaller chiefs were hostile to the King but afraid of his power. In particular the Wollo Gallas, a Muslim tribe around Magdala and ruled by a Queen, had been subjected to extreme atrocities by the King, and was ever in a state of confrontation with him. He had kept all the European prisoners in chains in his mountain fortress at Magdala deep in the interior of the country, except a few key prisoners who were held in his army camp at Debra Tabor.

By the middle of 1867, it was decided to despatch a strong expedition to Abyssinia, under Sir Robert Napier, Commander-in-Chief of the Bombay Army, to secure the release of the prisoners by force of arms. The expeditionary force consisted of four regiments of Indian cavalry (including the 3rd Regiment of Scinde Horse, the Belooch Horse under Major Briggs), four British and nine Indian infantry regiments (including the 27th Regiment, 1st Belooch Battalion, under Major Henry Beville, one of the oldest officers of the Battalion having joined in 1851), two batteries each of horse, field, and mountain artillery and six companies of sappers and pioneers. Later a detachment of naval rockets and 8 inch mortars were added. A very large establishment of logistical support was created as part of the expedition. The force was organized into two infantry brigades, an advance guard mainly of cavalry, and a Headquarters reserve. In preference to Massowah, a known port on the Red Sea, a small place called Zula (or Zela) in the Annesley Bay was selected as the disembarkation point and as a logistic base. Magdala lay nearly 400 miles to the south across a barren and trackless country of rugged mountain plateaux.

By middle of October 1867, the first brigade began landing at Zula and by mid-December the entire force had assembled with its advance guard pushed into the mountains and occupying the Senafe plateau, 8000 feet above sea level and 45 miles from the base. Zula became a vast military encampment, a huge logistic support base, and a busy centre for varied political and military activities, from where contacts were established with the King's adversaries, and their envoys invited for eliciting support for the expedition. In particular, the Wollo Gallas were contacted for military cooperation, against British assurance and support for their cause.

Within 20 miles of Zula, the abrupt ascent to the rising highlands began from Kumayli, along the dry bed of a ravine, which twisted painfully through the wild confusion of boulders and debris of stones washed down by the torrents from the precipitous walls of the mountain. Through this chaotic mass of hanging rocks and gloomy confinement, the road (nicknamed 'the Devil's Staircase') was driven up the sheer cliffs by the sappers and a wing of the hardy 27th Beloochis towards Suru Pass, which the force with its logistic train had to move through towards Magdala. As access to Suru and the highlands was gained during the early weeks of January 1868, the advance of the Expeditionary Force commenced in brigade echelons. The movement however remained slow due to increasing altitude of the passes and frequent traversing of deep gorges and ravines below, which dissected the highlands and invariably required extensive labour from the sappers. Throughout the long and tortuous march the Beloochis extended a helping hand to the sappers, and their cheerful shouting response ('Kai Kai') to the call of assistance echoed in the jagged mountains of Abyssinia. They felt at home in those wild environs which so much resembled their own in Balochistan; the scattered clumps of junipers and mimosas, and the mushrooms of thorny bushes, trickling water from the profusion of volcanic rocks, the roaming herds of ibex and 'markhor' and the cold wind sweeping the wilderness of the high plateaux all seemed familiar, and their officers observed a peculiar liveliness in their spirit and morale.[2]

By the end of March the advancing columns closed up with Magdala, where King Thedore was reported to have moved with his army and kept all the prisoners. At this time a wing of the Beloochis marched with the leading 1st Brigade and another formed part of the Headquarters force with the 3rd Scinde Horse. A double company had been left at Adigrat along the route for protection. They arrived through forced marches (its speed is claimed as 'unparalleled in the campaign')[3], a few hours too late for the first action of the campaign, but joined the Headquarters Wing which was eventually assigned to the 2nd Brigade for the final assault on the fortress of Magdala. On 4 April, the advance guard ascended the heights and seized the entrance to the Tolanta plateau. It was followed closely by the two leading brigades occupying the bed of Bashilo river and the forward edge of Aroge ravine, which had been Theodore's army camp a while ago and from where he had built a track to drag his guns to the massive ramparts of Magdala. The formidable fortress perched on the sheer heights of the jagged mountain range was now in full view of the British forces and the sight was indeed forbidding.

Across the Bashilo through extensive mass of broken ground, two massive spurs heavily dissected by ravines rose steeply towards Aroge plateau on the left and Gombage-Affijo plateaux on the right connected at the Aroge saddle (called 'the neck') and eventually joining the massive mountain range, with Fahla and Magdala forming the two flanking summits, both above 8000 feet from sea level. Between Fahla and Magdala rose another jagged peak of equal height called Selassie for the Church of Trinity, built on its summit and which was connected with Magdala by the saddle of Islamgie. Together they formed a crescent-shaped rampart of sheer cliffs and jagged rocks, which could be approached only through the natural saddles and at few places along the ravines. Magdala, the most towering height housed the fortress with palace, church and the army camp and had only two entry points or gates; Kokit-ber facing Islamgie, and Kaffir–ber in the rear along the Sangallat spur. To reach Magdala the approach was through Aroge plateau which was dominated by Fahla, and, strongly defended by Theodore, and where he had reportedly concentrated his guns. Fahla was the key and therefore to be captured first, and the preparations were initiated accordingly which also included measures to block withdrawal or escape from the rear of Magdala, through strong deployment of armed Wollo Galla tribesmen along Sangallat and its ravines.[4]

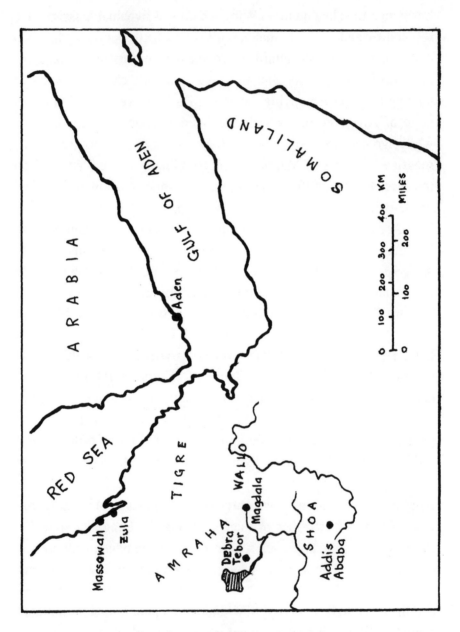

9. Abyssinian Campaign 1868

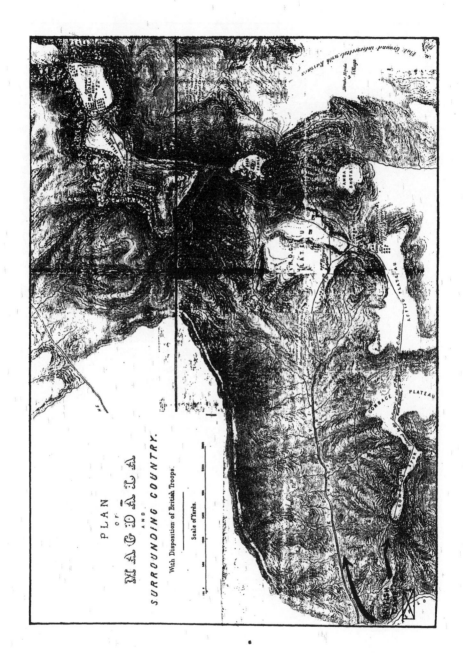

9B. Action on Aroge Plateau

9C. Attack on Magdala

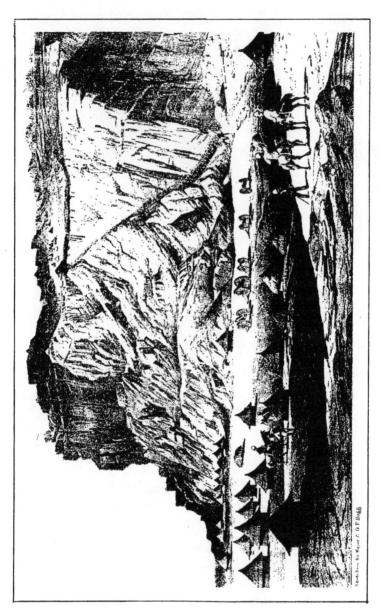

8. Ascent to Magdala

On the morning of 10 April, led by an advance guard and a company of pioneers, the 1st Brigade commenced its advance along the Gombage spur towards Affijo plateau, while the mountain batteries under a company escort, followed by baggage train, began their ascent to Aroge on the King's track (along Aroge ravine). By midday the Aroge neck was secured by the advance guard and the leading units of the 1st Brigade were pouring into Affijo plateau, but the artillery column was still below the Aroge plain. At this moment Abyssinian guns opened up from Fahla and swarms of Abyssinian soldiers, in thousands began to rush down from around Fahla towards Aroge. The artillery column and the baggage train were in imminent danger. The company of pioneers was immediately rushed towards the mouth of the Aroge ravine to cover the artillery column, the naval rockets were brought up from the Affijo to 'the neck' and hastily a wing each of the 4th Regiment and the 27th Beloochis were moved up to 'the neck' and formed into assault lines to meet the descending Abyssinians. The first salvo of rockets caught the Abyssinians in their tracks and the pioneers reinforced by the escort of the artillery column held the rushing Abyssinians, and after a close hand to hand clash repulsed the attack. An Abyssinian force skirting 'the neck' to attack Affijo was checked and pushed back by the cavalry elements of the advance guard, and yet another rushing on the baggage train was beaten back by its escort. Meanwhile the mountain battery had deployed itself in the ravine, and opened fire on Fahla and its forward slopes. There was much confusion in the already disorganized masses of the Abyssinians when the firing lines formed by the 4th Regiment and the 27th Beloochis began their advance into the Aroge plateau with loud cheers. In the ensuing encounter Abyssinians fought back stubbornly but suffered heavily from the new rapidly firing, breach–loading rifles of the Regiments, and began to fall back to Fahla and adjoining ravines.[5]

By evening, while it rained heavily, the 1st Brigade had fully secured Aroge, and its artillery and rockets were engaging Fahla.

While the British had suffered very lightly, Abyssinians had left 700 dead and twice as many wounded on the Aroge, including many chiefs of note, amongst them Fitaurari Gabri the Abyssinian army commander. There was visible disaffection and demoralization in the Abyssinian ranks on the misjudgement of their commanders of the strength of the enemy and the conduct of battle. During the night as the 2nd Brigade moved up to occupy Aroge, Theodore with his army was reported to have moved into the fortress of Magdala. During the next two days Theodore's offer for the release of prisoners was rejected and his unconditional surrender was demanded within 24 hours during which period hostilities were ceased. However there was no reaction from Theodore, and reportedly the Abyssinian army had begun to recover and was devoting much attention to the Magdala defences.

On the morning of 13 April the two brigades were formed in battle order and paraded in full view of the Abyssinians from all the commanding heights. The British plan was to secure Selassie and Fahla by the Second Brigade before attempting the final assault on Magdala. Accordingly the entire artillery had been brought up and deployed except the two mountain batteries which were to follow behind the 1st Brigade and deployed on Islamgie. At this moment a dramatic event had caused panic and disaffection in the Abyssinian ranks in Magdala. The temperamental King suddenly decided to escape from the rear but was stopped by his troops who challenged him to face the enemy. He returned to the fort but a large portion of his army had already begun leaving the ranks. Soon after, the advance of the British forces began. 'It was a fine sight to see; the long line of red, Royal Engineers (with scaling ladders), Sappers, 33rd and 45th Regiments, the 4th Kings Regiment in their grey Khakee, the Beloochis in their dark green, the Royal Artillery in blue and the mountain batteries on mules, winding up the steep and picturesque path that led to the Fahla saddle; while down the sides of the hills by every sheep track streamed the deserting soldiery of

Theodore and civilians with families seeking asylum in the Aroge. Sword and helmet sparkled in the morning sun, the banners were unfurled, the breeze was just enough to display their gay colours and the proud names woven thereon, and all nature seemed to contribute to the splendour of the pageant'.[6]

The first action was undertaken by a company of the Belooch Battalion, by climbing an accessible spur to capture Fahla, followed immediately by two companies of the 10th Regiment. Fahla fell without much fighting and the defenders surrendered. Meanwhile the 2nd Brigade led by an advance guard ascended the Selassie height and surrounding the Abyssinian positions, secured their surrender, upon which they were allowed to descend to Aroge. Together from Fahla and Selassie, it was estimated that about 10,000 soldiers had surrendered. The fall of the two strong positions before midday was unexpectedly too easy, and it seemed that the Abyssinians had lost their heart. Now, as the 1st Brigade advanced through Selassie, Theodore's attempt to pull back his guns from Islamgie into the fortress was thwarted by the advance guard and a heavy cannonade aimed at the gates of the fortress.

By midday the British forces had been deployed for the final assault on Magdala. The 2nd Brigade with three Indian regiments including a wing of the 27th Beloochis, and closely supported by three companies of engineers was to storm the fortress; the 1st Brigade following immediately behind for support and reinforcement. The attack commenced with heavy artillery bombardment of the gates and the adjoining walls of the fortress. The first assault was stalled as the engineers failed to blow up the gates or make a breach in the wall. However a company of the 33rd Regiment fanning out on the right managed to scale the wall through ladders, and secured a lodgement which allowed the whole regiment to pour in, and attack the gates from the flank. The Regiment soon fanned out in all directions, the gates were blown up, more troops including the wing of the 27th Beloochis[7] poured in, and within hours the impregnable fortress fell. Soon on learning that Theodore had killed himself, the Abyssinian army surrendered, and all the prisoners were released. On 17 April the fortress and its walls were demolished by the engineers, and the British force began its long homeward trek along the same route, 400 miles to Zula. The homeward march, however, was continuously threatened by the Abyssinian tribes, hovering on the flanks, forever waiting to seize opportunity for plunder, and the 'Beloochis' were constantly employed on rearguard duties for the protection of the columns.[8] Except for a few minor encounters the entire force managed to reach Zula during the first week of June 1868.

Thus ended the Abyssinian Campaign of 1868, which saw a remarkable logistic support organization, and a splendid display of soldiers' spirit of endurance and determination against extreme dangers and physical hardships. As Fortesque, the eminent British historian commented, 'the principal difficulty of the campaign was not the enemy but to reach him', which indeed was far more challenging than could be imagined.[9] For their excellent performance during the campaign, the 27th Regiment (1st Belooch Battalion) was made Light Infantry Regiment and given the battle honour of the campaign.[10] The indomitable Major Beville was promoted and awarded with C.B. General Napier presented the Battalion a magnificent silver trophy of 'Early Christian Cross' (taken from the Magdala Palace) as a memento of the 'storming of Magdala', which became a cherished centre–piece of its mess.[11]

It was during the Abyssinian campaign that the British officers were drawn towards the spirited shouts of 'Biya Baloch' and 'Kai Baloch' by the cheerful soldiers of the 27th Beloochis, during their long march to Magdala. These were traditional Balochi expressions of responding to calls of help. 'Biya' literally meant 'come' and indicated a call or invitation to assemble or move to help, while 'Kait' or 'Kain' ('t' and 'n' silent while pronouncing) in Balochi language meant 'coming or have come' and announced a built-in resolve or confirmation of the Balochi response to the call of help, either on their way or having arrived. 'Kai Kai' in Balochi tradition could be equated with 'labbaik' but with a peculiar connotation of responding to a distress call and of resolve 'to stay or not to return' till the cause of distress was overcome. It simply meant that 'we (the Baloch) have come (or are coming) to help (and will stay, or will not return till the help is fully rendered)'. Baloch 'lashkars' traditionally used this as a war cry to announce their arrival in the battlefield or when joining their allies or while charging the enemy or his encampment. The cheerful spontaneity of the slogan revealed the chivalrous Baloch character, and to the tradition-bound British officers it was aptly suited, and, highly appropriate to symbolize and represent the spirit of the 'Belooch' battalion and was readily patronized. On the Aroge plateau the battalion officers drew their sabres on the cheering shouts of the 'Beloochis' when the battalion was rushed forward to form up and meet the attack of the Abyssinian army. Although there is no record of its official recognition or adoption, the 'Kai Kai' Balochi war cry, like many unwritten (even unofficial) customs and practices, prevalent in the regiments, stayed as a tradition and spread to the other battalions of the Regiment.

Between the Abyssinian campaign and the Second Afghan War, there was a gradual deterioration of relations with Russia on the 'Eastern Question', and in 1878, another war appeared to be imminent. As a defensive measure, a small Indian contingent was moved to Malta to reinforce the British army. This contingent included the 26th Regiment (later the 126th Baluchistan Infantry and 2/10th Baluch Regiment). This was the first time when Indian troops crossed the Suez Canal, and were deployed in the Mediterranean. The war scare however was short lived, and the battalion returned after ten months stay on the island.[12]

Chapter Nine

The Second Afghan War 1878-80

Russia's southward expansion through Central Asia and its implied threat to India had been a haunting British bugbear. As the British extended their frontiers westward against the maze of barren mountain ranges that formed the turbulent boundary with Afghanistan, 'the Russian avalanche' slowly consumed the decrepit states of Central Asia; Samarkand in 1868, Bokhara, Khiva and Kokand between 1868-75, steadily moving towards the Oxus. Since 1858, within 18 years the Russians had come 600 miles closer to Peshawar.[1] Gaining domination and influence over Afghanistan, the only buffer state between the two great empires, became their primary political objective and the cold war that ensued came to be known as 'the Great Game'. An earlier British attempt in Afghanistan during 1839-42 to gain this objective through force had ended in the most astounding military disaster. The British also fought a short war with Persia during 1856-57, to force vacation of the provocative Persian involvement with Herat.

In 1878 the British again invaded Afghanistan precisely for the same reason as had been for the First Afghan War and suffered a painful defeat at Maiwand which reminded of the disastrous retreat from Kabul. However, the most interesting aspect of the Second Afghan War is the participation of all the Baloch battalions (including the two frontier battalions later integrated with the Regiment) and the affiliated Belooch Horse and Jacob's Mountain Battery, in this campaign.

On refusal of Amir Sher Ali to allow a British envoy in Kabul, the British government in India declared war on 20 November 1878, against Afghanistan. A Northern Army consisting of Khyber and Kurram Field Forces under Generals Sam Browne and Roberts, respectively, was formed with troops mainly drawn from the Bengal

Army and the Punjab Frontier Force. A Southern Afghanistan Field Force under General Donald Stewart was formed at Quetta with troops from both the Bengal and Bombay Armies which included the 3rd Scinde Horse (The Belooch Horse), the 29th Regiment (2nd Belooch Battalion), the 30th Regiment (Jacob's Rifles), and 2nd Bombay Mountain Battery (later 6th Jacob's). The three British armies poured through the passes and the early victories at Ali Masjid and Paiwar Kotal in the north and the capture of Kandahar in the south, forced the new Amir Yakub Khan to sign the Treaty of Gandamak on 26 May 1879.

During the advance of the Khyber Field Force, strong detachments had been deployed along the line of communication for protection against tribal disruption. In mid-April 1879, on hearing of the gathering of Mohmand tribesmen, a detachment of Mhairwara Battalion (138 all ranks) under Captain O'Moore Creagh was despatched from Dakka Fort (on the bank of Kabul River, five miles north of Haft Chah) to Kam Dakka, a mountain redoubt west of Shilman Pass. Captain Creagh presently on extra regimental duty was a Beloochi, belonging to the 27th Light Infantry (1st Belooch Battalion) which he later commanded and rose to the rank of General and C-in-C Indian army. It was here at Kam Dakka on the bank of Kabul River that on 22 April, he fought a gallant action against the swarming Mohmand lashkar, repulsing repeated tribal attacks with bayonet charges and won the Victoria Cross for himself and the Regiment.[2]

There was almost no opposition to the Southern Army. However in February 1879, a detached force under General Biddulph, operating near River Helmand was intercepted on its way back by tribesmen. Again, a strong detachment of 3rd Scinde Horse and a company of 29th Beloochis were attacked by a 1500 strong tribal lashkar near Khushk-i-Nakhud, which was beaten back after a fierce encounter. On 27 March, a gathering of the tribesmen near Kandahar was dispersed by a company of the 30th Jacob's Rifles.[3]

Treaty of Gandamak marked the end of the first phase of the war. However within six weeks of the assumption of office, the British Resident alongwith his staff and the escort were killed in Kabul by the mutinous Afghan troops and tribal mobs on 3 September. This signalled the beginning of the second phase of the war.

In the north, General Roberts with his Kurram Field Force rapidly advanced towards Kabul, defeated the Amir's army at Charasiah and occupied the capital on 9 October. In the south the Field Force, in the process of withdrawing from Kandahar was ordered to hold the city. From here a brigade which included the 29th Beloochis and a wing of 3rd Scinde Horse was moved to demonstrate on the Kabul road up to Kalat-e-Ghilzai, and was engaged in a major encounter with the Ghilzai tribesmen on 24 October[4]. The brigade returned after leaving the 29th Beloochis in garrison at Kalat-e-Ghilzai.

The British retribution against the massacre of its embassy, the deposition of the Amir, and the occupation of Kabul again led to general unrest and sporadic tribal uprisings in the north. On 11 December, Roberts' cavalry force was defeated with the loss of two guns, and again on 14 December General Baker's brigade was forced to retreat under Afghan pressure leaving two guns behind. Under the mounting pressure Roberts abandoned the city and Bala Hissar fort with its loaded armoury and magazine, and took refuge behind the walls of Sherpur cantonment. The British forces were besieged by the Afghan irregulars but their uncoordinated attacks were successfully repulsed with heavy losses to them. Disheartened, the Afghans raised the siege and withdrew on 24 December. On the same day a British brigade marched through the Khyber restoring the communications, and joined Roberts' forces.

While the north was seething with rebellious unrest, the south was relatively less agitated. To reduce pressure in the north, it was therefore decided to move a strong column from Kandahar to Kabul to reinforce Roberts as well as demonstrate British military power. Accordingly a force of 5000 – 6000 men under General Stewart marched to Kabul in April 1880. On 19 April, at Ahmed Khel near Ghazni, Stewart's column was attacked by a strong tribal 'lashkar' (estimated at 15,000). It was a violent engagement, in which 'for some considerable time the British forces could barely hold their own; in fact it was for a few moments touch and go'. A determined stand by the troops and heavy punishment by the artillery eventually broke the tribal assault, and Stewart affected junction with Roberts' forces near Kabul. This greatly improved the British situation in the north, and having offered Kabul to Abdur Rehman Khan, a nephew of the deposed Amir, British forces began preparation to vacate northern Afghanistan, thus bringing to a close the second phase of the war.

The departure of Stewart's column had weakened the garrison of Kandahar and was accordingly reinforced from Quetta and redesignated as Bombay Field Force under General Primrose. It retained the 3rd Scinde Horse, 29th Beloochis, 30th Jacob's Rifles, and the Jacob's Mountain Battery. The 29th Beloochis were still holding Kalat-e-Ghilzai and had been reinforced with a squadron of Scinde Horse, two companies of 66th Foot and two guns. Kandahar garrison was a relatively small force, keeping in view the tribal unrest that was sweeping the whole country. Indeed there had been numerous small outbreaks around Kandahar and communications through Khojak were continuously disrupted by Baloch tribesmen, forcing deployment of additional troops for its protection. The 24th and two companies of 26th Regiment (later 124th and 126th Baluchistan Infantry and 1/10th and 2/10th Baluch Regiment) were moved into Balochistan and deployed along the line of communication while the 27th Regiment (1st Belooch Battalion) formed part of reserve at Quetta. At this time the British government decided to separate Kandahar from Kabul and appointed a 'Wali' who was wholly unpopular with his people. They provided him with 6000 rifles and a huge quantity of ammunition to raise his own militia to defend himself against the growing threat from Ayub Khan, a brother of the deposed Amir and a contender for the throne.

Ayub Khan was the governor of Herat and since the British invasion, had raised a strong Afghan army of 7000 infantry (ten regiments), 1000 cavalry (four regiments) and 3000 irregular horsemen with 30 guns (six pounders). His army seemed to be well organized and armed, which by early July was reported to be advancing towards Kandahar.

To face the reported advance of Ayub Khan, the Wali's forces were moved out of Kandahar, into Zamindawar area enroute to Herat. On persistent requests from the Wali, mainly due to the

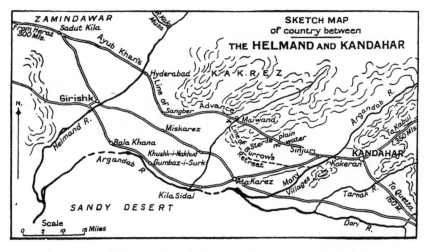

10. Second Afghan War 1878-80 (Southern Afghanistan)

unreliability of his own troops, a brigade under Brigadier Scott Burrows was despatched towards Girishk to provide the required support as well as to intercept the Afghan army's likely march to Ghazni. The brigade consisted of a battery of Royal Horse Artillery, half company of Sappers & Miners, 3rd Bombay Cavalry (300 sabres) and 3rd Scinde Horse (260 sabres), six companies of the 66th Berkshire Regiment, the 1st Grenadiers and the 30th Jacob's Rifles; in all 2500 men.[5] Burrows' brigade reached the Helmand River, 80 miles from Kandahar on 10 and 11 July. On hearing the approach of Ayub Khan, the Wali's forces encamped across the river, mutinied on 14 July; 2000 strong infantry seizing the guns marched towards Herat, the remaining mostly cavalry crossed the river to join the British Camp, but later galloped away towards Kandahar. A British cavalry detachment rushed out to intercept the deserting infantry, but could only recover a battery of guns, though without much ammunition. A counsel to retire to Kandahar was not accepted for fear of encouraging tribal uprising in the country which would only help Ayub Khan. However, to improve the supply situation the brigade retired to Khushk-i-Nakhud, at a distance of 46 miles from Kandahar and waited for the Afghan army.

On 23 July, forward elements of the Afghan cavalry were reported within four miles of the British camp and by 25 July, a patrol of Scinde Horse brought most accurate details of the Afghan army. On 26 July, the Afghan army duly reinforced with the Wali's deserters, had occupied the village of Maiwand 12 miles north of British camp and by its superior deployment had already outflanked the British forces while keeping clear the route to Ghazni and placed itself between the British brigade and Kandahar with the choice to attack either. Brigadier Burrows decided to leave his entrenched camp at Khushk-i-Nakhud and march to meet the Afghan army at Maiwand. On 27 July, the brigade covered the 12 miles during early hours and reached the village of Mahmudabad, which

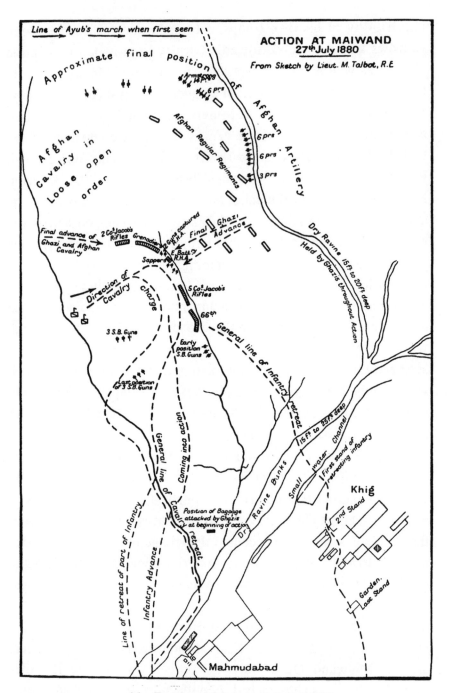

11. Battle of Maiwand July 1880

was occupied by Afghan cavalry but on approach of the British forces, fell back to its main position. The British commander decided to attack the Afghans immediately and as the sun rose high over the hot, dusty and deeply dissected plain of Maiwand, the action commenced at 10.15 a.m. with the fire of the two guns deployed on the flanks.[6]

The British had formed their assault line with the 1st Grenadiers (left) and the 66th (right) on either side of the guns, with Jacob's Rifles and the Sappers as reserve behind the guns, and the cavalry behind the centre and the left flank. The British discovered a deep nullah on their right flank affording easy cover to the Afghan artillery and the movement of infantry. This made the 66th to move inclined to its right flank which began to create a gap with its centre. Soon, the Afghan artillery came into full action and hit the British line with unusual accuracy, breaking its momentum and the ability to press the attack. With the forward movement the gap between the guns and the 66th increased, and was filled with five companies of Jacob's Rifles and the Sappers for the protection of the guns. When the Afghan irregular cavalry moved to threaten British left flank, the remaining two companies of the Jacob's Rifles were moved up with two guns on the left of the 1st Grenadiers. Now the British forces had no reserve except for three companies of the infantry regiments left behind with the baggage, and two cavalry wings separated by distance and inclined towards the right flank. The 1st Grenadiers and the two companies of Jacob's Rifles, being under constant artillery fire had already suffered heavily and after midday came under direct attack of the Afghan cavalry from the left rear. The guns having exhausted their ammunition had been pulled back and the other five companies of Jacob's Rifles under pressure of Afghan artillery had also tended to fall towards the 66th. As the Afghan cavalry attempted to surround them, a slow retreat on both flanks had begun. The only hope lay in a successful cavalry charge, to allow the infantry to re-form its line, but the British cavalry was divided and scattered and it could not be concentrated. However a gallant charge by a squadron of 3rd Cavalry on the left flank, helped the companies of Jacob's Rifles and the 1st Grenadiers to extricate themselves from the attacking Afghans. By afternoon the entire brigade was in full retreat toward Mahmudabad and Khig, and it was only due to a determined stand by the 66th and the Sappers that the brigade escaped complete annihilation and the Afghan cavalry was discouraged from further pursuit. Fortunately the Afghan army preferred to stay and loot the abandoned baggage and the exhausted brigade managed to retreat during the night towards Arghandab River where contact was established with the forward outposts of the Kandahar garrison. By afternoon of 28 July remnants of Burrows' brigade started straggling into Kandahar and the news of the disaster at Maiwand became public.

Although the British brigade at Maiwand faced a much stronger Afghan army, the conduct of the British commander was wanting in professional skill and maturity (for its poor decisions, much blame is thrown over the political officer by British writers). Yet the regiments and troops, despite heavy odds fought gallantly and for that they suffered heavily. An eye witness thus records the action of the Jacob's Rifles: 'among the heroes of the battle were a number of young sepoys in the Jacob's Rifles who were led by a young and recently joined British subaltern. They had not eaten since the previous evening and had little water. They did not know the unit on their right. On their front, flank and rear were the hordes of hostile Afghans. There had been a comforting battery of British howitzers near them but they had packed up and moved elsewhere, seemingly to the safety of the rear. It was an ordeal indeed for these young men, many merely boys, witness to the horror around them, caught in an action of which they understood little except their own peril; yet with rare courage they stood firm and did their duty'.[7] The losses of the Jacob's Rifles on the fields of Maiwand were three British and three Indian officers and 210 rank and file killed and one British and four Indian officers and 25 rank and file wounded (about 45 percent of the Battalion strength). At Maiwand, the total British casualties were; 20 British and 14 Indian officers and 908 rank and file killed and 8 British and 9 Indian officers and 151 rank and file wounded, (about 45 percent, most of it from infantry regiments).[8] Afghan losses were estimated between 1500 – 2500. With Maiwand the third phase of the war came to an end.

By 5 August, the Afghan army invested Kandahar, but the delay provided enough time to the British forces under Primrose to prepare its defences. Ayub's inability to storm the city began to wear off the Afghan unity as their tribal differences grew, and the British began to launch strong sorties against the Afghan army. By 23 August the siege had practically ended.

Immediately on receiving the news of disaster at Maiwand, a 10,000 strong army was organized at Kabul under General Roberts. His march to Kandahar covering 320 miles 'to rescue a besieged

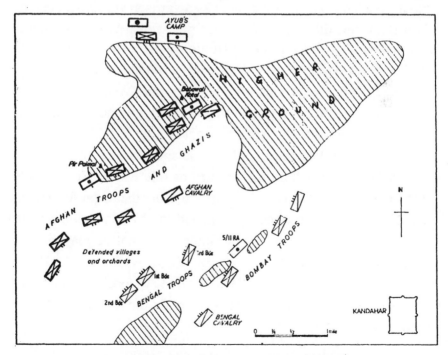

12. Battle of Kandahar - September 1880

garrison and avenge a humiliating defeat was stirring and caught the popular fancy' and has since been much dramatized. Simultaneously another smaller column which included the 27th L.I. Regiment (1st Belooch Battalion) marched from Quetta. On the way Roberts also picked up the garrison at Kalat-e-Ghilzai which now formed part of the British relief column. On 31 August, Roberts reached Kandahar and decided to attack the Afghan army, now much depleted due to dissensions and desertions. The situation had dramatically reversed and in the sharp and short encounter, Ayub Khan was defeated and his army dispersed. 29th Beloochis participated in the battle as part of Roberts' force, forming second line of the 2nd Brigade and was the first to enter Ayub Khan's camp. The column from Quetta reached Kandahar on 7 September after fighting its way through the Khojak against the disruptive attacks of the tribesmen. British government did not insist on having a Resident in Kabul and Roberts' force and British garrison at Kabul quickly withdrew into India. Kandahar was however held by a garrison which included the 27th Beloochis till April 1881, when the Afghan War was declared terminated. All the Belooch battalions, the 24th Regiment, the affiliated 3rd Scinde Horse, and Jacob's Mountain Battery earned the battle honours of Afghanistan 1878-79 and Kandahar 1880.[9]

The British for the second time were taught the lesson, which the Russians would also learn a hundred year later, that although Afghans can be defeated in open battle and cities can be captured, alien armies cannot hold the country or rule its turbulent people. British fear of the Russians continued to haunt them, but fortunately the anticipated war between Russia and the British in India never materialized and thus the Great Game could not be played to its sanguinary conclusion.

After the Second Afghan War, the three Belooch battalions and the 24th Regiment were stationed together for the first time in Sindh-Balochistan.

Chapter Ten

Smaller Campaigns and the Reorganizations 1881 - 1913

Campaign in Egypt[1]

Since the opening of the Suez Canal in 1869, European interest in Egypt had continuously increased. The Khedive of Egypt had been lent large sums of money by the European financiers at rewarding interest rates with Egypt as the pledge. From 1879, Egypt's financial situation steadily deteriorated inducing the Europeans led by Britain to have a stronger voice in the Egyptian affairs to protect their financial interests. This state of tutelage under a foreign power provoked a military coup in early 1882 under Colonel Arabi Pasha, who seized power in Cairo and formed a national government. It obviously posed a threat to the Suez Canal and the pockets of the holders of Egyptian bonds. In July 1882, the British decided to send a military expedition to Egypt under Sir Garnet Wolseley. It was a large expedition comprising of nearly 25,000 soldiers which included a strong contingent from the Indian army. The 29th Regiment (2nd Belooch Battalion) with an additional company from the 27th Beloochis, formed part of this contingent.

As the first step, Alexandria was heavily bombarded by the British fleet, its forts were reduced, and the city was occupied by a brigade. The main direction of attack was from the Canal at Ismailia to Cairo, by way of Tel-el-Kebir, where the main Egyptian army was known to be concentrated. The brigade at Alexandria was to feign an advance south and eastward to deceive the Egyptians of the assembly of the main British army and the direction of its attack. During the last week of August, the British and the Indian contingents of the main army began landing at Ismailia and Suez,

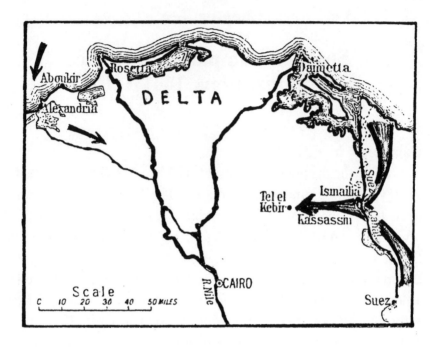

13. Egypt 1882

respectively, and immediately set out to establish their forward base at Kassassin, 21 miles southwest of Ismailia.

29th Beloochis having left three companies at Suez for the protection of the port moved to Ismailia on 30 August. Here the company from 27th Beloochis was detached to perform escort duties between Ismailia and Kassassin, which was twice attacked by the Egyptians, the last on 9 September, while the company was in the camp and had to defend itself. Both the Egyptian attacks were repulsed, forcing them to fall back to their entrenchment at Tel-el-Kebir. Assembly of the British army was completed, and on 12 September it moved out to attack the Egyptians. 29th Beloochis were deployed in the second line on the left flank of the attack, in support of the 20th Punjabis. With the first grey of morning on 13 September, the Egyptians were swept out of their defences, surprised, and overwhelmed. Tel-el-Kabir was a strong position and defended by 12,000 Egyptians, but surprisingly, the position was taken without much resistance and with very low casualties. Thirty six hours later the British cavalry appearing out of the desert before the gates of Cairo, received surrender of the city and its garrison. By the end of the month, all hostilities had ceased and the Khedive's authority restored under the aegis of British military presence. Egypt became a British protectorate.

29th Beloochis returned to Karachi in October and were later awarded the battle honour of 'Tel-el-Kebir'.

Campaign in Burma[2]

Despite previous wars and chastisement, the relations with the Burmese Court of Ava had continuously deteriorated since accession of King Theebaw in 1878. His flirtation with the French and mistreatment of a British trading company, finally led to another war with Burma in November 1885.

The plan of campaign was bold and simple. An army of 12,000 soldiers assembled at Rangoon, were to move on 55 river crafts up the Irrawaddy to Mandalay, the Ava capital, and depose the King. No great resistance was expected from the Burmese army and climatically the period chosen was highly suitable. On 15 November the British army commenced its 300 miles river journey and in less than a fortnight entered Mandalay. Theebaw surrendered and the British forces fanned out to secure the frontier as far in the north as possible. On 1 January 1886, Upper Burma was annexed and became part of British India.

Now the real trouble began. The Burmese army having been disbanded and dispersed, joined the lawless elements of the country and forming small bands, started a guerilla war,[3] spreading terror and anarchy in the entire length and breadth of Upper Burma. With varying intensity, this irregular war continued for nearly five years and at one time became so formidable and menacing that it drew

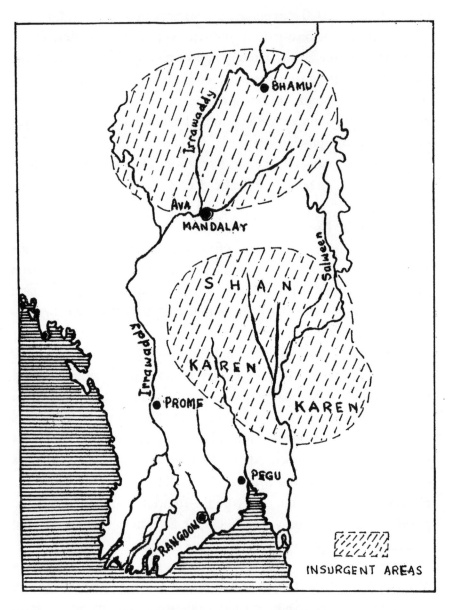

14. Campaign in Burma 1885-89

nearly 30,000 regular troops from India, including the 27th Beloochis. Thick and swampy jungles and impenetrable mountains, with unhealthy climate and non-existent communications, made British reaction slow, exhausting, and difficult. The British army followed the time honoured tactical formula of controlling the disturbed country with small fortified posts and reacting against hostile activities through strong flying columns. They managed to secure a large operational base between the river corridor north of Mandalay and laid a railway line along the Irrawaddy to ease logistic support problems. But despite fighting hundreds of small skirmishes, there was no qualitative improvement in the situation and the casualties from disease and sickness had mounted to twenty percent.

In September 1886, an Upper Burma Field Force was created from the massive reinforcements received from India, which swelled the strength of the British forces to nearly 30,000 troops. 27th Regiment (1st Belooch Battalion) reached Rangoon on 14 October under Colonel Sartorius and at once proceeded to Upper Burma, to join the Field Force which was to launch a major campaign during the winter. Based on increased number of fortified posts and larger and stronger number of flying columns and with improved communications, it was hoped to crush the insurgency. What followed was an intense warfare of moving columns and small posts in one of the most difficult terrains, where alertness, ability, and initiative at the lower levels of command became crucial to the success of the enterprise. 27th Beloochis' performance was rated as outstanding, particularly, the two companies which were converted as 'Mounted Infantry' under Lieutenant Micheal Tighe (Later General Sir), who greatly distinguished himself during the campaign. As it progressed, strong columns of foot and mounted infantry spread out into the great river basin and relentlessly hunted and pursued the insurgent bands and forced them to disperse or move out into deeper north. Even so, complete success was not in sight till the end of 1888 and even thereafter local outbreaks of disorder continued at intervals throughout the next two years, culminating in the Wuntho uprising in the spring of 1891, necessitating yet another major operation.

In 1888 the 27th Beloochis were moved into the Shan State and again split into small detachments, covering a large mountainous area of the state and remained involved in small operations against the dispersed insurgents. In December 1888, they joined the Karen Expeditionary Force with two companies converted as mobile infantry and participated in a major operation in the Red Karen country. It was here, during this operation that on Ist January 1889, the Battalion's medical officer Surgeon J. Crimmin, won the Victoria Cross (VC); the first for the Indian Medical Service.[4] During this campaign, the Battalion was issued with the new 'khaki' field uniform and wore it for the first time. On the termination of the operation the Battalion was moved to Rangoon from where it returned to Karachi in April 1889.

It was one of the hardest tenures of overseas field service, in which the 27th Beloochis, beside the VC for the Medical Service, earned three Distinguished Service Orders (DSOs) for its officers and five Orders of Merit (IOMs) for the men. The commanding officer was awarded the honour of CB and made a brevet Colonel. The Battalion was given the nickname of 'Capital Campaigners' and awarded the battle honour 'Burma 1885-87' for the campaign. The Battalion casualties during the campaign were one British officer, three Indian officers and eighty four other ranks killed and five British officers, four Indian officers and 153 other ranks wounded or sick.

First Reorganization

The process of army reorganization initiated after the Great Rebellion had continued. After the Second Afghan War it was again accelerated. As an economy measure, some reduction was ordered in the army, but the three Belooch battalions were not affected. However the 3rd Scinde Horse (Belooch Horse) disbanded in 1880, was re-raised in 1885 as the 7th Bombay Cavalry (later 37th Lancers) with old connections allowed to be maintained. In 1881, the 30th Regiment (Jacob's Rifles) was redesignated as the 3rd Belooch Battalion and officially joined the brotherhood of the Balochis.

During the seventies, under the Cardwell Scheme, an effort had been made to link two infantry battalions as pairs in brigade districts, with the intention of keeping one battalion at home for supplying manpower reinforcement to the other, when on field service or overseas duties. Besides heart burning in the regiments, the scheme tended to deprive the army of half of its infantry force. In 1886, a new system of linking the battalions in groups of two to five was introduced on the basis of common regional affiliations, experiences, history, and traditions.[5] Each group was allotted a regimental centre or depot and all recruits enlisted in one battalion were made liable to serve in any other battalion of that group. One battalion of the group was always to be located at the centre, with the object of providing reinforcements during emergency. This was the real beginning of the 'Regimental system', though still loose in its conception, it provided the foundation for the growth and expansion of the Regiments in the Indian army.

As a result, the three Belooch battalions were linked together as a group and took the first step towards the formation of the Baloch Regiment. The three Beloochi battalions had already become a brotherhood; now under the newly introduced system, their close association would get deeper and stronger, and the envisaged interaction would promote mutual dependence and understanding to foster the Regimental espirit de corps. Karachi was made the centre for the group and the 30th (Jacob's) Beloochis were the first battalion to assume the role of the centre. Although a good beginning had been made, the system still suffered from some defects; for example, the battalion at the centre was depleted of strength in providing reinforcements to the other battalions of the group and could not be available for emergency or war. Although it undertook enlistment of recruits to create a reinforcement pool, the demands from other battalions, particularly during war, took much of its own manpower. Yet the linked battalions were quite independent of each other and invariably left a self contained 'depot' behind, when proceeding on active service or overseas to function as recruitment and training centre for the battalion and to maintain records.[6]

On the same basis the 24th and 26th Regiments were linked together. In 1891 these were converted into frontier battalions as the 24th and the 26th Baluchistan Regiments, permanently relocated in Baluchistan at Quetta and Loralai and affiliated with the Baluch Group.[7] Quetta became its centre and with its conversion and relocation the recruitment of its manpower was also to be drawn from the traditional recruitment areas of the Baluchis.

In 1886 the enlistment for five years with option of extension was substituted for unlimited service, and a beginning was made in the formation of regimental reserves.[8] The recruitment in the Baluch battalions was generally from Sindh-Balochistan and its neighbourhood. With the introduction of enlistment under 'General Mixture', a large number of Punjabis and Pathans including some Sikhs were allowed to join the battalions. In 1885 it was again restricted to Baloch and Pathans from Zhob or trans-frontier, though this restriction due to decreasing number of Balochi recruits was not strictly followed. In 1882 the 'Class Company' composition finally replaced the 'General Mixture' and the class structure of the companies was laid down which extended the recruitment to Derajat, trans-frontier, the Punjabi Mussalmans and the Pathans, eliminating the Sikhs. But, unfortunately, this also almost severed the original connection of the battalions with Sindh and Balochistan.

In 1891 the Staff Corps of the Presidencies were amalgamated and became the Indian Staff Corps, followed by the abolition of the posts of the C-in-C of Madras and Bombay armies and withdrawal of their control from the Presidency's governments. In 1896 Presidency armies were abolished and all regiments and battalions became part of one army: the Indian Army. The old armies were reorganized into four army commands, each with a number of military districts, but their structure was not disturbed and the evolving system of the regiments was preserved. The union of the armies and the final adoption of 'Class Company' system profoundly affected the outlook of the regiments.

In 1900 the infantry throughout India was assimilated on the model of the British and the Continental armies, by converting eight company battalions into four 'double company' battalions. For the purpose of internal administration, the eight companies remained organized as before, under their respective Indian officers, but on parade and in the field the double companies were commanded by a British officer. Each infantry battalion was accordingly authorized four British officers for the double companies (instead of two previously for the wings) and four British company officers.[9] Although the strength of the companies and battalions continuously varied, at the turn of the century the strength of a company was 96 and that of the battalion 815 all ranks.

During this period, the 27th Baluchis provided armed escort to Robert Sandeman, Viceroy's Agent in Balochistan and under his guidance, Lieutenant W.M. Southy compiled the first provincial gazetteer of Baluchistan. In 1884, the 29th Baluchis received the new Colours at Hyderabad. The Duke of Connaught was appointed its 'Honourary Colonel' and the Battalion was officially permitted to use 'Duke of Connaught's Own' as part of its designation. In December 1889, the 24th Regiment received its new Colours and in 1895, after conversion, it was also permitted to use, 'Duchess of

Connaught's Own' as part of its new designation. In 1902 the 27th Baluchis represented the Regiment at the great Delhi Darbar.[10]

During this period there is the first mention of regimental bands in the records; the 24th and the 26th Baluchistan Regiments on conversion were authorized pipe bands in 1891 and wore distinctive uniform.[11] A passing reference in the records of the Abyssinian Campaign of 1868 indicates that 'a band of about sixteen buglers and drummers had accompanied the 27th Beloochis'. Buglers and drummers were found in every regiment, but their formation into a band was not a common practice. It came into existence in certain regiments on individual whims and fancies of the commanding officers and as it was the trend, was soon followed by others. Maxwell has recorded his regrets when the regimental 'brass band' of the 3/10th Baluch Regiment (old 27th/127 Baluchis) was abolished in 1929, after being in existence since 1877. Similarly 5/10th lost its brass band in 1935.[12] It seems all old Balochi battalions had brass bands which were replaced with pipe bands during 1930-40.

Enigma of the Frontier[13]

Since the annexation of Sindh and the Punjab, the British had come into direct contact with the territory called the 'tribal belt', extending from the snow covered Chitral in the north to the burning hills and deserts of Nushki in the south, a stretch of 700 miles of mountainous region of peculiar barrenness and severities, with depth varying between ten to a hundred miles. It became one of the most turbulent frontiers of the British empire, and where the tide of British conquests in India was finally stemmed. It was inhabited by the fierce and marauding hill tribes, who resisted all encroachments into their territories, and where every man was armed and a law unto himself. The harshness of their rocky valleys and wind swept

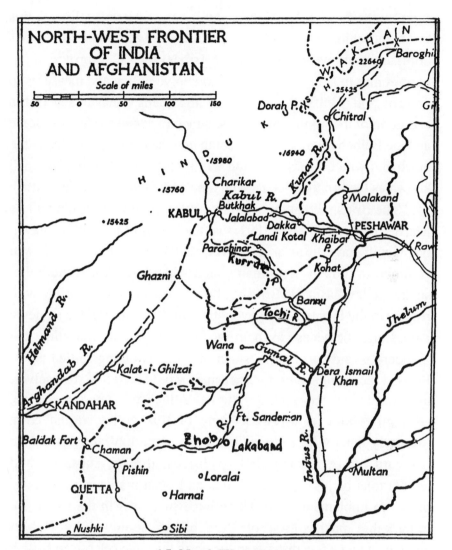

15. North West Frontier

mountains providing the barest necessities of life (perhaps only
wife, rifle and a horse), frequently brought them out on plundering
raids into settled areas to seek the rest. They followed their own
tribal codes, often at war with each other, were stubborn, vicious
and possessed of remarkable endurance. The British concern over
the status of Afghanistan and the control of numerous passes
through the territory; the traditional routes of invasions, led them to

fight two wars with the Afghans, by forcing their entry through this turbulent region. It not only involved them in an almost continuous confrontation with the frontier tribes but also provided an opportunity to study them closely to evolve policy and measures to control and pacify them. One of the many measures was the evolution of the frontier regiments, which included the Scinde Horse and the Baloch Regiment in the south and the Corps of Guides in the north and which over the period will include those colourful units, known as the Frontier Scouts with their romantic lore and legends.

The British did not inherit any settled boundaries and it will be nearly fifty years later, in 1891, that the Durand Line will be drawn, but it will have little or no effect on the tribal belt, which will continue to remain 'a no man's land where only knife and bullet spoke the law'. But the British followed a well-defined policy with respect to the Frontier. They would retain the control of the strategic passes and the access to them by force and would not allow the plundering raids of the tribesmen into the adjoining settled areas. Beyond these objectives, the tribesmen would be left to themselves, in whose affairs however, no external influence or interference (i.e, Afghan) would be allowed. Tone of this policy varied from 'masterly inactivity' to 'conciliatory intervention' and aggressive 'forward policy'; using flattery, bribes, threats, subsidies and temptations of jobs, punitive raids and even major campaigns as means to implement them. There were successes in the south, the remarkable pacification of Balochistan achieved by Robert Sandeman and a few districts in the north by some celebrated British political officers, like Robert Warburton. These, however did not prevent the endemic eruption of tribal violence inducing British military intervention.

From the time of the First Afghan War till Independence, a period of over a hundred years is strewn with the tales of encounters, raids, ambushes, small and big expeditions, and wars; all bearing the peculiar mark of the Frontier, exhausting and fearful, demanding vigilance and endurance. Between 1839 and 1913, a period of increased confrontation, more than seventy four punitive expeditions were undertaken by forces ranging from a few hundred to many thousands. On six occasions, roughly a division strength took the field and in the biggest of all, the Tirah campaign of 1897, practically an army corps was employed. From these emerged the romantic stories and the lore of the Frontier which for decades captivated the imagination of young British officers. Yet, behind the romance lay the cold truth of daring, determination, and endurance of these frontier battalions and regiments,[14] who time and again proved their mettle against the often clever, bold, and equally skillful tribesmen. 'The little wars of the Frontier, became the staple fare of the Indian army'[15] and set a pattern for the training and operational outlook, which to its detriment would stifle the initial performance of the Indian army during the Great War. The 'Khud race'[16] an innovation of the British frontier experiences, survived till our own time. The concept of frontier operations and numerous customs and traditions formed during the period continue to be followed by our Frontier Corps even today.

Frontier Operations[17]

In 1889 the 29th Baluchis were moved to Loralai. Next year trouble began with tribal restlessness and soon converted into dispersed acts of lawlessness. Khiddarzai clan of the Shirani tribe objected to the British exploration of Zhob Valley and instigated the other clans into hostility and armed defiance. 29th Baluchis were deployed in the disturbed areas for protection of communications and installations.

Meanwhile a Zhob Field Force was constituted at Quetta, which included the 30th (Jacob's) Baluchis from Hyderabad. The aim was to move in strength, through the disturbed areas, demonstrating power and resolve to get the submission of the hostile tribe, and if resisted, to take appropriate punitive action. The Force marched from Quetta in September 1880; 30th Baluchis joining the column at Khanai on 7 October. Apozai was reached on 2 November, from where the Force split in two columns and entered the Shirani territory, in conjunction with a third column, advancing from the Derajat. Submission of the tribe was obtained on 9 November, without major opposition.

A highlight of the termination was the scaling of Takht-e-Sulaiman summit by fifty men each of the 29th Baluchis and the Yorkshire Light Infantry, with full field equipment under the respective commanding officers, in full view of the tribal jirga and large tribal spectators.

In 1896 eastern Sindh witnessed a serious outbreak of lawlessness by the Hurs. A wing of the 27th Baluchis was drawn from Hyderabad to quell the disorder. Coincidentally, after fifty years in 1942, it will again be a Baloch battalion; the 6th, which will be called to crush a more formidable uprising of the Hurs in Sindh.[18]

During 1897, a British survey party from Kalat was attacked and looted by Baloch outlaws from Nausherwani tribe in Mekran area, in which quite a few members of the team were killed. It caused a stir in the area. A strong contingent consisting of 250 men of 30th (Jacob's) Baluchis with detachments of mountain artillery (two guns), cavalry and sappers under Colonel Mayne, was landed at Pasni on 13 January 1898. The forts of the Baloch Sardars were attacked and demolished and the outlaws were hunted and killed. Within one month the disorder was overcome. For this action Colonel Mayne was awarded CBE, a British and an Indian officer of the 30th Baluchis earned DSO and IOM, respectively.

During 1901 the coastal areas of Mekran, near the Persian border again came under a spell of serious disorder, perpetrated by the lawless elements particularly the notorious gun-runners, who were joined and supported by a few Baloch Sardars of the area. On 30 November 1901, two companies of the 27th Baluchis under Major Tighe were moved by steamer to Gwadar, from where they marched to Turbat. Here, they were joined by a detachment of the Battalion, already in the area on escort duties. On 16 December, this small force was ordered to attack and capture the fort of Nodiz, reportedly the stronghold of the hostile Baloch sardars. With the help of two guns sent from Quetta under escort of 26th Baluchistan Regiment with a detachment of engineers, a breach was affected but the first assault of the Baluchis was checked by intense fire from the defenders and the bravado of the Baloch swordsmen. The guns were brought up for point blank fire and the second Baluchi assault was carried through under strong resistance and the fort captured. With the surrender of the hostile sardars, order was restored in the area, though these companies remained employed for most part of the next year against the gun-runners in support of the 24th Baluchistan Regiment. For action at Nodiz Fort, Major Tighe was promoted brevet Lieutenant Colonel, the engineer officer and one from 26th Baluchistan Regiment were awarded the DSOs and a Havildar from the Battalion earned the IOM.

Campaigns in East Africa[19]

The British East African Protectorate was administered from the off-shore Island of Zanzibar, through a Counsel General and a British Prime Minister to the Sultan, but the main trade activities were centred at the mainland ports of Mombasa and Malindi. The growing trade with inland territories and increasing number of trade caravans, soon brought plundering raids from predatory tribes and lawless elements. Trade activities were seriously disrupted and the law and order situation deteriorated to warrant a military action.

In April 1895, the 24th Baluchistan Regiment,[20] under Colonel A.A. Pearson (later General Sir), was moved to Mombasa to restore the situation, which was much similar to Burma, except that the lawless elements here were not well armed or trained. Immediately on arrival, the Regiment deployed itself in strong company posts along the main trade routes; Kismayu on to Juba, on the border of

156

Italian Somaliland, inland from Malindi, Shimba, along the river forming border with the German Protectorate and along the coast, thirty miles south of Mombasa. Flying columns and escorts were provided from these bases, which built up the requisite pressure and the lawless activities gradually began to decline and eventually shifted further north to the Italian border. In a little over one year, the situation had been fully restored and the Regiment returned to Quetta in July 1896. The Regiment was granted the battle honour of 'British East Africa 1896'.

Soon there was another call to the Baluchis for service in East Africa. The territory known as Uganda, had been for sometime in a state of serious strife and internal wars. Despite severe actions taken by the British Chartered Company of East Africa, fighting continued with Kabbarega, the ex King of Unyoro and the Arab princes of Nazrumi family. In 1895, the territorial control of Uganda was

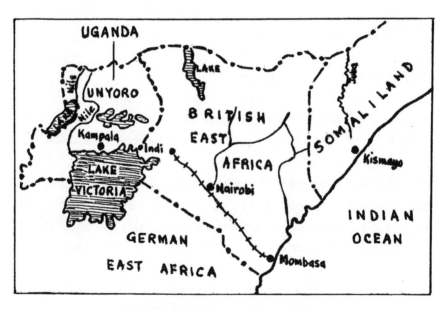

16. British East Africa 1895-97

assumed by the Crown and the old company forces, which consisted of Sudanese and Nubian soldiers and a strong component from India were taken over by the British officers. In 1897, the Sudanese soldiers mutinied and having killed their British officers, joined the ex chiefs of Uganda: Mwanga and Kabbarega. Soon a Muslim tribe called Waganda rose in rebellion. The situation suddenly became serious.

27th Baluchis under Colonel W.A Broome were immediately despatched to East Africa and reached Mombasa on 12 December 1897. Leaving a company behind, the Battalion moved by rail to Indi, thence in company detachments by road to Kampala on Lake Victoria Nyanza, 561 miles from Indi. The first two companies reached there by 30 March 1898. As the Battalion continued to assemble, the companies were pushed into Unyoro district to reinforce the hard pressed troops of the East African Protectorate and regain its control. Again a war of defended posts and small columns began in which the Battalion had done so well in Burma and the experience came in handy. The rebels were well armed and the Sudanese were particularly good fighters. The climatic conditions and the dense tropical forests were worse than Burma and the conduct of operations became extremely arduous and painstaking. During the one year of operations, the Battalion remained continuously involved in serious combat of varying intensity and despite extreme severities of terrain and climate and often with scant and uncertain food supplies, almost single handedly, succeeded in crushing the disorder and dispersing the rebels.

On 26 April Captain Southy with two companies, intercepted a large assembly of the rebels on the east bank of the Nile and in a fierce encounter, having inflicted heavy casualties, dispersed them. Southy lost one British officer and thirty seven men. In another action on the west bank of the Nile, at Jeruba, Major Price on 4 August in a surprise night raid captured a rebel stronghold. A small column while searching a dense forest near village Kitaba, was attacked by a strong rebel force on 10 October. In the initial surprise, the British officer was seriously wounded and the column suffered thirteen casualties. The Indian Officer (VCO) took over the charge and fighting a skillful rearguard action retired to a defended post at Kisalize, 21 miles distant, while carrying the wounded officer, with thirty men; half of them with some wound or injury. The rebels followed the column upto Kisalize. The Indian officer won the IOM.

At this time, large concentrations of rebels were reported and the Battalion was assembled to attack these rebel forces and disperse them. This entailed marching by numerous detachments and companies from distances as far as 150 miles in five days for the intended operations. The Battalion advanced in three strong columns; two moving in an enveloping fashion against the major rebel concentrations along the two rivers and the third directed against another rebel assembly in the north. On 27 October, the rebels were surprised at Kidweri on the Kapa River. Another column had attacked and dispersed the rebels on 25 October in Kinjanguti district across Maanja River. On 21 December the two columns joined to secure the cleared areas. The third column cleared and dispersed the rebels in Budonga Forest in the north. By 21st January 1899, Unyoro district had been cleared of the rebels and brought under control. The Battalion posts were soon relieved by the newly raised Uganda Rifles and the Battalion concentrated at Kampala, from where it moved by rail to Mombasa by 20 April. From here, two companies were detached as immediate reinforcements and sailed to Kismayu and took part in the ongoing campaign against the Ogaden Somali rebels in Jubaland and went through ten months of hard fighting with the troublesome rebels. The Battalion returned to Karachi in May 1899. During the campaign in Uganda, the Battalion suffered twenty percent casualties, most of them due to exhaustion and tropical sicknesses. Major Price earned a DSO and eighteen IOMs were awarded to the rank and file. The

Battalion was granted the battle honour of 'British East Africa – 1897-99'.

Expedition to China[21]

In the summer of 1900, rise of a Chinese sect known as the Boxers, soon became a highly militant, national and anti-foreign movement, with violent eruptions in Shantung and Chihli provinces. In mid-June, the capital was seized and all foreign legations were invested, resulting in urgent appeals for relief. An attempt by a composite naval brigade from Tientsin proved premature, as the port city itself was threatened and had to be supported from Taku. A strong contingent from India under General Gaslee was immediately

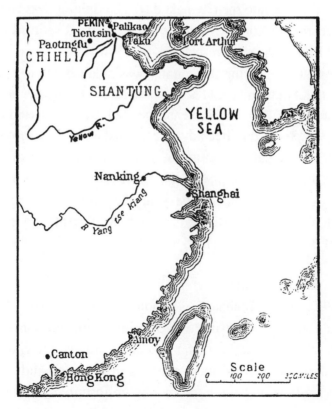

17. China – 1900

ordered to China, which included the 26th Baluchistan Regiment[22] and the 30th (Jacob's) Baluchis and arrived at Shanghai by mid-July.

An international Allied army (comprising eight nations) was constituted for rescue of the besieged Europeans in Peking. While retaining a strong component for the protection of Shanghai, which included the 30th (Jacob's) Baluchis, the British contingent for the Allied army was 4000 strong (including the 26th Baluchistan Regiment). The 20,000 strong Allied army was assembled at Tientsin by end July and the ill-organized and ill-equipped rebel army was defeated just outside the city and again a few days later at a place called Yang Tsun. Here the British troops took leading part in the fighting. By 14 August the Allies had reached the walls of Peking and broke into the city next day. The fighting was heavy and continued for 36 hours, when the rebels were dispersed and the besieged Europeans were rescued.

The task of clearing the country was delayed due to bickering amongst the Allies and could not be undertaken before the next year. The Boxer Rebellion, in the meantime, had died down and a much delayed two pronged Allied advance against a reported assembly of rebels at a place called Paotingfu, 80 miles south west of Peking, found no rebels in the area and the effort proved merely a military promenade. By the end of the year the Indian contingent had returned home. The 26th Baluchistan Regiment and the 30th (Jacob's) Baluchis were granted the battle honour of 'China 1900'.

Second Reorganization

In 1902, Lord Kitchner was appointed Commander-in-Chief of the Indian army and despite his ongoing confrontation with the Viceroy, initiated a series of far reaching military reforms. These became the harbinger of many changes in the army and led to its complete unification, and, in promoting uniformity in its standards. All cavalry and infantry regiments were formed into an overall

Indian army cavalry and infantry lines, and, re-numbered, with Bengal units taking the precedence, thus breaking all links with the old Presidency's armies. Old Bombay Army units were allotted new numbers beginning with hundred and the Baluchis became, 127th, 129th and 130th Baluchis and the other affiliated units were redesignated as 124th and 126th Baluchistan Infantry.[23] The Indian Staff Corps was abolished and henceforth all officers were to be gazetted direct to the regiments, which revived the old practice and strengthened the bonds with the regiments. The regimental groups formed by linking the battalions were allowed to grow and the 'class company' composition was maintained with clear softness for one class battalions.

These reforms were followed with the reorganization of the army's command structure, with greater operational orientation. All Indian army units were grouped into tactical formations of ten divisions, each comprising of two or three brigades, and the additional four independent brigades. As a standard, each brigade consisted of three cavalry or infantry regiments. These formations were grouped into four army commands; the divisions numbered from one to nine; the 10th was called the Burma Division. These were permanently located in major cities, which also became part of their designations; i.e, the first being located at Peshawar was designated as Ist (Peshawar) Division.[24] A significant departure from the old practice, affected by the restructuring of the army, was periodic rotation of the units for service throughout India. Though one battalion from each regimental group was allowed at the designated station of its centre, the others were rotated in different formations. This provided the infantry battalions greater interaction with other regiments and helped to develop regimental outlook and spirit in the new competitive environment. The 127th and the 129th Baluchis were the first battalions to be moved out of their home province to new stations; Poona and Ferozepur in 1909 and 1912, respectively.

In Kitchner's perception, the threat to India continued from Russia and therefore the strategic orientation of the reorganization and relocation of the army was to defend the north west frontier and internal security was relegated to a low priority. The whole army was trained accordingly and a tenure on the Frontier for every infantry battalion became almost mandatory. In his drive to modernize the Indian army, he equipped it with newly introduced 303 magazine rifles and new mountain guns and built arsenals for reserve stocks. Fear and discrimination in equipping the Indian regiments with better weapons had gradually eroded, but the financial constraints still affected its quality. Some improvements (provision of air-cooled Lewis guns) were made during the Great War. But it will be only after 1942, that a major refitting of the Indian army would be undertaken for campaigns in Burma, North Africa and Italy; at par with the regular British regiments. Century long fixation towards the north west Frontier would eventually die out only on the eve of Independence.

Kitchner's new policies brought about distinct improvements. He promoted sports, provided better rations, and encouraged regimental clubs and institutions. He laid down rigorous training standards and instituted an army efficiency competition.[25] A Staff College was founded in 1905 at Deolali, which shifted to Quetta next year. In the stupendous competition set by Kitchner in 1906, to test the efficiency of the units of the Indian army, the 130th (Jacob's) Baluchis topped the list and won the honour for the Regiment.[26] On the Viceroy's initiative an Imperial Cadet Corps was instituted with schools at Meerut and Dehra Dun to train Indian officers for the Indian components of the army and the state forces. The intakes were restricted to sons of princes and nobles only. The idea was not popular amongst the British officers, and those who graduated were not well treated in the regiment and could not rise above the level of company and squadron. However small, this was the first step towards the 'Indianization' of the army,[27] against the rumblings of discontent, which had begun with the formation of Indian National Congress and open protestations of its leaders on British discrimination. Nonetheless, for all the major changes and improvements brought about in the army, it was still found highly inadequate to fight a World War.

During this period, the 127th Baluchis were visited by the Prince and the Princess of Wales in March 1906 at Chaman, presented with the new Colours by the Princess and permitted to use 'Princess of Wales' Own' as part of its designation (later changed to 'Queen Mary's Own'). In 1909 the Battalion proceeded to Somaliland, in anticipation of an outbreak of war, which did not materialize and the Battalion sailed back the next year. The 129th Baluchis spent a three years overseas tenure at Hong Kong from 1905 to 1908 and on return were located at Karachi. In May 1911, the 124th Baluchistan Infantry proceeded to China and stayed in garrison at Tientsin and returned in May 1914. During the tenure, it participated in an international field exercise in November 1913. In 1912, the 126th Baluchistan Infantry also moved for an overseas tenure to Shanghai and returned on the outbreak of the Great War. In 1906, the 130th (Jacob's) Baluchis were given the 'Plume' as a mark of distinction by its Colonel-in-Chief, the Prince of Wales and again in 1910, it was awarded the 'Imperial Cipher' as an honourary distinction. In 1911, the Battalion represented the Regiment at the Coronation of King George V and received Coronation Medals. During this period, the class composition of all three Balochi battalions underwent change with the introduction of Mahsud Pathans as a result of which all Balochi and Brahui soldiers were transferred to the two battalions of Baluchistan Infantry, whose composition was also modified to include two companies of Sikhs.

An Overview

The fifty years following the Rebellion of 1857, were a period of great consolidation. The British were firmly established in India and perceived no threat from within. Their main military concern remained fixed towards the north west Frontier with the scare of Russian invasion, despite demarcation of the Durand Line and the signing of Anglo-Russian Border Treaty in 1907. It was also evident that the military focus was not on India but on the expanding empire. There had been much material and institutional improvements in India: road and railway networks had further expanded; development of canals and irrigation system in the Punjab and Sindh had revolutionized the agricultural growth and local economy; administration was fair, firm and efficient; and new universities and colleges had opened up windows on western education and knowledge. The British had gradually replaced the old fluid and fluctuating system of despotic rule with new political and administrative institutions predicated on precise boundaries, laws and regulations, under a highly authoritarian white bureaucracy which operated with the willing support of the feudals and local intermediaries. There was peace and order throughout and the people had reconciled to the cold realities. The British Raj in India seemed to have acquired a halo of permanency. Indeed, 'India became the jewel for which the whole empire existed and equally the pillar by which it was sustained'.[28]

British confidence sprang from the quality of its military power. The Indian army had reorganized itself, fought successful campaigns from China to Abyssinia and East Africa, gained valuable experience and emerged as the decisive instrument of British policy in Asia and Africa. Its prowess seemed unmatchable. The British officers often wondered about the mystique of the Indian army they had created and most took its credit upon themselves and their superior leadership. Self-deluding cliches of their indispensibility as leaders and patrons of the regiments were commonly believed. There was indeed some truth in it, but more it reflected the psyche of the ruling elite. However, most readily agreed to the superior fighting quality of the Indian soldiers and their regiments which deserved superior leadership by their own right.

There was nothing new in the British idea of 'martial races of India'. It had always existed in the social milieu of India. Militarism had always been integral to Muslim identity and the stratification of Hindu caste system made Kashtriyas; the Jats and the Rajputs, born warriors and fighting, a business of faith. The British had long discovered the martial passion of these classes and the sterling virtues of courage and a peculiar sense of honour, it bred. They knew that 'unlike English soldier who did not come to the ranks because it was the most honourable career; the Indian soldier did. To him, the military service was always a matter of honour and prestige'.[29] Surely economic pressures and other tangible benefits of military service were strong inducements, but his courage and sacrifice in face of acute dangers and death far away from his home and hearth could not be reckoned in cash. General O' Moore Creagh, the British C-in-C (1909-14) had observed that the Indian soldier generally enlisted for a career in a regiment which he considered honourable, but for his deep sense of pride, he should not be taken for granted. He was not a common hireling who sold his services to the highest bidder; on the contrary as long as his employers were honourable and befitting and kept faith with him, he kept faith with them with sincerity and devotion.[30] The British had learnt their lessons and also found the answer.

The source of military vitality of the Indian army was its regiments, whose structural and professional growth had now stabilized, and matured through numerous reorganizations and varied and rich experiences of many wars and campaigns. Regiments provided a collective identity to soldiers in whose common experience of toil and hardship and of glories and achievements, they saw the reflection of their martial sentiments and virtues. This generated the pride in the regiments as a symbol of their own honour which permeated into every facet of their professional activities: sports, professional competitions, training exercises, even personal conduct and discipline. Their regiment was, or ought to be, the best; they were no less and it had to be kept that way; a moral imperative, as John Jacob had perceived; created and borne by a strong collective consciousness of professional obligations and responsibilities. This regimental spirit or 'espirit de corps' was shared by the officers with the same emotional intensity; best illustrated by John Masters in his book, 'Bugles and a Tiger'; 'Fourth (4th Royal Gurkha Rifles), an honourable number. I soon came to believe with a passion worthy of a religion that there was no other regiment on earth like it'. Indeed, generations of British officers took soldiering with a religious fervour and to most, their regiments were nothing less than living temples.[31] The Indian regiments attracted more dedicated and professional officers than the British regiments in Britain as Lord Roberts lamented, 'all the best men at Sandhurst strive to get into the Indian army'.[32] The Indian regiment had become quite an institution.[33]

But it will be wrong to conclude that the soldiers only identified themselves with the regiments. Their religious beliefs and social and cultural perceptions also asserted in different contexts, often more powerfully than the regimental spirit and deeply influenced their psyche and responses. These were well understood and fully respected. The British were careful in not exposing the Indian troops to situations which could strain their religious sensitivities or create doubts in the wisdom and generosity of white men.

It was also a period which saw the growth and blossoming of peculiar military culture within the army, which for decades shaped and influenced the attitude and conduct of its officers. In the highly competitive environment, ancestry and wealth gradually lost their advantages and professional excellence became the decisive factor. It created a military order with its own code of professional morality and behaviour. A deep concern for honour was the common virtue which was shared by both; the officers and the men. It demanded courage, professional devotion, and exactitude in the performance of duty. But from the officers it demanded much more, and the entire process of grooming and education was geared to creating a class of officers distinguished by its peculiar ethos of excellence as professional leaders and gentlemen. An officer was expected to be bold and plucky but also to be truthful, fair, and modest. Within the confined social environment the officers lived in the small world of their regiments and the messes, with its colourful parades, field exercises, 'shikars' in the wild jungles, noisy polo tournaments and pompous dinners surrounded by dazzling silver and trophies. But for all its apparent display of opulent arrogance, the life of an officer in the regiment was hard and demanding. His pay was never enough and except for those who survived the oppressive Indian climate and the never ending wars of the empire and rose to higher ranks, mostly ended up in debts. Yet, it provided constant opportunities to test oneself, and earn distinction and glory. It was not uncommon to find every second officer in the regiment to be a veteran of many campaigns and decorated for valour. Many of them rose to higher ranks through sheer hard work.

The new military culture bred and groomed many customs and traditions in the service, some creation of individual eccentricities, but most conditioned by military values, which dominated the attitude and conduct of officers and men alike, both in professional and personal spheres. Devotion and loyalty to the regiment was supreme and officers took special pride in belonging to the regiment. Anything, that brought the regiment to disrepute was shameful and dishonourable. Regimental service was preferred and frequently higher promotion outside the regiment, declined. Officers did not sacrifice their regimental position by taking more lucrative and prestigious civil or staff appointments and those away, invariably joined their regiments, particularly for campaigns or in wartime to share the glory with the regiment. Many officers left large endowments for the welfare of the regiment such as Beville Welfare Endowment Fund in the 127th Baluchis (3/10th Baluch Regiment). Long uninterrupted service in the regiment was common. Already the second and third generations of old Balochi officers had begun to join the regiment, as was the tradition amongst the men. Relative peace and stability had converted the officer's messes into living institutions where young officers were groomed under the stern guidance of the old. It was here that they learnt the code of military behaviour: dignity, uprightness and exactitude. Some of the rigours and virtues of these traditions and customs were diluted by the unusual expansion of the army during the two great wars and the subsequent transformation into national armies of the two independent states. But their puritanical influences continued to regulate the regimental lives for a long time and their distant and nostalgic reflections still survive in the old regiments.

The breed of this peculiar culture is best described by Younghusband in his story of a regimental officer from India on leave in England, asking for a first class ticket with the army concession to which officers were entitled. 'How do I know you are an officer?' enquired the clerk. 'Look' was the prompt reply as the officer lowered his stern face to the level of the booking window. There was no more argument.[34] Such stories abound in many books and memoirs by officers and other writers giving a graphic description of life in the Regiments: its glamour as well as its hardships.

Soldier's life in the regiment was simple, austere, and orderly. Senior officers often rebuked the British soldiers for their shabbiness and quoted Indian regiments as examples for emulation. As the regiments got better organized, bulk of their manpower was required to live in the lines as against the old practice of living with the families under own 'bandobust'. Although the practice varied in the three armies, Bombay Army followed the British system. A certain proportion of the families were accepted 'on the strength' of the regiment and space for married quarters was provided for them within the regimental lines. Leave was usually granted on generous scale; two months every year and six months furlough every third year. Soldiers from far flung areas were granted additional leave to cover the long journey. Religious and social occasions were celebrated with great fanfare as regimental festivals and were fully participated by the officers. Ordinary working day usually started at the first light and finished before noon, followed by sports activities late in the evening. It would be amusing to note that a hundred years ago, soldiers followed almost the same routine, even the same bullshit – 'Chuna and gairi'. But one and all acknowledged the soldier's cheerfulness and high morale and his sense of duty and devotion to his regiment. The organization and discipline of the regiments were so good that the officers often boasted of comparing it with and even beating the 'old Prussians'. Indian soldier's 'nobility' and 'simplicity' were highly prized and the British officers 'idealized' the 'chivalry' of their men. Soldiers were good in musketry and shooting and their physical fitness was remarkable; their ability for long marches, incredible. Balochi soldiers had acquired a reputation as 'prodigious marchers' and 'swift as the cavalry'. The campaign records are full of astonishing feats of physical endurance and determination, for which the Balochis earned ungrudging admiration from all.

It is impossible to accommodate all events that fill the regimental diaries, reflecting its peculiar life and activities during campaigns and between the campaigns at peace locations, which for its exclusive sentimental value must continue to remain a part of the battalion history. Two such histories, those of the 124th Baluchistan Infantry (later 1/10th and now the 6th Baloch Regiment) and the 127th Baluchis (later 3/10th and now the 10th Baloch Regiment), have come down to us and must be mentioned for their prolific details.

Professionally, this was the best period, free of inner conflicts and external pressures. Soldiering combined the rigours of campaigns with the romance of distant lands. Successes reinforced the soldier's pride in his regiment and fortified his faith in the army. The service conditions, economic benefits, and the official patronage were good and inviting. Loyalty and hardwork were well rewarded with land grants, an old Mughul practice. The soldiers considered themselves different if not superior to other Indians and the ego worked to enhance their devotion and performance. The charisma never worked better.

But it was also a period of subtle changes in the broader Indian context. Western education, knowledge and ideas were breaking the traditional barriers and inhibitions. The wave of British liberalism was encouraging and friendly to its colonial subjects and critical of the Imperial system. There was a hesitant and uneven shift in policy towards a still distant goal of self rule.[35] The new educated Indians were fast expanding into a vocal and politically conscious middle class. There was a growing feeling of frustration which regarded the British rule as oppressive and stifling. The efficient and highly organized British civil administration was actually teaching the Indians, how to govern their own country, which they were unjustly denied. The desire for greater Indian participation in their own affairs was becoming stronger and the dispersed and divided socio-political sentiments were beginning to acquire coherence and a national form. By the turn of the century, sporadic acts of political violence had been on the increase, giving a radical character to the simmering Indian upsurge. But it was not wide spread and had hardly touched the countryside. As yet, there was no serious internal threat to the British rule in India; certainly not from its soldiers. As the dark clouds of war gathered over Europe, the soft rumblings of discontent were becoming louder in India, an ominous warning of the approaching new watershed – the end of Pax Britannica.

24th Baluchistan Regiment, c. 1897

26th (Baluchistan) Regiment of Bombay Infantry.

LANCE NAICK.	LANCE-NAICK.	JEMADAR.
(Afghán : Durráni).	(Pathán : Wazíri).	(Baloch : Brahúi).
REVIEW ORDER.	MARCHING ORDER.	REVIEW ORDER.

26th Baluchistan Regiment, c.1897

129th Baluchis in France – October 1914
Hollebeke-Wytchacte Sector

129th Baluchis in France – October 1914
Hollebeke Sector

127th Baluchis, Pune 1909, Mobilization for Somaliland

A Baluch Battalion on Parade, Quetta 1911

124th Baluchistan Infantry in Isfahan (Persia),
September 1916

Sepoy Khudadad Khan, V.C.

Baluch War Memorial, Karachi, c. 1920

Regimental Band, 10th Battalion (Centre) Karachi - 1936

Mess Ante Room, 130th Baluchis (Jacob's)
Hyderabad Sindh, c. 1905

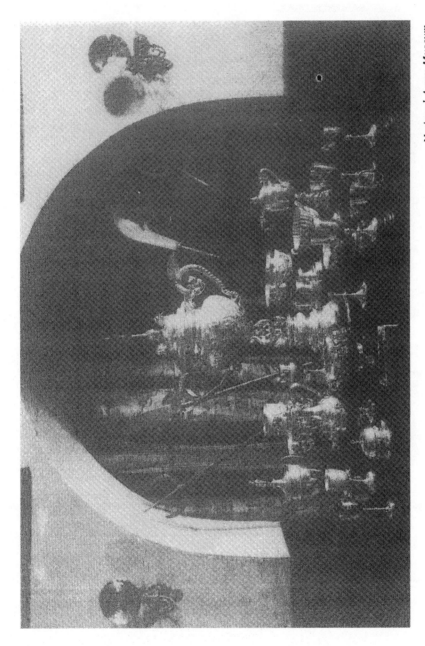

Mess Silver, 130th Baluchis, c.1905

Chapter Eleven

The Great War 1914-18

In July 1914 Europe plunged into a war which for its scale and dimension in violence and attrition spread over four years and three continents would become 'the Great War' in the annals of warfare. As the war began, the powerful right wing of the German armies swept through Belgium and on 20 August appeared before Namur, the last landmark before crossing the Meuse into France. Meanwhile in a hasty response the French had launched an offensive against the German centre into Upper Alsace, which with some initial setback had succeeded in reaching the Rhine. Suddenly the gravity of the German threat along the Meuse forced the French to reel back from the Rhine, into their defensive fortifications. Another French offensive through the Ardennes to threaten German flank in Belgium was stalled. The French now faced a difficult situation. Four British divisions landed in France and moved upto Mons on 22 August for an advance into Belgium but were held back due to the recommencement of the German offensive.

The Germans made their first strategic blunder by prematurely wheeling inward to envelop the French left flank and in the process exposed their own right flank. The French quickly regrouped a strong reserve north of Paris and on 6 September struck at the exposed German flank and in the fiercely contested Battle of the Marne, succeeded in stemming the German tide. It proved decisive. The exhausted German forces reeled back to close the gaps and regroup. Although they were able to reknit their right wing, and stand firmly on the line of Aisne, the strategic dimension of the offensive had been lost. The war from here onward stagnated into tactical movements, encounters, and battles, in successive attempts by both sides to envelop or overlap in a setting of preponderant defensive power. Yet the Germans had won a decisive victory against the Russians at Tannenberg in Eastern Prussia and still retained sizeable strategic reserves which could combine for a fresh offensive in the West. The German threat continued to loom large and the critical situation before the Marne had not fully stablized. Additional troops were urgently needed by the Allies to bolster the long thinly held defences, and reinforce their reserves.

The first major Allied contribution to the war in Europe came from the Indian army, the largest in the empire. Immediately on the outbreak of war, the Indian army was mobilized and an Indian Corps consisting of two infantry and one cavalry divisions (each division of two infantry or cavalry and one artillery brigades) were despatched to France. Simultaneously, and anticipating Turkey's entry into the war, it was followed with a mixed force to East Africa, a brigade (later increased to a division) to the Persian Gulf and six infantry and a cavalry brigades to Egypt. By the end of 1914, 23,500 British and 78,000 Indian troops from the Indian army had joined the war and eschewing their previous false notions, the British, for the first time used the Indian soldiers against their white enemies for the defence of their own people and homeland. As the war will prolong and spread and its attrition and wastages will multiply, the number of Indian troops employed in the war will cross the mark of a million by the end of 1918.

During this period, the Indian soldiers would fight in France and Belgium, in Gallipoli and Salonika, in Egypt, Palestine and Mesopotamia, in Persia and East Africa[1]. In addition to these major theatres of war, they would be required to assist in many minor scenes of fighting from West Africa to North China and furnish many garrisons. It would be a challenging experience in many dimensions, for an army trained to fight on its northwest Frontier and still suffering from organizational deficiencies. It will subject them to extreme severities of terrain and weather, pressures from better organized, armed and trained opponents, the terrible effects of new weapons of war and the emotional strains caused by inner conflicts. That they acquitted themselves of these challenges so honourably, is a tribute to their professional devotion, fighting spirit and remarkable endurance.

During this war all the battalions of the Baloch Regiment were employed and fought on all major fronts and theatres of war, four of them on more than one front. To meet the pressing demands of war five new Baloch battalions were raised and there was much inter-mingling of officers and men amongst the battalions, at times at the cost of battalions' own efficiency. Their exploits and achievements during the Great War on its various fronts are detailed in the following narrative.

Western Front - The Flanders

The 129th Baluchis (later the 4/10th Baluch Regiment), under the command of Lieut Colonel W.M. Southy, as part of the Ferozepur Brigade of the 3rd Lahore Division, moved with the first Indian Corps and on 26 September 1914 landed at Marseilles; the first Indian regiment to step in Europe[2]. Before sailing from Karachi the Battalion had received a double company from the 127th Baluchis (later the 3/10th Baluch Regiment) to make up its manpower deficiencies. At Marseilles, amid scenes of much excitement and cheers of 'les Indians', the Battalion received new rifles and ammunition and moved on by train to Orleans on 30 September. Here it stayed in camp till 17 October, was issued with woollen garments and as the northerly wind blew, had its first feel of the European cold weather. On 17 October, the Battalion with the Division, entrained for the front and after 39 hours of journey, entered the war zone at Arques. Here the troops saw for the first time aeroplanes flying overhead. On 19 October, as the troops were detraining at Arques, the Germans launched their attack on Ypres, which with short pauses continued till 22 November.

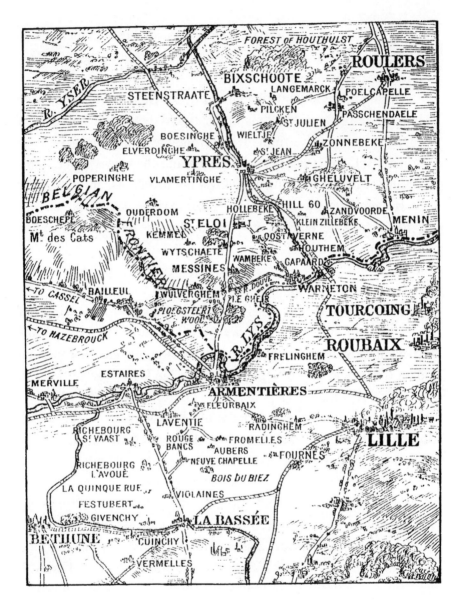

18. Flanders and France 1914-15

'This was one of the most momentous and critical periods of the war. The British army was fighting for its very existence and was close to breaking point from exhaustion and heavy losses'.[3] Arrival of the Lahore Division was the first major reinforcement and the most welcomed. At Arques, the Ferozepur Brigade was placed under the 2nd Cavalry Division, while the remaining alongwith the Meerut Division moved on to reinforce the 2nd Corps at Estaires. The same evening the Battalion joined the 3rd Cavalry Brigade and next morning took over a portion of the 'firing line' (forward defended locality or FDL) which extended irregularly, for approximately 2500 yards from Hollebeke in a southerly direction. The trenches were hasty improvisations and had not been well developed. The Cavalry Corps was holding an important stretch of country in southern Belgium, north of River Lys, which included a part of the ridge, whose capture would force evacuation of Ypres. The 2nd Cavalry Division was holding a 4 miles stretch between canal bridge east of Hollebeke and Messines, with 3rd Brigade on its left. Although heavy fighting was going on further in the north, the Cavalry Division was continuously kept engaged by artillery shelling and on the very first day the Battalion lost five men.

On 25 October all elements except the machine gun detachments of the cavalry support in the Battalion area were withdrawn for an offensive operation. Next day, with little warning, the Battalion was ordered to attack German positions west of the Canal. The Battalion attacked with three companies from the direction of Poplar Grove (see sketch map of Hollebeke Sector), keeping the fourth in reserve behind Jardines Farm and placing the machine gun section forward of the Farm for flanking support. The area was flat and open and the

176

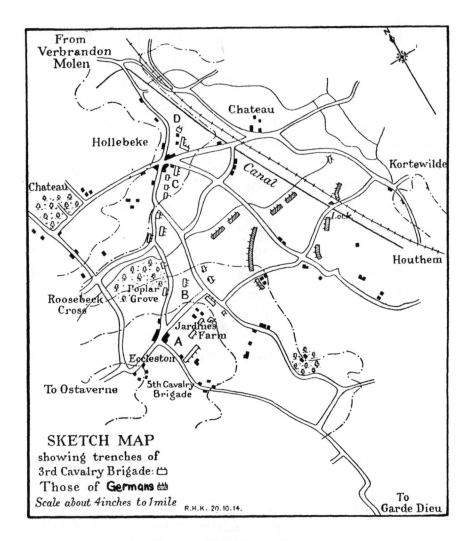

19. Flanders (Hollebeke Sector)

distance to be covered was over 600 yards. At 3 p.m. the attack commenced, and when the first line was within 300 yards, it came under heavy German machine gun fire and was pinned down. Fire fight continued for an hour, without any progress, during which period a company commander was mortally wounded, six men were killed and 40 wounded. The attack was called off and the Battalion was pulled back to the Chateau. As darkness fell, two jawans of the company sneaked in to search within 200 yards of the German lines and brought back the wounded company commander, who later died[4] in the hospital. Both the jawans were awarded the Indian Order of Merit (IOM) for courage and devotion.

On 29 October, with two companies in the old firing lines, the Battalion was moved to Klein Zillebeke to form part of the Ist Army Corps reserve[5]. Next morning, the whole weight of a German offensive came against the Cavalry Corps with the heaviest artillery fire concentrated against the 3rd Cavalry Brigade. When the German attack started, the two companies in the firing lines were being relieved by their double companies. In the ensuing confusion, one company managed to withdraw but the other was pinned down on the way and was temporarily lost. As the German pressure increased, the withdrawing company first held the Chateau, then fell back in the evening to a rear line of defence. During this period, the two companies holding the old firing lines, bore the brunt of the German attack and were subjected to very heavy artillery shelling, but despite suffering severely (company commanders of both the companies were mortally wounded) the companies stuck to their positions. In the afternoon the companies were ordered to fall back, but they were almost surrounded by the Germans and very few men could rejoin the Headquarters that night. Lieutenant Lewis, who took over one of the companies after his company commander was severely wounded, returned with the survivors of his company to describe[6] the day's infernal battle and the courage and tenacity with which the Balochis endured the German onslaught. In particular the courageous conduct of the two machine gun crews under Captain Dill,[7] who kept their guns in action throughout the day and when one was knocked out, the other kept on engaging the Germans, till they were swept over by the German assault and every man was either shot or bayoneted at his post. Of these devoted men only one survived. Sepoy Khudadad Khan, who being severely wounded was left for dead and managed to crawl back during the night and joined the Battalion. For his heroic conduct he was awarded the Victoria Cross; the first Indian to be so honoured.[8] The other members of his crew: Havildar Ghulam Mohammad and Sepoys Lal Sher, Said Ahmad, Kassib and Afsar Khan, were also awarded with the Indian Distinguished Service Medal (IDSM) and the IOMs.

Next day there was a rush of French troops arriving in the area as reinforcement, which caused some confusion of identification at night, as a result of which, a German platoon sneaked into a farm occupied by a company, and captured it without opposition. The regimental doctor with wounded officers and men inside the farm were made prisoners, while the company outside fell back to block all routes of escape. Within hours, another company was brought in and the farm assaulted and recaptured. Ten Germans were killed and 27 taken prisoner.

On 4 November the Battalion handed over its lines to the French cavalry and marched to rejoin its parent Ferozepur Brigade at Estaires. Thus ended the first ten days of the war, in which the 129th Baluchis sustained themselves honourably against a major German offensive, now remembered as the First Battle of Ypres. Their casualties were three British officers killed and three wounded, three Indian Officers killed and two wounded, and 93 men killed and missing (mostly dead) and 149 wounded.

The Battalion stayed with the Brigade for the remaining period in France, except for a short spell in April 1915, when it was again moved to Ypres. Ferozepur Brigade was part of the weak and exhausted Indian Corps, which was holding an eight miles stretch from north of Givenchy, passing through Festubert, west of Neuve Chapelle, past Mauquissart to Rouges Blanc and had seen some heavy fighting since their arrival and also suffered considerable casualties. On 5 November the Battalion was moved into the firing lines at Rue de Bacquerot, an area described as 'a dismal dead plain, dotted with farmhouses, occasional clumps of trees and flooded shell holes forming pools of water'. The water table was high, which made digging deep trenches very difficult and living in them even worse. As the winter set in with the depressing spells of cold and wet weather, 'the discomfort was quite undescribable'. The troops endured the hardships with quiet fortitude and fell into the routine of duties in the trenches and relief for a few days in the billets. The Battalion strength despite drafts from India had come down to ten British and fourteen Indian officers and 520 other ranks. The Germans continued to harass them through artillery shelling.

On 23 November the Germans attacked all along the front. Against the Indian Corps, the main attack came upon its centre and made considerable gains. An imminent breakthrough was prevented by a quick redeployment of two companies by the Commanding Officer of the 129th Baluchis to plug the gap in depth. Their determined stand not only checked the German penetration but also saved their own brigade positions getting outflanked.

During the night of 16 December the Battalion marched to Givenchy where it was to participate in local operations as an auxiliary to a French offensive. Ferozepur Brigade was assigned the task of capturing two German 'saps' (trenches for approaching or undermining the enemy positions) opposite the 15th Sikh's position in the neighbourhood of Givenchy and then extending it to the German main trenches. The 129th Baluchis were to lead the assault at dawn and secure the space of 25 and 35 yards before daybreak. Due to limited space in the forward trenches, the assault was made on two platoon frontage in two lines against each sap. Leading assault lines captured the saphead and the major portion of the sap but by the time the second line moved up, the day had broken and these men trapped in shallow trenches came under heavy cross-fire of the German guns. The Balochis withstood 12 hours of savage attempts to dislodge them but eventually due to heavy casualties were gradually pushed back to the saphead. As darkness fell, the exhausted men were relieved by the 15th Sikh. The Battalion suffered 53 men killed and 65 wounded for 40 yards of German sap.[9]

On 20 December the Germans launched a major offensive against the Indian Corps. Their heaviest bombardment and the main thrust of infantry attacks were directed against Givenchy and La Quinque Rue. On the 129th Baluchis' front the earlier lost 'parallel' was recaptured. The unit on its left flank was assaulted and driven back and soon its right flank came under heavy shelling and was overwhelmed. With both flanks gone, the centre gave way and the Battalion under mounting pressure began to fall back. The German shelling was so intense that most of the rear trench system had been practically destroyed which resulted in a lot of confusion. While isolated fighting continued by trapped pockets, the falling back companies and stragglers were rallied by Colonel Southy, to the count of 5 British and 4 Indian officers and 210 men. Under the German onslaught the entire division had been pushed back to area Pont Fixe, where the Battalion now marched to occupy yet another firing line.

By the end of the year Battalion had lost 13 British and 16 Indian officers and 800 men; practically the whole battalion that set out from India only three months ago.[10] Such was the attrition of trench warfare during the Great War. Due to the slaughter and exhaustion suffered, the Battalion was pulled back for rest and recovery, until early March 1915. During this period the Battalion received fresh drafts from the 124th Baluchistan Infantry (later the 1/10th Baluch Regiment) and the 127th Baluchis and by 1 March its strength was made up to 10 British and 21 Indian officers and 704 other ranks.

With the coming of the spring the Indian Corps had planned an offensive in the area of Neuve Chapelle. On 10 March the offensive was launched by the Meerut Division but it soon ran into snags. The Ferozepur Brigade was moved up and during the next 48 hours continuously marched and counter marched around Neuve Chapelle without getting any definite operational mission, till the offensive petered out. On 13 March the Battalion again moved into trenches at Rue du Bois and fell into rotational routine of trench duty and rest. On 24 April the Brigade was suddenly ordered to Ypres.

The Second Battle of Ypres began on 22 April and ended on 25 May 1915 and was as critical as the first one, and strained the British forces as much. During early April, the British line had been further extended, resulting in thinning out of Ypres front which was now defended by two French divisions. On 22 April the Germans' first gas attack was directed against these divisions, who were taken by complete surprise and the front collapsed. The Germans moved through the gaps and reached the road Poelcappelle-St Julien and were checked by the Canadians in depth positions. The gap created was very large and the approach to Ypres was wide open. The British made a series of desperate and expensive counter attacks, but most failed to make any gain.

The Ferozepur Brigade reached Ypres on 26 April after a long and exhausting journey and was deployed in the La Brique - St Jean area. The same night, a major offensive was being launched on a large frontage, which involved the British, the French, and the Indian Corps. The mission assigned to the British Division, under whose command the Ferozepur Brigade had come, was 'to attack northwards and assault the enemy's trenches wherever met with, the first objective being a frontage from Oblong Farm to the Longemarck road'. The attack was to be led by two brigades (Ferozepur left and Jullundur rigth) each on 500 yards frontage. The

129th Baluchis formed the right forward assaulting line of the Brigade. A little after midnight, the brigades advanced through 1700 yards of open and rolling ground to reach their assault line. As they closed up, the leading lines came under heavy German artillery fire, 'which practically knocked out whole platoon at a time and casualties fell literally in heaps'. The assault began to falter when the Germans used gas against the French on the Brigade's left flank and soon after, the attack collapsed. All the brigades fell back in confusion and disarray, leaving behind a ground strewn with the dead and wounded. Yet the Battalion had advanced steadfastly and had reached within 200 yards of German positions when the French collapsed on its flank and it was also affected by the gas attack. For individual bravery during the assault two British officers were awarded DSO and MC and two sepoys earned the IOM and IDSM. During the next two nights, the reserve brigade was put 'through the same dance of death and failed' with equal slaughter. On 1 May, the Brigade marched back to join the Indian Corps at Doulieu. At Ypres, the Battalion casualties were 275 all ranks, killed, wounded and missing and the Battalion strength had come down to six British and eight Indian officers and 233 other ranks.

The Second Battle of Ypres was the last major action in France in which the 129th Baluchis participated. During the next six months the Battalion rotated between duties on the firing lines and billets, at times forming brigade and divisional reserve. The manpower deficiencies were steadily made up through drafts from sister battalions, mainly the 124th Regiment and the 127th Baluchis. The period was generally uneventful except for the daring exploit of Naik Ayub Khan, who went into the German lines under cover of defection and brought back valuable information for which he was awarded the IOM.[11] On 4 November the relief of the Indian Divisions in France began and by 10 December the Battalion reached Marseilles from where it moved by ship to Egypt and thence to Aden. On 1 January 1916, the Battalion sailed to Mombasa in East

Africa.

During its nearly fifteen months stay in France the Battalion had served in the War Zone for most of the period with long spells in the firing lines and fought in four major battles. During this period 41 British and 48 Indian officers and 2547 other ranks served in the Battalion; of these, 8 British officers were killed and 15 wounded, 8 Indian officers were killed and 25 wounded and 265 other ranks were killed and 944 wounded. Of the original battalion, only 4 British and 5 Indian officers and a handful of men had survived.[12] The men of 129th Baluchis were generally remembered for their high morale and cheerfulness, in particular 'the Mahsuds who specially seemed to revel in the fighting'.[13] The Battalion earned nine battle honours and 46 gallantary awards (including the first VC to an Indian), and the unique distinction of being the only Indian Battalion to bear the honour of both the battles of Ypres on its Colour.[14] It carries the 'Menin Gate' silver trophy as a highly esteemed memento of its great sacrifices at Ypres, where even today its name is inscribed on the Great War Momorial. Sepoy (later Subedar) Khudadad Khan's name went into the annals of history and is adorned on the walls of National Army Museum at London.

War in Mesopotamia

The Persian Gulf had always been important for the British interests in the region, particularly for the security of India and for which her involvement here had almost been continuous over the last two centuries. In the World War, with Turkey's entry on the German side imminent, the Gulf assumed greater importance. Besides, the German influence in Mesopotamia was considered highly threatening to British interests, particularly the Persian oil which could only be obtained by approaching through Turkish waters. In October 1914, the 16th Brigade from Poona Division was despatched to the Gulf to provide support to Mohammerah and Abadan. When Turkey joined the War, this Brigade captured the

Turkish port of Fao on 6 November and followed it with the capture of Turkish positions at Saihan and Sahil, which led to the evacuation of Basra and its occupation by the British troops on 22 November. During this period the entire Poona Division had landed in Mesopotamia. An advance to, and capture of, Kurna, 50 miles up the river, brought the whole Basra District along with its oilfields under British control. Apparently, the Turks had been surprised.

The ease and brilliance of these successes offered much temptation for an advance to Baghdad but was wisely contained and even Kurna was vacated to form a more compact defence of Basra. The expected Turkish offensive came on 12 April 1915 against the British position at Shaiba, but narrowly missed the victory.[15] Another Indian Division, the 12th, had landed in Mesopotamia and following an aggressive policy, it was decided to advance to Amara, another 90 miles up the Tigris from Kurna. On 31 May Kurna was recaptured. On 25 July after three weeks of heavy fighting, Nasariyeh on the Euphrates was captured. As the successful advance continued, the objective was set for Kut-el-Amara, nearly 150 miles further up the Tigris from Amara. On 19 September, strong Turkish positions of Sunniyat and Es Sinn were contacted and on 27-28 September, in a fierce battle, these positions were overrun and Kut-el-Amara fell to the British. Now the fatal infatuation led the British columns to the strongly fortified Turkish position of Ctesiphon, south of Baghdad, which was attacked on 22 November. By morning of 24 November, the first line of defence was secured and all Turkish counter attacks repulsed. But the British had suffered 4500 casualties; nearly fifty percent of its infantry and could not press the attack any further. The British retreat began next morning, with the Turkish cavalry on their heels. Kut-el-Amara was reached after two days of hard marching by the exhausted troops and as they waited for recovery, all roads were closed and the British garrison

20. Mesopotamia 1915 - 18

was besieged. The British made desperate efforts to relieve Kut-el-Amara and the 7th Division returning from France was landed and pushed up, but failed to dislodge the Turks. On 29 April 1916 the British garrison surrendered.

After the fall of Kut-el-Amara, the British reorganized their forces in Mesopotamia, with reinforcements and new raisings, forming a new army of two corps, under General Maude, to renew the offensive against the Turks. It was under these new arrangements that the 124th Baluchistan Infantry, which had so valuably supported the 129th Baluchis in France with drafts from its own strength,[16] was ordered for field service in Mesopotamia and was destined to raise two additional battalions and fight on three fronts. It had been initially mobilized for the relief of Kut-el-Amara but due to disaffection amongst Muslim troops for fighting against the Turks, was diverted to Bushire, where it landed on 8 March 1916. In April, the Right Wing of the Regiment (later formed into 3rd/124th) was moved to Bunder Abbas for intended operations in Persia. In August, the Left Wing was raised to a battalion strength and redesignated as the 2nd/124th Baluchistan Infantry[17] (later the 10/10th Baluch Regiment), was moved to Basra in October from where it proceeded up the Tigris to join the 8th Brigade of the Lahore Division at Es Sinn, south of Kut-el-Amara.

During the first week of January 1917, the British decided to resume their offensive in Mesopotamia by attacking the Turkish defences at Khudiara on 9 January. Khudiara was a formidable defensive system anchored on the Tigris and formed part of the main forward defence line for Kut-el-Amara. It was organized in three lines of entrenchment dotted with strong points and well defended. The British forward brigades, the 8th and the 9th, were deployed barely 300-500 yards from the Turkish line and had with great labour and secrecy dug T-shaped trenches, ahead of their defences, for the movement and formation of assault line along the head of the T. The attack was to be launched by these two brigades initially on a narrow frontage of 200 yards supported with 72 guns and was to be expanded after securing the first line of Turkish defences. Simultaneously, diversionary attacks were planned in other sectors.

At 8.45 a.m. on 9 January, after intense artillery bombardment, 8th Brigade launched its attack, with three battalions drawn in three lines in depth; 2nd/124th forming the third line. The Turks were taken by surprise and their first line of defence was overrun and captured. Within hours the Turks counter attacked, which checked further progress of the British attack. In the afternoon, the Turks again counter attacked and were repulsed with the support of the 2nd/124th, which had been moved up and had taken over the captured area. The next day, attack was resumed which continued for two days. The Turks fought stubbornly and every British gain was fiercely counter attacked, inflicting heavy casualties and losses. The progress was slow and the attack was almost stalled. The assaulting brigades had suffered severely; the casualties of 2nd/124th alone stood at five British officers and 262 rank and file. Fresh troops were brought up and 2nd/124th was relieved and pulled back to Imam Ali Mansur in the rear.

With fresh regrouping and new reinforcements, the British recommenced their offensive in February and with great persistence, despite heavy casualties, pressed their attacks and succeeded in capturing the main Turkish defences at Sunniyat on 22 February. Simultaneously, the Khudiara Bend was cleared, outflanking Kut-el-Amara, which fell to the British on 25 February. The Turkish army fell back on Baghdad.

As the British resumed their advance on Baghdad, the 2nd/124th moved up on 20 March, to rejoin its Brigade at Baquba on a parallel axis further to the north east. Here two brigades had been formed into a force called Keary's Column, which had been tasked to follow up the retreating Turks from Kut-el-Amara. on 23 March the Column marched to Shariban, where contact was established with the Turkish defences in the Jabel Hamrin ranges, across the Haruniya and Ruz canals, where the leading 8th Brigade went into temporary defence. The Turkish forces facing the Column, belonged to the best Turkish divisions, which had fought at Gallipoli and were holding strong defensive positions with natural advantages. On 25 March the 9th Brigade was ordered to make an outflanking movement on the Turkish left, but it actually got involved in heavy fighting with the Turkish left flank and was subjected to artillery shelling and frequent counter attacks, which forced the leading battalions to fall back. During this engagement, the 2nd/124th was brought up to support the attack as the 9th Brigade reserve and actually assisted in the extrication of the leading battalions, initially by providing a fire base and later as the rearguard. In the process, it came under severe Turkish pressure and suffered heavy casualties with three Indian officers and 123 men killed and wounded. On 1 April, the Column again resumed its advance into Jabel Hamrin, but the Turks had withdrawn across River Diala. A little further to the north, the Column made junction with the Cossacks of the Russian army, operating from the north at Kizil Robat.

Meanwhile, Baghdad had fallen to the march of the main British army and the fighting extended to the north and north west around Samarra and Istabulat. During early April, the 8th Brigade was moved to Baghdad, from where on 14 April, it marched north to join Cobbe's Column, operating against the Turkish 8th Corps. The Brigade remained in reserve, with the 2nd/124th deployed for the protection of line of communication and did not participate in the capture of Samarra and Istabulat. By the end of April, the British army had secured most of Mesopotamia between the Euphrates and the Tigris, through hard fighting and settled down to a relatively peaceful period to pass the summer. During this period, the 126th Baluchistan Infantry (later the 2/10th Baluch regiment) had landed at Basra as reinforcement.[18] This Regiment on return from China in July 1914, had been despatched to Aden for its defence, where it stayed from 1914-17 and participated in an operation in Muscat against hostile Arabs. For a short period it was moved to Egypt as reserve. It had provided valuable drafts from its strength to 2nd/124th to make up their battle casualties. However the Regiment could not participate in active operations and remained a part of the army reserve in Mesopotamia.

On 23 October a strong Turkish force was reported advancing on the Tigris right bank towards Huwaislat. The 8th Brigade moved the same day from Istabulat and joined the 7th Division at Samarra. The Turkish position at Huwaislat was attacked the next morning with two brigades, 2nd/124th forming part of the attacking column, but the Turks had hastily withdrawn during the night. The Brigade returned to Istabulat.

The Turks had retired to a position at Daur, 16 miles north of Samarra. Cobbe's force resumed its advance and on 1 November the Turkish position at Daur was captured without much opposition. The Turkish forces had withdrawn to their stronger position at Tekrit, 11 miles further to the north. Tekrit was a walled town, located on a bluff on the right bank of the Tigris. The Turkish defences were laid a mile south of the town in a loop, anchored on the Tigris, in three lines with well sited strong points. A corps operation was planned involving the Meerut and the Cavalry divisions and the 8th Brigade from the 7th Lahore Division, for the capture of Tekrit. The attack was planned for 5 November, against Turkish left-centre, which was accessible by a night march to the infantry. The 8th Brigade was detailed to lead the attack.

The Brigade moved to its forward assembly area at Jibin Wadi and as darkness fell, the assaulting battalions, the 59th Rifles, the 47th Sikh and the 2nd/124th, commenced their advance through one mile of open area to the assault line. The Turkish artillery was already active. As the British guns opened up, the assault went in and with that the Turks also opened up with everything in hand. But the assault was carried through without a halt and the Battalion took

190

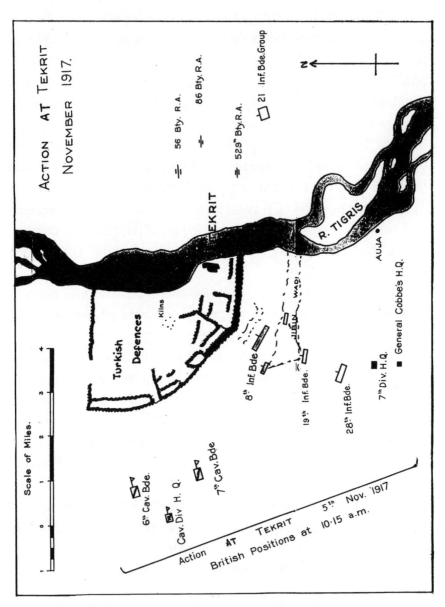

21. Mesopotamia - Action at Tekrit (November 1917)

the first two lines of trenches. There was close-in fighting and many casualties, and now the Battalion came under heavy enfilade fire from the machine guns sited in the strong points. Several attempts by follow-up companies to expand the lodgement failed under strong Turkish resistance. During the day, the Battalion was twice counter-attacked which were successfully repulsed. The casualties continued to mount and it was in the evening, when the strong point was reduced by a brigade attack that the Turkish pressure relented. Next day, the British resumed their attack on Tekrit, but bulk of the Turkish forces had already withdrawn and it fell to the British without further opposition. The Battalion had suffered heavily during the assault; three British officers killed and two wounded and 37 Indian ranks killed and 267 wounded. The Battalion earned, one DSO, four MCs (one to an Indian officer), five IOMs and five IDMS for gallantry in action[19] and was awarded three battle honours: Kut-el-Amara 1917, Baghdad, and Mesopotamia 1916-18.

This was the last major action of the Battalion in Mesopotamia. After spending a quiet winter in Samarra, the Battalion was moved to Basra in March 1918 and from there to Egypt, reaching Ismailia on the Suez Canal on 9 June, to participate in Allenby's drive through Palestine.

War in East Africa

Although the German East African territory did not pose a serious threat to British interests in the area, its small nuisance value was admitted and as a precautionary defensive measure, despatch of some troops was considered. But the hidden motive of aggrandizement was always present in these considerations, which eventually led to deeper British military involvement in a long and exhausting war in German East Africa, with heavy casualties and much suffering. In their calculations the British had completely underestimated the peculiar harshness of the terrain: dense bush country and the black cotton soil with hardly any communication and the oppressive climate; and the quality of German opposition, particularly its remarkable commander, Colonel Paul von Lettow - Vorbeck, who had arrived in the colony a little before the outbreak of war.

As a result of this decision, two Indian brigades; the 2nd and the 27th, were despatched to East Africa, with the main object of capturing Tanga, an important port in dangerous proximity of Zanzibar and Mombasa and the terminus of the German Northern Railway. Surprise as an essential factor was lost in the unnecessary delays in the landings, which helped in the reinforcement of German garrison at Tanga.Two battalions were landed on 3 November 1914, but soon after, their advance towards the town came under heavy fire and having lost several of their British officers, hastily fell back. Landings of other battalions continued and by 4th morning the entire British force had landed. In the afternoon, the British attacked in strength, but were repulsed with heavy casualties and pushed back to the beach. Next day the entire force was back on the ships. The British had lost six officers and 814 men; and one officer and six men, all wounded, were taken prisoner. A large quantity of weapons and ammunition fell into the Germans' hands. Thus the British campaign in East Africa commenced with this serious setback, which to the Germans 'called forth and revived the determination to resist all over the territory',[20] infused new confidence in the German askaris[21] and set the pattern for the war, for the next four years.

After the failure at Tanga, the British position through 1915 remained vulnerable, particularly its railway between Nairobi and Uganda, which passed close to the German border at a number of places. But the German effort in its disruption was not very effective except for the capture of Taveta salient east of Kilimanjaro which dominated the approach into German territory to Arusha and Kahe on the German railway. Amongst the earliest reinforcements from

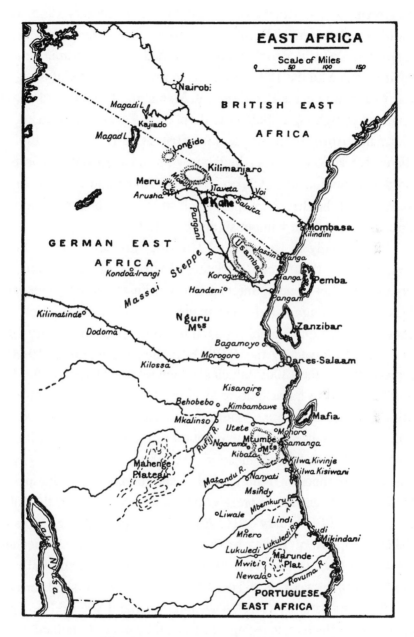

22. German East Africa 1915 - 18

India were the 130th (Jacob's) Baluchis (later the 5/10th Baluch Regiment) who reached British East Africa in February 1915. They had been detained at Bombay due to trouble with their Mahsud elements, the same people who had earned so much admiration for their valour with the 129th Baluchis in France and later at Rangoon due to a mutiny in the Battalion.[22] In March, the 130th Baluchis were engaged in fighting at Salaita Hill opposite Taveta, in blocking the German efforts to infiltrate into British territory possibly for disruptive actions. Earlier in January an effort to seize a German border plantation fort at Jasini north of Tanga had resulted in the surrender of the British troops.[23] Such small engagements continued throughout the year, without significant effects.

It was only in December 1915, after an East African Force consisting mostly of South African (SA) troops and formations, got organized under General Smuts that a coordinated military campaign was launched against the Germans. During the course of this campaign the 129th Baluchis joined in from France in January 1916 and were followed by the 127th Baluchis in September 1918 as replacement of the 130th Baluchis, which returned to India after two and half years of hard fighting in East Africa.[24] However, with the arrival of the SA forces, came the racist prejudices against the Indians, which affected the integration of the British forces. It took quite sometime before these racist white soldiers grudgingly admitted the superior fighting quality and remarkable endurance of the Indian soldiers. An impressive beginning was made by the 130th Baluchis on 12 February 1916. An attack by two SA regiments on Salaita Hill, east of Taveta was repulsed with heavy casualties and the falling back troops were further threatened from the flank by hidden German weapons. The 130th Baluchis were rushed forward and they attacked the German weapon post and silenced it. Then forming an effective covering fire base, they not only helped in the extrication of the shaken SA regiments but gallantly extended a helping hand in bringing in their numerous wounded soldiers.[25]

In the beginning of 1916 the German situation in East Africa was quite superior both in strategy and the effectiveness of its forces. But, cut off from the mainland from any support, von Lettow foresaw a long hard struggle against much stronger forces and the necessity of fighting a war, that would preserve his forces and be able to hold on to the German territory. He devoted much of his attention to the training of his troops in conducting the remarkable campaign ahead using every advantage of the familiar terrain in his own favour. He devised a defensive strategy of highly mobile operations on interior lines, almost akin to guerilla war; avoiding pitched battles and preserving his forces, with the main object of prolonging the war and exhausting the opponent. He held on to his objectives to the bitter end, and by any standard, quite successfully. At this time, the German forces in East Africa were estimated at 2000 German soldiers and 14,000 askaris, with 60 pieces of light guns, organized in companies of 150-200 men, each with two machine guns. They were well trained and excellently led.

Immediately on the assumption of command by General Smuts on 19 February 1916, preparations for the British offensive commenced.The immediate task was to recapture Taveta salient which offered the main entry into German East Africa through the gap between Kilimanjaro and Pare mountains to Kahe, astride the German railway. The main attack was to be delivered by the 2nd East African (EA) Division[26] (the 130th Baluchis forming part of its 1st Brigade), while an enveloping movement was to be executed by the 1st East African (EA) Division (the 129th Baluchis forming part of its 2nd Brigade) from the north, through Longido mountain, skirting Kilimanjaro and capturing Moschi and Kahe in the German rear. The enveloping movement started on 5 March and the main attack was launched two days later. As the enveloping column approached Moschi, the Germans realized the threat and withdrew from their positions in Taveta, which they had defended well against repeated attacks, and by 13 March the salient fell to the British. In this operation the 130th Baluchis were constantly engaged especially in the fight at Latima Reata on 12 March when a gallant night attack was made by the Battalion on the strong German positions.[27] On the 15th, junction was made between the two advance guards on the slopes of the Kilimanjaro.

A similar plan was launched on the 18th to capture Kahe; while the 1st Division was to attack from the flank, a cavalry column was to cut the Germans further south across the Pangani River, through a deep turning movement. The Germans had laid their defences very skilfully: a series of screens and outposts in depth ahead of main defences, with mobile detachments posted on the flanks and strong reserves held in the rear, ready to exploit every single mistake or weakness of the opponent. The object was to force frequent deployment, cause attrition and exhaustion before the attackers reached the main defence, where the process was repeated through counter attacks. The battle at Kahe was fought exactly as von Lettow had planned and the British had their first taste of the bush war and its terrible cost in attrition and exhaustion, difficulties of moving through trackless dense bushy terrain and attacking strong positions on restricted frontages. After every exhausting encounter and attack, the troops learned that 'the real fighting was yet to come'. Germans maintained strict fire discipline and frequently resorted to counter attacks giving little time to the attackers to settle down. The 129th Baluchis were employed twice for attacking the German positions, sustaining their first casualties of the campaign. On 24 March, when the main attack was launched by the Division, the Germans had already withdrawn. The turning movement by the Cavalry Column did not materialize due to difficult terrain conditions. This was the pattern of operations which dominated the entire campaign.

By end of March, the entire Kilimanjaro country had been captured. Now General Smuts launched his plan of driving the Germans south of the Pangani in the first phase, followed by the seizure of the Central Railway through encircling movements by the two divisional columns along the central axis of Pangani-Usambara to Handeni and Morogoro, with the Cavalry Column operating through the Massai Steppe on the western flank. His main object was to avoid direct attacks against prepared positions and to force the Germans to withdraw or get trapped in the pincers. In the process they were to seize large territory, limit Germans' operational freedom and deprive them of the areas from where they drew their supplies and and recruitment. A third column was to operate along the coast. But the plan owing to the difficult nature of terrain and practically non-existent roads, made heavy demands on the men's endurance, while increasing the problems of logistic support. To these were added the severe strains caused by the rains and tropical diseases. The two Balochi battalions formed part of the central column. The combined offensive began on 18 May. 'Throughout the advance there was little fighting, as Smuts' strategy had made it impossible for the Germans to hold their positions without the risk of being outflanked by the main column, but it was far from being a promenade'. There was always the risk of a surprise attack, of sniping and of being ambushed, requiring utmost vigilance, which made the march infinitely laborious and exhausting, through the dense cloud of dust and the glaring sun. The Germans following their own strategy, invariably managed to slip through numerous gaps. As the advance entered the swampy areas of the Pangani, troops were attacked with malaria and dysentry and such entries in the regimental diaries, 'about 300 men down with malaria and dysentry' became quite common. Soon the breakdown in the supplies forced the battalions on half rations and at times even close to starvation. By the time the column reached Handeni during the first week of July the fighting strength of 'the 129th Baluchis was reduced to 158 rifles'[28] and they were allowed a short respite to recover.

Meanwhile the focus shifted from Handeni to the south. The Cavalry Column operating from the Massai Steppe had cut the

Central Railway at Dodoma during the first week of August and the column along the coast had captured Tanga and Bagamoyo. The advance of the main columns was resumed to trap the Germans in Nguru mountains by securing Kilossa and Morogoro through the cavalry. Simultaneously, Dar-es-Salaam was to be captured through landing a brigade by ships. The 129th Baluchis formed part of this brigade and moving by train to Tanga, were shipped to Bagamoyo on 31 August. Marching in three columns, the Brigade entered Dar-es-Salaam on 3 September. There was no opposition. In mid September, the 129th Baluchis were shipped to Kilwa further south and came under the command of Brigadier Hannyngton, who was an old battalion officer and had commanded it in France.

On the central front although the Germans had been steadily pushed towards Rufiji River, their defeat or capitulation was nowhere close. Fighting on interior lines, they had conducted excellent rearguard actions, subjecting the British columns to severe attrition and delays and had invariably slipped out of the noose. During this period the 130th Baluchis operated with the 2nd S A Brigade and fought a major engagement at Mkalomo in which they suffered heavy casualties. Again they were involved in fighting through the Nguru mountains and the advance to Morogoro.[29] By the end of September, their losses in the actions and due to sickness almost rendered them ineffective and the Battalion was allowed a respite for rest and recovery. Meanwhile an Anglo-Belgian force initiated operations from the north-west to push the Germans towards Mahenge Plateau. Though the Germans had been confined to a comparatively restricted area, the troops of the advancing columns too were utterly exhausted with excessive marching and fatigue, constant exposure, insufficient rations, and sickness. 'Smuts had reached the end of his forces'. Any further advance would lead into the swamps of the Rufiji and the rains were imminent. A pause was needed for reorganization and a new strategy was to be evolved. Towards the end of 1916, von Lettow considered the situation quite favourable to his cause. The exhaustion and casualties had worn out the South Africans and most were going back home and 'other regiments like the 129th Baluchis who had fought in Flanders, were without doubt very good but they might not be expected to stand the fatigues of African warfare for a prolonged period'.[30]

At this stage the 129th Baluchis were ordered to march together with 1/2nd King's African Rifles (KAR) for Kibata, a small stone-built fort in the Mtumbe mountains, about 60 miles from Kilwa which controlled a few dirt roads and tracks. The Battalion left Kilwa on 10 October, following the Matandu river and was met with German resistance throughout its march. These were generally delaying actions, fought always from well-chosen and concealed positions. A frontal attack invariably entailed considerable casualties, and the flanking movements imposed delay and exhaustion. Just when the attack got underway, the Germans vacated their positions. Everything seemed to help the Germans in their tactics of endless small rearguard actions and the exasperated Battalion could not help but admire their skill and persistence. Very rarely did the Germans make mistakes. The hardships of the march are thus described by an eye witness:

'The men were crowded together and the day very hot, so that very soon they were drenched in sweat and parched and blinded with dust. The march was a succession of halts and slow advances which were also exhausting, as throughout the day there was no shade at all. Chumo was not reached till 3 p.m. by which time the almost total lack of water was making itself very severely felt and many of the men were staggering along like drunkards with blackened lips and tongues. Every now and then a man would collapse, to be helped up by his almost equally exhausted comrades, who shouldering his rifle and kit staggered themselves with their increased burden. Men suffering with malaria or dysentry would collapse unconscious on the road and were left to be succored later at night. So the interminable day seemed to prolong its weary hours for all'.[31]

On 14 October, Kibata was reached and unexpectedly found undefended and was peacefully occupied. Kibata was well worth all the toils to reach it. Situated at an elevation, it was cool and healthy, with plenty of water and good supply of fresh vegetables the troops had not seen in months. While leaving the 1/2nd KAR in Kibata, the Battalion was employed in the clearance of Matandu and Mitole areas. When German patrol activities were reported around Kibata, it returned to join the KAR, where it stayed till January 1917, during which period, it fought a memorable action and proved worthy of von Lettow's admiration.

The fighting at and around Kibata began on 6 December and continued till 13 January 1917, when the action near Mwengi terminated it. Kibata's importance as a junction and switching point had increased since the fighting in the Rufiji basin, which had also drawn the Germans' attention. 'Kibata has been described (refer to the sketch) as an inverted cup standing in a high-rimmed saucer, the rim in some places, as at Picquet Hill, overlooked the top of the cup. The main defences were on the rim, which it was essential to hold as any part of the rim held by the enemy would affect the other part through enfilade fire and afford good observation. The fort was located in the centre of this inverted cup. The 'redoubts'on the Picquet Hill were the highest points and key to Kibata defences, which however had ignored the possibility of artillery being used against it'. But as so often happened, the Germans did the impossible and brought up the guns, through dense bushes and precipitous hills, which surrounded Kibata. Perhaps, it was the experience on the Flanders of patiently enduring the slaughter of the guns, that helped the 129th Baluchis withstand the shock of its much lower intensity at Kibata.[32] When the fighting began, the strength of

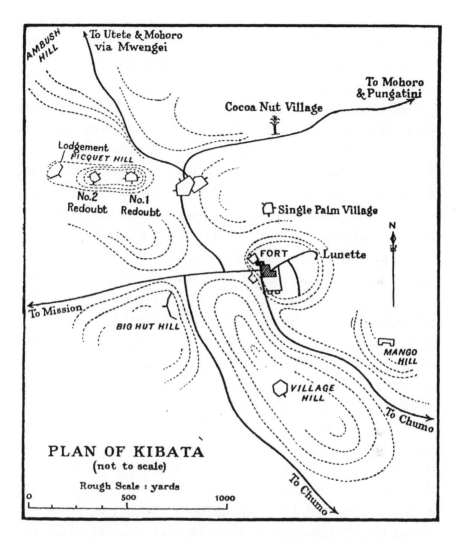

To Utete & Mohoro via Mwengei

AMBUSH HILL

To Mohoro & Pungatini

Cocoa Nut Village

Lodgement
PICQUET HILL

No.2 Redoubt   No.1 Redoubt

Single Palm Village

N

FORT   Lunette

To Mission

BIG HUT HILL

MANGO HILL

VILLAGE HILL

To Chumo

PLAN OF KIBATA
(not to scale)

Rough Scale : yards

0   500   1000

23. German East Africa - Action at Kibata (January 1917)

the 129th Baluchis was 8 British Officers and 240 Indian ranks and that of 1/2nd KAR, 17 British officers and 563 African ranks. All the positions were held by the 1/2nd KAR except the Picquet Hill which was occupied by 150 rifles of the 129th Baluchis, with a company each from the two battalions held in reserve. The 129th Baluchis were in overall command.

The German attack commenced in the afternoon of 6 December and developed into heavy fighting next day. The Germans approached from the direction of Ambush Hill and the forward posts in the area and the picquet at Cocoa Nut Village were pushed back, but an attack on the Palm Village, possibly a distraction, was repulsed. It was again attacked the next day in considerable strength, but the African picquet again held out. The same evening, the Germans engaged the Picquet Hill with artillery fire (possibly with five guns of different calibres), which caught the defenders with surprise and also engaged the positions with machine guns. The bursting shells completely demolished the shelters and 'sanghars' of the Frontier type and caused considerable casualties, but the expected attack did not come. Next morning the position was again shelled heavily for half an hour and the Germans were found entrenched on a knoll; an extension of Picquet Hill (called the Lodgement), from where they could effectively engage the fort areas. During the day German shelling continued on all picquets. In anticipation of the German attack, Picquet Hill was reinforced and additional troops from the 2/2nd KAR with a section of the 27th Mountain Battery arrived at Kibata and a Gold Coast Regiment was moved to Kitambi on the German right flank. During the next few days, while fighting from the trenches continued, it was decided to throw the Germans from the Lodgement. The newly arrived 2/2nd KAR were launched, but the attack failed and they were asked to relieve the 129th Baluchis to form the reserve for the attack. On 13 December Brigadier O' Grady arrived and took over the command, followed by a section of the Mountain Battery during the night. On 15 December as the Germans attacked the Gold Coast Regiment, the 129th Baluchis went into attack against the German position on the Lodgement.

It was a pitch dark night. The attack was led by Major Lewis from the Picquet Hill, using a line of 'bombers' who were to sneak into the defences and throw the bombs (kind of improvised grenades) across the obstacle of stakes and then pull out as many stakes as possible for the assaulting troops following at their heel. The explosion of the bombs was the signal for the artillery and the machine guns to open up with all vigour. The attack went in just as planned except for a little pandemonium while crossing the stakes. The position was overrun with bayonets and a feeble attempt to counter attack was repulsed. 40 German casualties were accounted for, in addition to five Germans and eight askaris taken prisoner. The Baluchis suffered ten killed and wounded. The Commanding Officer added a bar to his DSO, while Major Lewis and Lieutenant Thatcher received DSO and MC, respectively. Three IOMs were won by the Indian ranks. The Germans went on the defensive, though their positions were still considerably strong. Meanwhile the bigger pincers steadily progressing towards the Rufiji in the area of Mkalinso - Kimbambawe began to threaten German forces in the Mtumbe mountains and their positions around Kibata. The 129th Baluchis were ordered into action and in a series of strong patrol and company size attacks, cleared all the adjoining hills, bringing the Kibata episode to a successful end. During the six weeks fighting, the 129th Baluchis had lost two thirds of their strength to casualties and sickness. During the same period, the 130th Baluchis were back, and engaged in severe fighting, having 37 men killed in one action at Wiransi on Ist January 1917.

Before the main offensive could be conclusive, the rains came a little before the usual time and were peculiarly heavy, affecting the progress of the operations and allowing respite to the Germans, who while keeping a strong force in the Mahenge, moved out of the Rufiji towards the coastal areas of Kilwa and Lindi. Von Lettow had managed to preserve his forces in some strength and was still capable of posing a threat. Although most of the German territories had been captured, their forces had not been defeated and now the main object of the fighting during 1917 was to seek and destroy the German forces even at the cost of heavy casualties. Accordingly, two strong brigade columns were formed at Kilwa and Lindi, to advance along the rivers Matandu and Lukuledi, pushing the Germans westwards, while maintaining the pressure on the Mahenge from the north; in the process it was hoped that the German forces would be destroyed or driven out of East Africa.

The operations commenced in late July. The 129th Baluchis had been moved to Kilwa and formed part of Kilwa Column, which later in early September was also joined by the 127th Baluchis. Each column moved on multiple axes covering a wide frontage, each forming an enveloping arm for the other. There was constant fighting but none pitched or decisive, the Germans always managing to fall back to the next position. It was typical bush fighting, where Germans never presented a big target to the strong British forces and invariably the strong mobile patrols yielded better results. Von Lettow fought skilfully but had begun to suffer casualties, reportedly losing 35 percent of his force in actions against the Lindi Column. In November, Tafel the German commander in Mahenge had been driven towards Rovuma and was making an effort to join with von Lettow. On 18 November, after heavy fighting, Lutshemi was captured, where some 300 Germans and 700 askaris were taken prisoner and a large number of British prisoners were released. The noose was closing and 129th Baluchis with a cavalry patrol were despatched to Rovuma to intercept Tafel, but before he surrendered with his 2500 men on the 28th, the 129th Baluchis bumped into his force at Mwiti Water and lost 50 men killed and wounded. It was soon learnt that von Lettow with 2000 men had crossed into Portuguese East Africa, which abruptly brought the fighting to an end.

The four months of fighting during 1917, was the most exacting of its kind and quite fierce in nature and placed much demands on the troops, both in alertness and physical fitness. The 127th Baluchis, who entered East Africa in September, saw the most intense part of the campaign and remained continuously engaged throughout their short stay and gave a good account of themselves. Both the battalions were moved to Dar-es-Salaam from where they embarked for India, reaching Karachi in January and February 1918. During the Campaign in East Africa the 129th Baluchis lost 5 British and 7 Indian officers and nearly 400 other ranks killed in action or died through sickness.[33] 129th and 130th Baluchis respectively earned 15 and 22 gallantry awards. All the battalions were given the battle honour of 'East Africa 1915-18'. The Balochis had lived upto the compliment given by one of the most remarkable adversaries, who himself deserved no less.

War in Palestine

Initially the main British concern in the Middle East had been the protection of the Suez Canal, for which, right from the outset they had maintained strong forces in Egypt which also became a major staging area for the Western Front. During early 1915, the British made two unsuccessful attempts to capture Gaza, then fell back to purely defensive measures. But as the war progressed through 1917, the Turks were defeated in Mesopotamia and an Arab rebellion had been successfully organized in Syria and Hejaz which was causing severe attrition on the Turkish resources and became a potent threat to their line of communication. Taking advantage of the deteriorating Turkish situation, the British made a cautious advance into Palestine and seized Jerusalem and a portion of Jordan Valley. From here preparations were initiated for the final offensive to drive the Turks from the Middle East.

Three Baloch battalions: the 2nd/124th Baluchistan Infantry, the 2nd/127th Baluchis[34] and the 130th Baluchis, participated in the final offensive in Palestine. The first formed part of the 3rd Indian Division (8th Brigade) and the other two of the 60th Infantry Division (179th and 181st Brigades respectively). The plan was to create an opening in the Turkish defences along the coast using six infantry divisions, then pour through it three cavalry divisions, racing across the Plains of Sharon, seize the passes through the Carmel Range and thereafter in a turning movement capture Deraa in Jordan and Damascus in the north, thus bagging the entire Turkish forces in Palestine, Jordan and Hejaz. The key role was played by the Arabs and the Air Force in completely paralysing the communication and command network of the already demoralized and severely depleted Turkish armies. Simultaneously, successful deception measures were taken to conceal the direction of the main breakthrough.

'On 19 September 1918, at 4.30 a.m, 385 guns opened up on the selected frontage. After 15 minutes of intense bombardment the mass of infantry advanced under cover of a rapid lifting barrage. They swept, almost unchecked over the stupefied defenders and broke through the two trench systems, shallow and slightly wired by the Western Front standards. Then they wheeled inland, like a huge door swinging on its hinges. On this door, the French contingent and the 54th Division formed the hinged end, 3rd, 75th and the 7th Divisions, the middle panel and the 60th Division by the sea the outside panel; the last reached Tul Keram by nightfall'. Within their respective brigades, the 2nd/124th was assigned the objectives of Byar Adas and Tell Manasif, the 130th, the village of Qulunsawe and the 2nd/127th remained in reserve. Out of the two assaulting Balochi battalions only the 130th met with strong opposition, which was overcome with the usual grit and dash.[35] After overcoming the first line of defence, owing to complete confusion and paralysis in Turkish ranks, there was no opposition worth its value and it was marching through open spaces towards the final objectives. Only the 3rd Division met with some resistance near Nablus. As the infantry formations wheeled inward, the cavalry divisions broke out to seize their assigned objectives in depth. El Afule and Beisan were reached at 8 a.m. and 4.30 p.m. respectively; the latter 70 miles in 34 hours by the 4th Cavalry Division. On 1st October, the 5th Cavalry Division had reached Damascus. For Turkey the war was over.

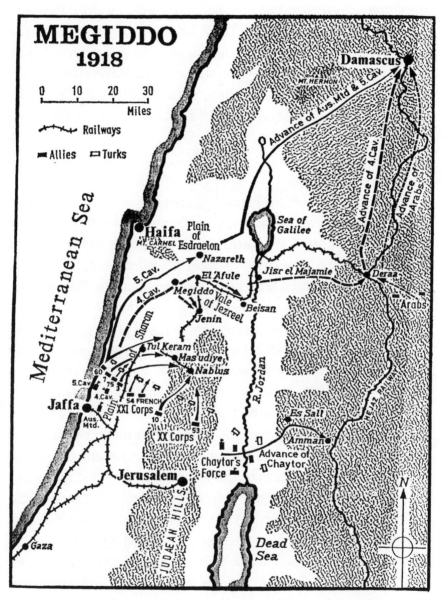

MEGIDDO 1918

0 10 20 30
Miles

Railways

Allies Turks

Mediterranean Sea

MT. HERMON

Damascus

Advance of Aus. Mtd & 5 Cav.

Advance of 4.Cav.

Advance of Arabs

Haifa
MT. CARMEL

Plain of Esdraelon

Sea of Galilee

Nazareth

5.Cav.

El 'Afule

Jisr el Majamie

Deraa

4.Cav.

Megiddo

Vale of Jezreel

Beisan

Arabs

Jenin

Tul Keram

Mas'udiye

Nablus

Plain of Sharon

60
7
75
5
5.Cav.
A.Cav.
54 FRENCH
XXI Corps

R. Jordan

Es Sall

HEJAZ RAILWAY

Jaffa
Aus. Mtd.

10

53

XX Corps

Amman

Advance of Chaytor

Jerusalem

Chaytor's Force

JUDAEAN HILLS.

N

Gaza

Dead Sea

24. Allied Offensive in Palestine September 1918

The 2nd/124th earned one CMG, one MC and two IDSMs and the 130th, two IDSMs and both battalions were awarded the battle honour of 'Palestine - 1918'. These battalions stayed in Palestine and Egypt till next year and returned to India in July and August 1919. Although the Great War was over in November 1918, a Baloch battalion, the 3rd/124th Baluchistan Infantry (late Left Wing) continued to fight in Persia and was soon joined by the 127th Baluchis.

Campaign in Persia

Situation in southern Persia had always been disturbed due to strong tribal influences and the weakening hold of the central authority. Since 1907, the British and the Russians had respected a tacit demarcation of respective areas of influence in Persia; the Russians to the north of line Hamadan - Herat and the British in the Persian Gulf. The lower triangle, forming southern Persia was left neutral. This large area stretching from Isfahan to Seistan consisted of a vast plateau, rugged and heavily dissected, generally dry and barren and with poor communications. It included the ports of Bushire and Bunder Abbas and the main towns of Isfahan, Shiraz and Kerman, besides dispersed small mud-hut villages. The entire area formed the grazing grounds of the powerful and well-armed nomadic tribes: Bakhtiaris, Kashgais, Arabs, Tangistanis and further to the east Balochis. Persians did not exercise any administrative control over these tribes, who frequently resorted to banditry and lawlessness. Persian effort to raise a Gendarmerie under Swedish officers to control the south had not succeeded and its remnants frequently in mutiny, now formed part of the weak Persian army and were located in the north. As the war broke out, Turkish and German agents moved into southern Persia to instigate the tribes against the neutral Persian government and the British. Tribal chiefs were provided with finances and large quantities of weapons. The German consul at Bushire, Herr Wassmuss, was particularly most active amongst the Tangistanis and Kashgais and greatly succeeded in creating serious tribal unrest, which gradually involved nearly a division strength of British troops in exhausting operations for two years.

Besides maintaining their influence in Persia, the British were highly concerned with the spread of tribal unrest into Balochistan and Afghanistan and its serious security implications. A small force under General Dyer (later called East Persian Cordon) had been raised at Quetta and was deployed along the Persian border in Balochistan. It was now decided to provide a small force of Indian troops, to Sir Percy Sykes, the British representative in southern Persia, to assist him in raising a Persian force (to be called South Persian Rifles or SPR), equipped and trained on the lines of Indian Frontier Corps for restoring order in south Persia. The Persian government willingly consented and the proposed ceiling of the SPR was fixed at 6000 (later increased to 11000). The Indian troops placed under Sir Percy Sykes, were the Right Wing 124th Baluchistan Infantry under Lieut Colonel E.F. Twigg, squadron of 37 Lancers, the old Baluch Horse (later 15 Lancers) and section of 23 Mountain Battery. These had assembled at Bunder Abbas on 16 April 1916.

Raising and training of the SPR Battalion for the protection of Bunder Abbas was undertaken immediately. It was however felt that occupation and control of major towns was essential for organizing the security and communication in the area. Kerman being closest to the Indian border, was chosen to be occupied first. The Indian force at Bunder Abbas was organized into two echelons; 124th forming the second, for march to Kerman through Tang-i-Zindan. It was the longest route (280 miles) as compared to the usual direct route (125 miles) and was adopted to avoid the hostile tribes. The march commenced on 17 May and proceeded without major incident except for heat and scarcity of water, and Kerman was reached on 11 June. Leaving a small nucleus for raising a SPR brigade at Kerman, preparations (including acquisition of large number of Persian mules) were made to resume the march to Shiraz. Again the longest route via Yezd (460 miles) was chosen as against the direct route (335 miles). The march was resumed on 27 July and Yezd was reached on 14 August. Soon after arrival, it was learnt that the mule convoy following the column was under attack of tribesmen. The squadron of Cavalry with a company from 124th (mounted on mules) were despatched to succour the convoy 64 miles distant. The convoy was saved and escorted back within 36 hours.

While at Yezd, gradual withdrawal of Russians from Persia, had begun to affect the political situation and Bakhtiaris who had been kept under check by them, on instigation and physical support from the Germans were threatening Isfahan. The town had the British consulate with its residential colony and a large Armenian population and was defended by 600 Russian Cossacks with two guns. The other hostile tribes, the Kashgais and the Arabs, were waiting on the wings for the first major debacle, to exact their own plunder. In view of this new threat, it was decided to march on to Isfahan, which was reached on 11 September. Arrival of this new force imposed caution on the Bakhtiaris who reportedly retired into their country. During the stay in Isfahan, negotiations were undertaken with the Kashgai chief, Saulat-ud-Daula and the Arab chief, Qawwam-ul-Mulk, for conciliation without much success and armed escorts were provided for the movement of commercial convoys for protection and punitive action against bandits.

On 20 October the march was resumed to Shiraz, thus completing the first thousand miles (not counting the extra side shows which could be closer to 500 miles). Shiraz was reached on 12 November. Enroute, near village Kumisheh, a company of 124th supported with cavalry undertook a successful operation against a noted brigand of the area, whose stronghold was attacked and his gang rounded up. At Kumisheh, some German prisoners had been taken over from the friendly tribesmen, who were now escorted

211

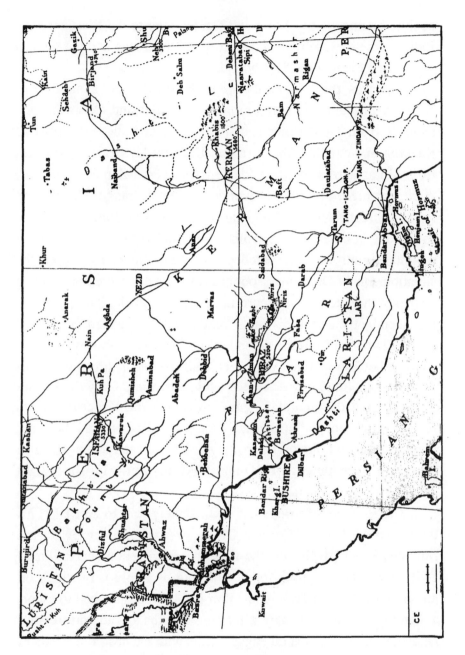

25. Campaign in Southern Persia 1915 - 19

back to Isfahan by the 124th and handed over to the Russians. The Indian force settled down at Shiraz for a longer stay and got busy in raising and training the SPR brigade for Shiraz area.

Towards the end of the year, Nasir Diwan, a notable of Kazerun probably on instigation from Saulat and Qawwam and support from Gendarmerie officers, attacked the SPR post at Kazerun and expelled the garrison. Kazerun lay nearly 100 miles from Shiraz across two formidable passes: Pir-i-Zan and Dukhtar, 7000 feet high, in a thickly wooded mountain range. Despite the lurking threat from the Tangistanis, a composite force of cavalry squadron, company each from 124th and SPR and section of mountain guns were despatched on 22 December to restore the situation. On 24 December, foot hills of Pir-i-Zan were reached and next day the attempt to secure the pass was made. The pass was defended by the Kazerunis and several attempts to gain access failed under heavy fire from the defenders and the troops fell back with a wounded officer and many soldiers. Half the SPR soldiers were lost in the woods (probably deserted) while retreating. Only the gallant support from the mountain guns prevented the Kazerunis from following the troops. Further advance was called off and the force marched back to Shiraz. The artillery officer and an Indian officer of the 124th were awarded DSO and IOM, respectively, for gallant actions during the operation.

The shortage of troops had been acutely felt. In April 1917 a divisional staff under Colonel Orton, with a squadron of Burma Mounted Rifles (BMR) and the 16 Rajput Regiment reached Shiraz. 124th also received a reinforcement draft of a company which on arrival at Bushire on 16 July last year had been despatched to escort a convoy to Kerman and after ten months of adventure and hardships involving several engagements with the hostile Bochakchi tribes and Baharlu Arabs, rejoined the Regiment.[36] In may 1917, Lieut Colonel Twigg was recalled to India where in August he raised the 1/124th. During the same period, Lieut Colonel B.F.R.

Holbrooke raised another battalion; the 3/124th, at Karachi (with large number of Baloch recruits from Derajat) which was eventually to absorb the Wing 124th in Persia.

In July, a company of 124th with a squadron of BMR, attacked the fort of Kafta and the encampment of a hostile Kurshuli tribe, 30 miles south west of Dehbid. The fort was captured and the tribe was dispersed. In September a strong force including the Wing of 124th understook a punitive expedition against the hostile Lashani tribe in the area of Khawja Jamali east of Shiraz - Dehbid road and after an encounter dispersed them into the hills. During October-December, the Wing 124th remained on constant march in area Dehbid-Marvas-Saidabad engaging and dispersing the hostile tribes, which brought some peace in the area and the Wing camped at Saidabad for the winter.

The Bolshevik Revolution in Russia brought about a qualitative change in Persia. All Russian troops had been withdrawn by the beginning of 1918. This created a vacuum in the northeast, requiring alternative steps to provide support to the Persian government as well as protect British consulate at Meshed, and its interests at large. Consequently, a Military Mission was established at Meshed and the area of East Persian Cordon was extended beyond Birjand. A brigade size Moveable Column of Indian troops was moved to Meshed to restore order in Khurasan and watch over the northern borders. Simultaneously, southern Persia was reinforced. In April 1918, the 3/124th landed at Bushire, as part of a major reinforcement to Persia. The Battalion marched to Shiraz, where in early May it was joined by the old Wing of 124th to form the complete battalion: 3/124th Baluchistan Infantry.

During May a section of the Kashgais attacked a SPR column and besieged it at Khan-i-Zinian northwest of Shiraz. A large force of Kashgais and Kazerunis were reported moving from Kazerun towards Shiraz, while another strong Kashgai force under Saulat himself was encamped south west of Shiraz. The situation seemed serious and the Shiraz force moved out of camp to face the threat. It was obvious that the Kashgais were expecting to draw the British towards Khan-i-Zinian, for the relief of the besieged column and to involve them with the strong Kazeruni force, providing Saulat, the British rear and an open access to Shiraz. The British instead decided to screen the Kazerunis in Khan-i-Zinian at Deh Sheikh with mobile troops and launched the 3/124th to secure a series of heights in Koh-i-Phan, which effectively dominated the Khan-i-Zinian road to Shiraz and Saulat's encampment. Most of these heights and their slopes were held by the Kashgais and were captured with heavy fighting including bayonet charges at a number of places. By evening all the heights were captured and Saulat's camp was now under the effective range of the Lewis guns. The 3/124th had lost one officer and eight men while the Kashgai casualties were estimated at 600.[37] Next morning, 26 May, Saulat had retired into the hills, his camp was burned by the cavalry and the Shiraz force returned to Deh Sheikh and thence to Shiraz.

Next weeks witnessed the peak of Kashgai opposition along with the danger of mutiny in the SPR. The neighbouring heights were occupied, and Shiraz and the movement along roads were constantly sniped. Flying sorties were regularly launched 'to tip and run'. A major assembly of Kazerunis was attacked at Ahmedabad on 16 June and dispersed with heavy casualties, before it could combine with Saulat's Kashgais at Deh Shiekh. This action firmly discouraged Saulat from attacking Shiraz. On 8 July a strong column under the 3/124th, attacked Saulat's camp behind Chinar Rahdar south of Shiraz and forced them to disperse. At this time a post at Abadeh was besieged by the Kashgais. A relief column with two companies from 3/124th, two squadrons of BMR and a section of mountain guns, through forced marches covered the distance of 180 miles in 169 hours and rescued the post. With continuous reverses, the Kashgais around Shiraz had melted away. In October the whole of Shiraz force less 16 Rajputs moved out to Firuzabad, 75 miles south of Shiraz where on the 23rd, a Kashgai force under Saulat was attacked and dispersed with heavy casualties. This was the last action against the Kashgais and also of the 3/124th.

Soon after the attack, the entire force was hit with influenza. On 30 October, out of 800 men of the Battalion only six were fit. From 6 November, small columns of relatively better and recovering men were despatched and by 2 December the whole battalion assembled at Shiraz. The Battalion lost one British and four Indian officers and 169 men to influenza, while there were 700 casualties from the entire force. It was a depressing situation and the only good news was that of Armistice on the 18th November.

In November 1918, the 127th Baluchis landed at Bushire and marched 55 miles to Daliki to join Brigadier Elmslie's (or Elsmie) force and was employed in securing the passes and opening the road to Kazerun. On 28 January 1919, the Battalion marched to Kazerun and stayed there till 7 April. During its stay, it remained employed on road making and construction of strong points. With squadron of 37 Lancers, the Battalion was moved to Shiraz, where on 11 April, it relieved the 3/124th Baluchistan Infantry which returned to Karachi in May. The 127th Baluchis remained garrisoned at Shiraz without any major operational employment until March 1920, when all Indian troops were withdrawn from southern Persia and this lingering episode of the Great War finally came to an end. The Battalion returned to Karachi on 20 May and was moved to Multan.

While an improved situation in southern Persia led to the withdrawal of British troops, the situation in north eastern Persia had come under strain due to aggressive Bolshevik attitude. The troops at Meshed were therefore retained. In November 1919, the 1/124th Baluchistan Infantry was ordered to Meshed as a relief of 19th Punjabis. The Battalion reached Meshed after a long train and road journey in mid-February 1920.

During its six months stay, the Battalion was successfully employed on the border near Kushan to discourage the Bolsheviks from attacking a Persian post at Bajgiran through carefully planned and executed deception and movement. Besides, it undertook one punitive operation against a Persian brigand and two relief operations to border posts.[38] During August, British evacuation of north eastern Persia was ordered and by mid-October the Battalion reached Dalbanddin in Balochistan.

Thus ended nearly three years of involvement of three Baloch battalions in Persia, which tested their professional abilities and physical endurance to the utmost. All the three battalions were raised during the war and had seen much field service without the advantage of old veterans. Two of these were soon disbanded, but the Regiment was allowed to carry the battle honour of 'Persia 1915-18', which was so deservedly earned by all.

Chapter Twelve

Between The Two Wars: 1919-39

The Third Afghan War

Following a period of anarchy, the turbulent situation within Afghanistan had been brought under control by the Afghan General Nadir Khan. However the religious sentiments aroused against Aman Ullah's liberalism soon transferred to 'Khilafat's' cause, in whose sympathy, the Indian Muslims had also united in a movement. The new Afghan rulers, taking advantage of the British involvement in the Great War, launched a religious campaign in the Frontier to agitate the tribes into rebellion against the British and succeeded in great measure in the Tochi and Gomal valleys, the strongholds of the Mahsuds and the Waziris. The Third Afghan War commenced on 6 May 1919. The Afghan army, mostly composed of irregulars, advanced into Kurram and Tochi valleys and made minor gains in areas of Para Chinar and Miran Shah. As the British brigades at Bannu and Dera Ismail Khan moved forward and a stronger force under General Andrew Skeen was assembled, the Afghans already under pressure decided to pull back, bringing abruptly in August, the Afghan intrusion to an end. But the tribal rebellion and violence unleashed by the preceeding events spread and continued for considerable time, and consumed much larger resources, time and energy to control it.

In the north the initial shock was absorbed by the two forward brigades and segments of Frontier Corps, which had stood firm against heavy odds, but a large number of its border posts and administrative centres in the area had been overrun by strong lashkars of the hostile tribes. Movement was completely disrupted, there was no law between Tochi and Gomal and the violence was spilling across into Zhob valley. While the assembly of a strong strike force under General Skeen was underway, as part of immediate reinforcements, the newly raised 1/124th Baluchistan Infantry was moved to Hangu in Kohat District, where it stayed from 30 May till mid-July and then moved to Mardan, from where it returned to Lahore in October. During its stay at Hangu it took part in operations against the Afghans in Paiwar Kotal and suffered 20 casualties. This battalion since its raising in August 1917, had already been employed in Frontier operations against the Mahsuds and Bhittanis in Jandola area.[1]

In the south the Baluchistan Field Force was constituted. The 3/124th Baluchistan Infantry which had just landed at Karachi on return from Persia, and the 129th Baluchis that was already at Quetta, were ordered to join the Force. The 129th Baluchis reached Chaman on 18 May and formed part of the force assembled on Toba Plateau and participated in the capture of Afghan border fort of Spin Baldak on 27 May. Loss of the fort imposed caution on the Afghans and limited their options in the south. The Battalion stayed at Chaman till September, when it was moved to Harnai to join the Zhob Field Force (created in place of Baluchistan Field Force in August) and later in November became part of the garrison at Fort Sandeman.[2] Meanwhile the 3/124th had reached Quetta where its left Wing was despatched to Shelabagh for the protection of the Khojak tunnels and the right Wing moved to Loralai, via Harnai, where it reached on 10 June. Simultaneously a column had been moved from Quetta through Zhob under Brigadier O'Grady, who was to command the Zhob Field Force, and restore order in the area. The right Wing 3/124th, with a squadron of Patiala Lancers and 30th Mountain Battery was moved to Lakaband, where it reached on 30 June and went into a perimeter defence. Here during the next six weeks, the right Wing 3/124th came under the most severe pressure of the tribal violence which it sustained with tenacity and courage.

During the night of 14 July the camp was attacked by 200 tribesmen but was prevented from closing in by a well placed piquet. In the fight, Lieut Colonel Holbrooke was wounded and the command was taken over by Captain Munn. Before dawn two companies sallied out of the camp, attacked, and drove out the tribesmen occupying the neighbouring Zhara hills. By midday a logistic convoy was provided an escort and despatched towards Fort Sandeman (now Zhob), to be handed over to another escort at Milestone 98. During the night large movements of hostile tribesmen had been reported in the area which had considerably delayed the despatch of the relieving escort from Fort Sandeman. After an overnight stay at Dilwal (here 40 men under an officer were left to cover the retirement of the main escort), the convoy moved to Babar and having found that the relieving escort had not reached, pressed on towards Fort Sandeman. Soon the convoy came under heavy fire from the hills and was attacked by a strong tribal lashkar. In the ensuing fight the officer and 35 men were killed. The remnants were rallied by the two Indian officers who after securing whatever was left of the convoy, fell back to Babar, and put up a spirited defence against a thousand strong lashkar. Late in the evening the delayed relief from Fort Sandeman arrived and dispersed the tribesmen. Meanwhile the detachment left at Dilwal (mainly of Patiala Lancers) instead of rallying towards Babar had galloped into Lakaband. The same day another small escort bringing the British telegraphists from Thana was attacked and badly hurt. It was quite a trying day for the Battalion. It had lost one officer and 80 men.[3]

The reported number of hostile tribesmen was constantly increasing and in view of an impending threat of a major attack on the open camp, the Wing 3/124th moved into the Lakaband Fort and deployed to defend the 'thana' (Police Station) and the 'sarae' (Public rest area) as well. During the last week of July Fort Sandeman was twice attacked, besides reports of numerous attacks on the convoys. During the first week of August an attack on Lakaband was imminent by 2000 strong lashkar, which prompted special measures for its defence, including improvised mining and booby traps. On 6 August, the lashkar closed in and occupied the surrounding hills and engaged the fort defences with firing. At night a number of sneaking parties were blown up by the exploding bombs and the others were effectively repelled. The fort remained surrounded and subjected to firing from the hills for the next two days but on 8 August these positions seemed vacated. A sortie was immediately launched to demolish all the dangerous 'sanghars' and when the tribals reappeared, it moved back under the cover of the Lewis guns. During the next three days the lashkar gradually dispersed.[4]

On 17 August the Wing 3/124th was relieved by the 2/153rd Punjabis at Lakaband and was moved back to Quetta to join the other Wing, which had successfully defended the Khojak tunnels without any incident.

It took another eight months and a major operation into the heart of Mahsud and Wazir country by a powerful strike force under General Skeen that the tribal rebellion was brought under control and some semblance of order restored. But the Frontier maintained its tranditional pattern and continued to exact its toll of sweat and blood.

Arab Uprising in Iraq[5]

During 1920 a serious Arab uprising in Iraq hit the occupying British forces largely dispersed into small garrisons due to the vastness of area. The depleted British army was also guarding a number of Prisoners of War (POW) camps and providing protection to numerous refugee camps, and the movements along lines of communication. The rebels were estimated at 130,000 with 60,000 rifles. These began to attack smaller isolated garrisons, while larger rebel forces resorted to besieging town garrisons in the hope of exhausting them to surrender. Due to shortage of troops, relief of the beleaguered garrisons could not be promptly undertaken, which was causing serious distress to many despite their spirited defence and endurance. The situation called for immediate reinforcements from India.

Amongst the reinforcements despatched was the indomitable 3/124th Baluchistan Infantry, which landed in Basra on 16 September 1920. It moved by train to Ur and joined the brigade at Nasariyeh.

Sammawah was under rebel siege. The railway line from Nasariyeh had been cut, an armoured train derailed, and most of its occupants massacred. Efforts to send provisions through gun boats had failed. A brigade had now been formed to force its way to Sammawah. The advance commenced on 23 September, and despite persistent rebel resistance it managed to reach Sammawah, and the garrison was relieved on 14 October. During the advance the 3/124th was deployed enroute to protect the brigade rear and its line of supplies. It joined the brigade on 11 November at Sammawah and took over the defence of the city. On relief on 24 November it joined the brigade in its mopping up operations and later in the capture of Rumaitha. On 11 January 1921 it returned to Nasariyeh and participated in an operation along the Shatt-el-Hai. During February it was deployed for the protection of railway line near Basra.

By now the Arab uprising had subsided and the country was brought under control. In April, the Battalion was relieved and moved back to Karachi, where unfortunately, it was required to be disbanded. It was quite a disappointment for the 3/124th, since its performance throughout had been praiseworthy. However, the bulk of its manpower was absorbed by 1/124th and 126th Baluchistan Infantry against deficiencies and some were distributed between other battalions. Thus the pride and rich experiences of this magnificent Battalion were transferred and lived thereafter.

Impact of the War

The Great War had been one of the longest and the most exhausting armed conflicts and left a strong impact on the entire world. It changed the political maps of Europe and West Asia, leaving deep scars to fester in pain and agony. World economy was badly affected and an anti-imperialist surge began to gather strength. From the Soviets, a new socialist dogma was stirring the minds of the oppressed in the shaken colonial empires. Nearer home, the Indian National Congress had become increasingly vocal and had been accusing the British government of exploiting India for imperial purposes at the cost of the Indians and their resources. But it had softened its earlier condemnation of the Indian regiments and its soldiers in the hope of extracting some political concessions against their contributions to the War.

The British campaigns against the Turks in Mesopotamia and Palestine were considered threatening to the Muslim interests and beliefs, which resulted in anti-British agitations and the launching of the Khilafat Movement. Although it naively ignored the fact of the Arab Revolt and the growing strength of the Young Turks against the Ottomans, the movement aroused the Muslims in India, adding a new dimension to their political consciousness and struggle. It also affected the Muslim soldiers and resulted in mutinies in the 5th Light Infantry at Singapore and the 130th Baluchis in Rangoon during 1915 and the 37th Lancers in Basra during 1916, besides some desertions from Egypt and Mesopotamia.[6] It imposed caution on the British in the employment of Muslim regiments against the Turks, but generally the army's discipline and cohesion as a fighting force remained intact.

The anti-British character of the Khilafat movement was also exploited by the Indian National Congress for its own nationalist agenda, by increasing its opposition to the 'martial races theory', demanding to open recruitment for the non-martial areas and for the 'Indianization' of the army. Through this new thrust, it sought to change the composition of the Indian army (predominantly from the north and north-west) and hoped to gain its control through Indian officers. It had realized that the key to political power in India was the Indian army![7] Hindu flavour of the nationalist movement led by the Indian National Congress, convinced more and more Muslims of

India that it was not for them and consequently the All India Muslim League began to assert itself and acquired new political strength and stature. It was during this period that a native of Karachi (Sindh) and a barrister of repute, practicing at Bombay; Mohammad Ali Jinnah, acquired prominence as a promising Muslim leader of ability and vision. He began his political career from the ranks of the Indian National Congress, but was soon to be disillusioned by the Hindu mentality and their dubious character and was destined to lead the Muslims of India to freedom and a new homeland. Despite hesitations and uncertainties, Muslim leadership had begun to emerge and an awareness of things political was fast growing.

A significant impact of the war, in military context, not well emphasized, was the growth of a new awareness of identity amongst the soldiers of the Indian army. Fighting alongside a host of nations and nationalities they were frequently identified as Indians and soon began to feel as one, with a pride of distinction, borne of their excellent performance during the war. For the first time, it germinated common nationalistic sentiments outside the ethnic or racial class and regimental identity. But in the peculiarly harsh environment of the war, the regiments remained the rallying points for the soldiers, as symbols of strength and honour, and a compelling necessity for survival. In France and Great Britain the Indian soldiers had come across the common white people and from closer distance did not find them any superior, nor did the war help in sustaining the old British 'pretensions;' which had frequently collapsed under the German pressure. Yet there was much to learn from the peculiar experiences amongst the ordinary white people. When the Indian soldiers returned home they had become more confident and Indian-conscious.

India's contribution to the war effort was considerable. By the end of 1918, over 1.1 million Indian troops had served overseas and provided valuable assistance to the hard pressed British forces, and in many campaigns were responsible for the British victories. They paid a heavy price in human losses and suffering: 62,000 killed and 67,000 wounded.[8] Their performance had surprised the world and had been heart warming to the common Britons. There were official statements of appreciation, even flattery. In August 1917 a promise of political concessions was made by Edwin Montagu, the Secretary of State for India, for 'an increasing association of Indians in every branch of administration and gradual development of self governing institutions for an eventual realization of a responsible Indian government, as an integral part of the empire'. It was followed by Montagu-Chelmsford Report of July 1918 which laid down steps towards this direction. In 1919, a system of 'dyarchy' was setup, which for the first time gave a feel of political power to the Indians. It was still much short of the Indian expectations, but it provided an opportunity to air their views and influence the British policies.

In deference to nationalist criticism, the British replaced 'martial races' with 'martial classes' and later to simply 'enlisted classes', but their policies on military recruitment from specific areas and classes did not change. In this, the British were openly supported by the Muslim League, who found the recruitment policy favourable to the Muslims' interest and a deterrent to Congress' mischief. Sivaswamy Aiyer's resolution for opening of military recruitment to other areas was defeated in the Legislative Assembly. The demand for the Indianization of the army was strongly opposed by the British officers, and reluctantly accepted under political pressure. The British soon began to assert themselves; passage of Rowlatt Act was followed by the 'Massacre of Jallianwala' in April 1919. Meanwhile reorganization of the Indian army was taken in hand both for considerations of military efficiency as well as economy.

Reorganization after the War

The Great War had ended in November 1918, but the British forces, particularly a large component of Indian army had remained engaged on active service in Mesopotamia and Persia and nearer home, on the Frontier, till September 1920. This involved five Baloch battalions. However by end 1920 all subsidiary conflicts and fighting had ceased, and bulk of Indian troops (including all the Baloch battalions) had returned home. Indian army and its regiments had fought for the first time a long and exhausting war of an unfamiliar dimension, for which it was neither trained nor equipped. The advent of mechanisation, automatic weapons and aircrafts had profoundly affected the nature and concept of war, and, the organization of the armies. There had been rapid expansion in the army, which had brought additional officers and men often with different ideas and background. These and the heavy attrition exacted by the war had severely strained the traditional pattern of the regiments. That these survived despite the accompanying problems was mainly due to the strong institutional character of the regiments which infused the new entrants with the old spirit of the regiment and maintained the tradition of professional devotion and sacrifice. There was, however, much to learn from the war experiences and plans were already in hand to implement major reorganization and structural changes within the Indian army.[9]

The first immediate step was the reduction of the army which resulted in the demobilization and disbandment of many regiments and battalions, both old and those raised during the war. Some of these had greatly distinguished themselves during the war: the 3/124th Baluchistan Infantry, being one from the Balochi group. During the war five new Baloch battalions had been raised;[10] most had seen active service on the fronts overseas. Out of these only one battalion, the 2/124th Baluchistan Infantry, was retained and the remaining: the 3/124th Baluchistan Infantry, the 2/127th, 2/129th and the 2/130th Baluchis, were disbanded during 1920-21. Some of the good manpower from these was however absorbed by the old battalions.

The link battalion system introduced in 1886 could not be employed as envisaged and its depot system not only broke down but became highly extemporized and isolated, resulting in wasteful duplication of efforts and mismanagement. Similarly the old silladari system (mainly concerning the cavalry regiments and partially the 130th Baluchis) could not cope with the new demands of a world war and had already disintegrated under its pressures. A new 'Regimental System' of four and more, better integrated battalions, was introduced in 1921-23, with a 'training battalion' on a permanent basis, solely responsible for the recruitment and training of manpower for the Regiment and for maintaining records centrally. This really created the Regiment for the first time and provided the foundation for its subsequent development and expansion.

Under the new system every Regiment was authorized a 'Training Battalion', which was to act as a permanent depot for all its active battalions, both in peace and war. It contained a training company for each battalion, who were responsible for providing it with the prescribed command, and training and administrative staff. This nucleus was also to perform depot (record) duties, when battalions were mobilized for active service. The liability of service by recruits and trained soldiers in all battalions of the Regiment was made more effective, enhancing opportunities of interaction and interchange between battalions, leading to greater association and better integration of the Regiment. The 'Training Battalion' was given a permanent location, which in time grew into a nursery for all battalions and became the 'Home of the Regiment'.[11]

Maintaining the old associations of the 'Link' and 'Affiliated' system, all the active infantry battalions in the army were grouped into twenty regiments (Gurkhas were formed into ten separate regiments) and numbered progressively according to a seniority formula (not very convincing to many old hands). The grouped battalions were numbered serially, strictly according to the seniority from the dates of raisings and the training battalion was numbered as the tenth. Thus the 10th Baluch Regiment came into existence with five of its old battalions grouped and numbered from one to five and the tenth being the training battalion. This inevitably destroyed the old numbers which had continued with minor changes, almost unaltered since the raising and with which, the officers and men had developed great pride and affection. Karachi was made the permanent location of its Training Battalion, which with a few temporary dislocations continued till 1946. The redesignated composition of the Regiment, given below, continued till 1940, when new raisings during the Second World War considerably enlarged it.

1/124th (DCO) Baluchistan Infantry	- **Ist Battalion (DCO), 10th Baluch Regiment**
126th Baluchistan Infantry	- **2nd Battalion, 10th Baluch Regiment**
127th (QMO) Baluch Light Infantry	- **3rd Battalion (QMO), 10th Baluch Regiment**
129th (DCO) Baluchis	- **4th Battalion (DCO), 10th Baluch Regiment**
130th (KGO) Baluchis	- **5th Battalion (KGO), 10th Baluch Regiment**
2/124th Baluchistan Infantry	- **10th Battalion, 10th Baluch Regiment**

With the institution of the new regimental system the class composition of each regiment was reviewed and further rationalized, and the organization of all infantry battalions was standardized. The class composition approved in 1923 for the Baluch Regiment was Punjabi Mussalmans, Pathans (Khattaks and Yousufzais), Balochis and Brahuis.[12] This completely eliminated the 'Sikhs' from the Ist and the 2nd Battalions (old 124th and 126th). However the recruitment from the Baloch and Brahui classes had been consistently declining and against increasing difficulties in obtaining suitable recruits, these classes, though regrettably, were replaced with Dogras (Brahmins) in 1925-26. This brought the Hindu elements in the Regiment for the first time since its raising. The designated areas of recruitment for the Regiment included the Punjab (less Ambala District), Hazara, NWFP and the State of Jammu and Kashmir. The establishment of the infantry battalion was fixed at 12 British and 20 Indian officers (Viceroy's Commissioned Officers or VCOs) and 742 Other Ranks, while that of the training battalion was fixed at 9 British officers, 14 VCOs and 636 Other Ranks.[13] Each infantry battalion had a standard organization. A Battalion Headquarters was provided with a Headquarters Wing, consisting of signallers and band, machine gun crews, provost, mess and transport personnel, tradesmen, artificers and followers. The battalion comprised of four companies, each of four platoons of 3-4 sections (one was the Machine Gun section). Each company was commanded by a British officer with a company officer.[14] War increments were clearly defined. New reserve liability and rules governing the establishment of reserves and their training were laid down.

New badges and insignias for each regiment were designed and approved. The badge chosen for the 10th Baluch Regiment was a Roman 'Ten' within a crescent, a crown above and title scroll below.[15] For the most part, the other ranks did not wear the badge on the head dress (pugree), till the induction of berets during the Second World War, but shoulder titles were worn on the tunics or shirts. Officers were authorised a maroon emboss with a Roman 'Ten' in silver on the peaked caps and side caps usually worn with service dress. There is no historical background to the design of the emboss in the official records. But from the recollections of the old

Balochi officers, the emboss symbolized and honoured the 'frozen blood' of the soldiers killed in battle. 'Khaki' had already been in use as the standard colour of uniform.[16] However old regimental pattern uniforms were allowed to be worn by the officers, VCOs and the band personnel on ceremonial occasions and official functions to maintain the continuity of regimental history and old traditions. The reforms of 1921-23 profoundly affected the old structure of the Regiment and provided a new and modern beginning on which it has grown and expanded in its present state.

At the higher level, the army was organized into four commands: Northern, covering the Punjab and the NWFP; Western, in Sindh-Balochistan and Rajputana; Eastern, in the United Provinces and Bengal; and Southern, covering the Indian Peninsula. Each command (equivalent to corps areas) consisted of 3-4 divisional districts. The troops within these commands were assigned the role of field army, covering troops and internal security. The field army consisted of four divisions and five cavalry brigades. The covering troops of twelve infantry brigades were essentially a frontier force, constituted and deployed to deal quickly with minor disturbances and to act as screen in the event of an invasion, behind which the field army could mobilize. The internal security troops mostly consisting of regular British regiments were intended to free the field army to operate as a mobile strike force.

As the nationalist movement gathered momentum in the 1920s and 1930s, the internal security forces were frequently called upon to support the civil administration and at times had to be assisted by the field army. In the late thirties and during the Second World War, the bulk of the regular British troops in India were virtually locked up in internal security duties.

Indianization

The demand for the 'Indianization' challenged many of the cherished legitimizing myths of the colonial enterprise and the sharp

British reactions exposed their fears as well as pretensions in this respect. To many of the British elite it was almost unthinkable that even educated Indians could make good officers and only the British groomed in public schools, possessed the right combination of courage and intelligence, who could win the respect of the martial races in India and lead them to victory.[17] Deep behind these self-deluding assertions lay the fear of gradually losing control of the army, which was the main lever of colonial power and a loss of grip upon it would force them to relinquish its monopoly. Traumatic memories of the Great Rebellion were not forgotten, in which only the lack of professionally trained rebel leaders had allowed the British their victory. The process of 'Indianization' had therefore been accepted very grudgingly. But its implementation was continuously delayed, frequently with very absurd recommendations and proposals, clearly biased and discriminatory, even unintelligible. Although the process was initiated, the British succeeded in keeping the number of the Indian officers to only a few hundred till the beginning of the Second World War, when they had to pay rather ashamedly for their lack of grace.

Indian medical graduates had already been inducted in the army's Medical Corps as King's Commissioned Officers (KCOs) and served with great distinction during the Great War; a few winning gallantary awards. In 1923, 150 Indian doctors were holding King's Commission. In 1917, as an immediate relief against Indian protestations, seven Indians were given the King's Commission[18] and ten vacancies were reserved for the Indian cadets at the Royal Military Academy (RMA), Sandhurst. In 1919, 35 cadets from the Cadet College, Indore, were made KCOs.[19] Meanwhile eight Indian regiments were nominated for 'Indianization' and rigorous rules were framed to regulate the process, which, to say the least, made it very slow; only 141 Indians graduating from the RMA by 1932. In this year the Indian Military Academy (IMA)was established at Dehra Dun, on the Sandhurst model for a regular annual intake of 60 Indian cadets.[20] In 1932, eight more regiments were nominated for 'Indianization', which included the 5th Battalion of the 10th Baluch Regiment. The Battalion received its first Indian officer 2nd Lieut Syed Ibne Hasan on 18 July 1932 (Later transferred to the political service).

The initial intakes for the RMA were mostly from the princely and feudal families, who invariably could not survive the rigours of military training. To minimize wastage, the selection was broadened to upper and middle classes, which policy was also followed for the IMA. But despite the rigorous selection and training, Indian officers had to endure British racial prejudices and social discrimination in the regiments. Most of the British officers refused to serve under an Indian officer and a proposal to replace the VCOs with KCOs was considered and partially implemented. The idea of segregated 'Indianized Units' was not popular and even the Indian officers refused to be posted there. The whole scheme suffered from British insincerity. Later, General Auchinleck would comment on this episode:

'The policy of segregation of Indian officers into separate units, the differential treatment in respect to pay and terms of service as compared with British officers and the prejudice and lack of manners by some – by no means all, British officers and their wives, all went to produce a very deep and bitter feeling of racial discrimination in the minds of the most intelligent and progressive of the Indian officers'.[21]

D.K. Palit, commissioned in the 5/10th Baluch Regiment during 1939 who rose to become a Major General in the post-independence Indian army, has given a vivid account of life under those conditions in his article 'Indianization - A Personal Experience' *(Indo-British Review 1989)*. Significantly, however, Indianization did little to undermine the military dominance of the martial races and the Muslims and Sikhs invariably made up the bulk of the cadets for training and induction as KCOs.[22] A good proportion of these cadets came from the sons and relatives of the serving and retired VCOs and NCOs of the Indian regiments, who were preferentially recommended by the British Officers and for whom the Army had opened a number of military schools and training wings in the Government Colleges.

The process however tardily, was continued and between 1932 and 1939, the 5th Battalion had received 18 Indian officers as KCOs (eleven Muslims, five Hindus and two Sikhs). Out of these Muslim officers, Lieutenants Muhammad Usman (later Brigadier), M. Habib Ullah Khan (later Lieutenant General), Gulzar Ahmed (later Brigadier), Fateh Khan (Later Brigadier), Syed Ghawas (later Major General) and M.A. Latif Khan (later Brigadier), rose to prominence in the post-Independence Pakistan Army, and two amongst them held the honour of being the Colonel Commandants of the Regiment. As the Second World War broke out, all Indian Regiments were opened to the KCOs (now called the Indian Commissioned Officers) and the discriminatory and invidious features of 'Indianization' were swept away. Suddenly the critical needs of survival found Indians quite capable of commanding troops and leading them to victory, nor did the British feel slighted serving under Indian officers.

Between the Two Wars

After the reorganization, the five battalions of the newly formed Regiment settled down to resolving large audit objections and accounting mess caused during the war and routine training at peace stations. During the next twenty years, these battalions frequently served in the Frontier (the Ist, 3rd and 5th Battalions having two tenures) mostly in the Waziristan Agency. During one of these tenures, the Ist and the 3rd Battalions in 1930, reoccupied Wana and were instrumental in the construction of the 'Wana Huts'. The 5th

Battalion participated in the 'Mohmand Operations'[23] during 1935. The 3rd and the 5th Battalions had a year of overseas service in Burma and Aden during 1931 and 1927 respectively during which the 3rd was actively employed against the Burmese insurgents and earned a MC and an IDSM. In 1929, Sir William Birdwood, the Commander-in-Chief, awarded Colours to four Balochi battalions (the Ist, 4th, 5th and the 10th) at a magnificent combined parade at Karachi. The 3rd, 4th, 5th and the 10th Battalions were authorised pipe bands and the old Balochis, with much regrets had to part with their brass bands. As the Regiment recovered from the strains of the Great War and the Reorganization, its traditional character began to reassert itself in the rapidly changing socio-political conditions of India. Much of the old charisma still worked, but it could not escape the wind of change sweeping through the country.

1920 marked the moment of political change in India. Jallianwala and the assertive British repression 'swept aside the forces of pragmatic conservatism with a new radicalism' that was to dominate the next decades. India between the two wars was a scene of continuing political turmoil and agitation, civil disobedience, 'satyagrah' and much violence (Moplah insurrection 1921-22 and Bengal disturbances 1930). Congress leaders were frequently jailed and political dialogues and debates intensified. Behind the succession of these events India moved closer to the realization of its demand of 'Swaraj' (Self government). Throughout, Indianization of the officer corps and the costly and demeaning presence of British troops in India remained the focus of strong nationalist criticism. These carried more than simple military considerations and clearly reflected the ambition of the Indian National Congress to control the Indian army. The British understood the game and firmly refused any Indian interference in the military matters and those concerning the Indian army.

Under its fast expanding power base, the Congress leaders insisted on being the sole representative political party for India and refused to accommodate the legitimate interests and special status of the Indian Muslims. It led, Dr. Sir Mohammad Iqbal, a Muslim poet and visionary from the Punjab to propound his theory of the 'two nations' during his historical address at the annual session of the Muslim League at Allahabad in 1930, in which he pointed out the irreconcilable differences between the Hindus and the Muslims and proposed a separate state for the Muslims in areas where they were predominant. The same year, during the Second Round Table Conference in London, Jinnah demanded recognition of the Muslims as a 'distinct national group'. In 1933 a radical Muslim student, Chaudhry Rehmat Ali published a pamphlet in London proposing a name for the independent Muslim state; Pakistan. The Muslims in India were closing up with their political destiny.

The Government of India Act of 1935 granted self rule to India. Following the elections in 1937, Indian National Congress formed governments in nine out of eleven provinces which soon revealed its communal Hindu face. In the shadow of Hindu delusion and impatience the Muslims found themselves seriously threatened by the overwhelming Hindu majority and its manifest religious and cultural challenges.[24] The communal arrogance of the Hindu Congress infused greater unity amongst the Indian Muslims and the All India Muslim League under the capable leadership of Mohammad Ali Jinnah emerged as their sole representative. In 1937 at Lukhnow through a resolution, Jinnah declared that 'Muslims could not expect any justice or fair play from the exclusively Hindu Congress' and demanded 'the establishment in India of full independence in the form of a federation of free democratic 'states' in which the rights and interests of the Musulmans were paramount'.[25] With a firm resolve to resist the Hindu domination and fight for the political rights, the battle lines were now drawn and with every passing day the possibility of conciliation with the Congress diminished and the gulf between the two communities widened.

The inevitable Hindu-Muslim divide and the growing

confrontation forebode some anxiety but amicably fitted into the British political web of 'divide and rule' and the policy of concession and repression. The Princely states and the landed feudals felt threatened by the growing political awareness of the people and the socialist trends of the Congress and eagerly sought British patronage and protection. They continued to be the most reliable allies of the Raj. Except for the usual pattern of Frontier turbulence and the gradually increasing political and communal violence there was nothing alarming in the emerging political situation in India. None could perceive the end of the Raj within the decade.

The Indian army regiments securely placed in the insulated confines of the military cantonments and frontier garrisons, remained engaged in the usual peace time training and administrative routine. These were disturbed by periodic rotational tenure of duty on the Frontier or other stations and occasional deployment against political disturbances. Although Indian soldiers did not like acting in aid of civil power, no Indian regiment refused to put down a public disorder. There was no unrest within the army despite repeated Congress effort towards its subversion, and the Indian soldiers mainly drawn from areas still dominated by the feudal and tribal culture, were generally unaffected by the political radicalism of India's urban middle class. The British were very careful in the choice of Indian troops for employment against internal violence and disturbances, and it was believed that the ingrained discipline and loyalty of the regiments would withstand the internal pressures, and, continue to be the trusted arm of the imperial authority.

The growing political rumbling was not a new factor. India had always been sultry, noisy and chaotic. Internal friction and turmoil in some form had been endemic to the Indian situation. With the self governing institutions functioning satisfactorily and the disciplined army under effective British control, the rulers could continue to bask in the twilight of India's imperial splendour. As the dark clouds of yet another Great War gathered over Europe, regimental parades, range firing, sports and the popular polo tournaments followed in placid succession in the clean and calm military garrisons and cantonments throughout India. In the evenings, the jawans in neat regimental 'muftis' laughed, chatted and argued at wayside pubs and in the noisy bazaars of 'Lal Kurti', while the corridors of messes and clubs echoed with the officers' shouts of 'koi hai'. Following the bugle calls from the quarter guards announcing the passage of dusk, the gathering gloom was scattered by the seductive gaiety of the Indian nights with the perpetual rounds of dinner parties, dances and theatricals, gossips, flirtations, and philandering. And so it went on, the never ending pattern and routine of military life in the cantonments of British India until 1st September 1939, when the German armies marched into Poland and initiated a long and exhausting war which would consume the world and bring about changes of profound political consequences. Within a few years of the termination of war, the British colonial empire would almost disintegrate and the sub-continent would wade across the gloom of centuries of imperial despotism and colonial repression and see the dawn of independence. The veteran Indian army would transform into two national armies of the emerging sovereign states of Pakistan and Bharat. At last the soldiers' professional virtues would get blended with patriotic sentiments.

Appendix I

Genealogy of
The 10th Baluch Regiment

Ist Battalion

1. 1820   12th Regiment, Bombay Native Infantry
   (Raising) 2nd (Marine) Battalion
   1823   12th Regiment, Bombay Native Infantry
            (2nd Battalion)
   1824   24th Regiment, Bombay Native Infantry
   1891   24th (Baluchistan) Regiment,
            Bombay Infantry
   1895   24th (The Duchess of Connaught's Own)
            Baluchistan Regiment, Bombay Infantry
   1902   124th (The Duchess of Connaught's Own)
            Baluchistan Infantry
   1922   Ist Battalion (The Duchess of Connaught's
            Own), 10th Baluch Regiment

2nd Battalion

2. 1825   2nd Extra Battalion,
   (Raising) Bombay Native Infantry
   1826   26th Regiment, Bombay Native Infantry
   1891   26th (Baluchistan) Regiment,
            Bombay Infantry
   1902   126th Baluchistan Infantry
   1922   2nd Battalion, 10th Baluch Regiment

3rd Battalion

3. 1844   Belooch Battalion, The Scinde
   (Raising) Beloochi Corps
   1846   Ist Belooch Battalion

1858	Ist Belooch Regiment
1859	Ist Bombay Belooch Regiment
1861	27th Regiment (Ist Belooch Battalion), Bombay Infantry or 27th Beloochis
1869	27th Regiment, Bombay Light Infantry (1st Belooch Battalion) or 27th Light Infantry
1901	127th Baluch Light Infantry or 127th Baluchis
1909	127th (Princess of Wales' Own) Baluch Light Infantry
1910	127th (Queen Mary's Own), Baluchis
1922	3rd Battalion (Queen Mary's Own) 10th Baluch Regiment

4th Battalion

4.	1846 (Raising)	2nd Belooch Battalion
	1859	2nd Belooch Regiment
	1861	29th Regiment (2nd Belooch Battalion), Bombay Infantry
	1885	29th (Duke of Connaught's Own) Regiment (2nd Belooch Battalion), Bombay Infantry or 29th Beloochis
	1902	129th (Duke of Connaught's Own) Regiment or 129th (Duke of Connaught's Own) Baluchis
	1922	4th Battalion (Duke of Connaught's Own) 10th Baluch Regiment

5th Battalion

5. 1858   Ist Belooch Rifles or Ist Jacob's
    (Raising)   Rifles
    1861   30th Regiment (Jacob's), Bombay
                     Infantry
    1881   30th Regiment (3rd Belooch Battalion),
                     Bombay Infantry
    1891   30th Regiment (3rd Baluch Battalion)
    1902   130th (Jacob's) Baluchis
    1906   130th (Prince of Wales' Own) Baluchis
    1910   130th (King George's Own) Baluchis
                     (Jacob's Rifles)
    1922   5th Battalion (King George's Own)
                     10th Baluch Regiment, (Jacob's Rifles)

Disbanded Battalions

6. 1858   2nd Belooch Rifles or 2nd Jacob's Rifles
    (Raising)
    1861   Disbanded
7. 1858   3rd Extra Scinde or Belooch Battalion
    (Raising)
    1860   Disbanded

10th Battalion

8. 1916   2/124th Baluchistan Infantry
    (Raising)
    1922   10th Battalion, 10th Baluch Regiment

Disbanded Battalions

9. 1917   3/124th Baluchistan Infantry
    (Raising)
    1921   Disbanded

10.	1918	2/127th Baluchis
	(Raising)	
	1921	Disbanded
11.	1917	2/129th Baluchis
	(Raising)	
	1922	Disbanded
12.	1918	2/130th Baluchis
	(Raising)	
	1920	Disbanded

Affiliated Regiments

1.	1857	Belooch Horse or Macaulay's Horse
	(Raising)	
	1861	10th Scinde Silladar Horse
		3rd Scinde Horse (Disbanded in 1880)
	1885	7th Bombay Cavalry (Jacob Ka Risallah)
		(Reraised)
	1886	7th Bombay Cavalry (Belooch Horse)
	1890	Bombay Lancers (Belooch Horse)
	1903	37th Lancers (Baluch Horse)
		(Amalgamation)
	1922	15th Lancers (Baluch Horse)
2.	1858	Jacobabad Mountain Train
	(Raising)	(Manned by Jacob's Rifles)
	1876	2nd Mountain Battery
	1889	6th (Bombay) Mountain Battery
	1903	26th (Jacob's) Mountain Battery
	1927	6th (Jacob's) Mountain Battery

Appendix II

Campaigns and Battle Honours

Title	Compaigns	Battle Honours
Ist Battalion (DCO), 10th Baluch Regiment	Persian Gulf (Aden) 1839, The Great Rebellion 1857 (Central India), Second Afghan War 1878-80, East Africa 1896, Mahsud Blockade 1900, Persia 1915-1918, Third Afghan War 1919.	Aden 1839, Central India 1858, Afghanistan 1878-80, East Africa 1896, Persia 1915-18, Afghanistan 1919.
2nd Battalion, 10th Baluch Regiment	Sindh 1838, Persia 1856-57, China 1900 The Great War (Aden, Egypt and Mesopotamia) 1914-18.	Khooshab 1856, China 1900, Aden 1914-17
3rd Battalion (QMO), 10th Baluch Regiment	The Great Rebellion 1857 (Delhi, Oudh and Rohilkhand), Abyssinia 1868, Second Afghan War 1878-80, Burma 1885-87, East Africa 1897, Somaliland 1898, Mekran 1901, The Great War 1915-18 (East Africa), Persia 1919.	Delhi 1857, Abyssinia 1868, Afghanistan 1878-80, Burma 1885-87, British East Africa 1897-99 East Africa 1915-18.

Title	Compaigns	Battle Honours
4th Battalion (DCO), 10th Baluch Regiment	Persia 1856-57 SecondAfghan War 1878-80, Egypt 1882, Frontier (Zhob) 1890, The Great War 1914-18 (France and East Africa), Third Afghan War 1919.	Reshire, Bushire, Khooshab, Kandahar 1880, Afghanistan 1878-80, Tel el Kebir, France and Flanders 1914-15, Messines 1914, Ypres 1914-15, Neuve Chapelle 1915, East Africa 1915-18, Afghanistan 1919.
5th Battalion (KGO), 10th Baluch Regiment	Second Afghan War 1878-1880, Frontier (Zhob) 1890, Mekran 1898, China 1900, The Great War 1914-18 (East Africa and Palestine).	Afghanistan 1878-80 China 1900, Kiliman-jaro, East Africa 1915-18, Megiddo, Palestine 1918.
10th Battalion 10th Baluch Regiment	The Great War 1914-18 (Mesopotamia and Palestine).	Mesopotamia 1916-18 Kut-el-Amara 1917, Palestine 1918.
3/124th Baluchistan Infantry (Disbanded)	Persia 1915-1918, Third Afghan War 1919, Arab Uprising (Iraq) 1920.	Persia 1915-18 Afghanistan 1919
2/127th Baluchis (Disbanded)	The Great War 1917-18 (Egypt and Palestine), Waziristan.	–

Title	Compaigns	Battle Honours
2/129th Baluchis (Disbanded)	Third Afghan War 1919 Arab Uprising (Iraq) 1920.	–

BATTLE HONOURS
OF THE BALUCH REGIMENT

ADEN 1839, PERSIA 1856-57, RESHIRE, BUSHIRE, KHOOSHAB, DELHI 1857, CENTRAL INDIA, ABYSSINIA 1868, KANDAHAR 1880, AFGHANIS-TAN 1878-80, EGYPT 1882, TEL EL KEBIR, BURMA 1885-87, BRITISH EAST AFRICA 1896, BRITISH EAST AFRICA 1897-99, CHINA 1900, AFGHANISTAN 1919.

MESSINES 1914, Armentieres 1914, YPRES 1914-15, Gheluvelt, Festubert 1914, Givenchy 1914, NEUVE CHAPELLE, St. Julien, France and Flanders 1914-15, Egypt 1915, MEGIDDO, Sharon, Palestine 1913, Aden, KUT EL AMARA 1917, Baghdad, MESOPOTAMIA 1916-18, PERSIA 1915-18, N W Frontier, India 1917, KILIMANJARO, Behobeho, EAST AFRICA 1915 - 18.

Uniforms, Badges and Buttons

Uniforms

Soon after the raisings the two 'Belooch' (Baloch) Battalions had adopted a colourful uniform for themselves which keeping in the general trends and practices in the Indian army was also as gorgeous and exotic. It was recorded in 1851 as 'dark green tunic with red collar and cuffs, the rest of the coat being quite plain, scarlet pantaloons and red kilmarnock bonnets'. Kilmarnock bonnets were soon replaced with 'Pugree' (turban), of the same colour as tunic and worn in the tribal style of the soldiers. The colours of the uniform were improved to rifle (or drab) green and cherry and the 'pugrees' of the soldiers got standardized around a red 'kullah'. But the Indian officers wore a 'pugree' more elaborate and ornamented with gold lace. The British officers wore British pattern tunic and breeches in regimental colours and frequently wore the Indian officers' 'pugree' instead of British pattern helmets. Sometime, the 'pugree' was wrapped around the helmet.

The Bombay Gazette of October 1862 laid down the regulations for the Belooch uniform. 'Coat-tunic, rifle green with red facings, same pattern lace as for infantry officers. Buttons-bronze, regimental pattern. Helmet – for Ist Battalion – rifle green felt with red pugree, 2nd Battalion scarlet with green pugree. Trousers – rifle green with red stripes and welt. Sword belt – black patent leather, infantry pattern. Waist plate – bronze with large regimental pattern. Pouch belt – black patent leather. Cartouche box – black patent leather. Frock coat – rifle green cloth or any other light material for hot weather, stand up collar rounded in front, edged all round with black braid. On each side of the breast four olivets and loops of black cord, plain pointed cuff trimmed with black cord forming a knot extending from the edge of the cuff.

Forage cap – rifle green with red band and regimental devices. Shell jacket – infantry pattern rifle green, red facings, collar and cuffs edged with narrow black braid. Waist coat – rifle green edged with one row of narrow black braid'.

In May 1865 minor changes were effected. Tunic lace was to be edged with narrow black braid, buttons and waist-belt plate of gilt and the device on the cartouche box and forage cap was to be rifle green with black silk oak leaf braid. Officers carried swords with metallic scabbards. During the Abyssinian campaign, the 'pugrees' of the soldiers were much larger with two ends hanging on either shoulders (a typical Baloch style). After 1888 the dark green pugree acquired a 'shamla' and a cherry kammarbund under the leather belt. By the end of the century, Indian Officers' 'pugrees' had two upstanding ends over the red 'kullah'.

Although the uniform of both the battalions was laid down, they maintained some distinctions with each other. The Indian officers of the 2nd Battalion wore the green tunic with collars and cuffs edged with gold lace. The soldiers wore white gaiters over the trousers. The British officers wore a green silk 'pugree' wound around their helmets with the top fold scarlet and chin chain showing red leather between the links. When the 3rd Battalion joined the ranks of the Balochis, it also adopted the same pattern of uniform, with a distinctive dark green 'pugree' which had a green fringe and a red 'kullah'.

When the 24th and the 26th Regiments were converted into frontier battalions, they adopted the Baloch pattern uniform but substituted a drab coat and 'pugree'. The facings were red and the lace gold. The khaki and red 'pugree' had a red 'kullah'. The scarlet 'kullah' of the Indian officers was embroidered with gold. The 'kammarbund' was red with stripe edged green. The 26th wore the same 'pugree' with white ends.

The tropical helmet became the full dress headwear for the officers. The narrow white helmets gave place to the broad Wolseley pattern and the 'pugree' was added as well as a spike. British and Indian officers wore their ranks on the tunic collars. The Regiment did not have an insignia or a badge and in some battalions the soldiers wore its number as an identity on the 'pugree' but it was not a standard practice, However, every battalion and regiment had distinctive tunic buttons.

Khaki (or dusty) uniform had come to the fore during the Great Rebellion but despite its approval by a commission, it was not accepted by most Indian regiments. Even the Guides who chose this innovative colour brought about a variation with a pinkish tinge called 'drab'. However in 1885, khaki drill was adopted as the universal service dress by the Indian army and the Regiment gradually changed to the new colour, retaining the old pattern for ceremonial occasions. The Great War swept aside all the magnificence of the old uniform, which survived only in the regimental bands and the officers' mess dresses. With the khaki uniform, 'puttees' were added as a part of the legging and the 'kammarbund' disappeared. The officers wore more comfortable, light pith hats and carried swords hung on 'Sam Browne' leather cross belts. After the creation of the the 10th Baluch Regiment, a maroon emboss was authorised on the peaked caps and side caps, with a Roman 'Ten' in silver.

Regimental Badges

For the first time a regimental badge or insignia was approved in 1922, when all the old Baloch battalions were grouped under the 10th Baluch Regiment.

For British and Indian Officers   For Other Ranks

Regimental Buttons

Distinctive regimental buttons were worn by all the battalions, which underwent periodic changes in shape and design. The finally adopted buttons for the 10th Baluch Regiment were plain ball-shaped in silver, as being worn by 129th Baluchis (4/10th Baluch Regiment) and the 130th (Jacob's) Baluchis (5/10th Baluch Regiment)

124th Baluchistan Infantry

1861   1891   1903

126th Baluchistan Infantry

1861   1891   1903

127th Baluch Light Infantry

1861   1871   1903

129th Baluchis

1846

References and Notes

Chapter One

1. Mughuls have been variously spelled (Moghuls and Moghals, etc). Here the spelling as used in the *History of the Freedom Movement* has been followed.
2. Percival Spear, *Nabobs*, p.xv (reference is to the Rebellion of 1857).
3. William Irvine, *The Army of the Indian Moghuls*, p.61. The figures have been drawn from *Badshahnama* ii, Bernier's account and Rustam Ali's *Tarikh-i-Hindi*.
4. Ibid, p.11 *(Mirat-i-Ahmadi*, ii, 118, has been quoted as source).
5. Ibid, p.112.
6. Ibid, p.57 (quote attributed to a Mughul Prince-1712).
7. Ibid, p.11.
8. Ibid, p.119 and Philip Mason, *A Matter of Honour*, p.47. In preparation for a battle in March 1712, three heavy guns were reportedly moved from Lahore to a camp merely 3-4 miles distant in ten days, each gun being dragged by 250 oxens and aided by 5-6 elephants! In contrast, until well into the nineteenth century, the biggest siege guns used by the British were 24 pounders.
9. Irvine, p.119.
10. Ibid, p.119 and *History of the Freedom Movement,* I, pp.390-91 (Abbr HFM)
11. HFM, I, p.27, also Mason, pp.44-49.
12. Ibid, I, p.62.
13. Mason, pp.54-55.
14. Irvine, p.298.
15. Ibid, p.234, Also Mason, p.39.
16. Refer to Ghalib's famous couplet;

صوفیشت سے ہے بے پیشئہ آبا سپہ گری
کچھ شاعری ذریعہ عزت نہیں مجھے

17. Spear, *A History of India,* II, pp.109-111.
18. HFM, II (1), pp.260-262.
19. Ibid, I, p.63.
20. Spear, II, p.60.
21. Ibid, p.75.
22. HFM, I, p.25.

Chapter Two

1. SM Burke & Salim Qureshi, *The British Raj in India*, p.4. In 1586 Mughul emperor Akbar in a letter lamented his inability to undertake 'the destruction of the Farangi infidels, who had stretched out the hands of oppression upon the pilgrims to the Holy places'.
2. Michael Glover, *An Assemblage of Indian Army Soldiers and Uniforms*, p.1.

3. A trading post consisted of a fort, one or more factories or warehouses for transit storage of goods and a small settlement or residential colony. Some of these posts grew into large towns and eventually into mega cities.

4. Historians consider the Mughul leniency was mainly due to British sea power, which could threaten trade and the pilgrim traffic.

5. Mason, p.31. The battalion consisted of one officer and 113 men; with periodic reinforcements was designated First Bombay Fusiliers; disbanded in 1922.

6. Ibid, p.31. The mixed composition included 'mestees', 'topasses' and 'sepoys'. The first two categories almost disappeared during nineteenth century.

7. Ibid, p.31. The Company had enrolled a few companies of Rajputs and Madrasis during its brief confrontation with the Mughuls (1687-91), but disbanded them soon after.

8. Clive also held the rank of a brevet captain in the Company's army (reserve list).

9. Ibid, p.107. A grossly exaggerated case of atrocity had been propagated by the British historians, commonly referred to as the Black Hole of Calcutta.

10. Spear, II, p.83. Forty million sterling were said to lie in the Nawab's treasury at Murshidabad!

11. Some historians also claim the panic was caused by a thunderstorm followed by a heavy downpour, which destroyed the gun powder storage.

12. Very light casualties; British 23 killed and Nawab 400-500 killed and wounded.

13. Ibid, p.84.

14. Mason, pp.18-19.

15. Spear, II, pp.106-108.

16. Alan J. Guy and Peter B. Boyden, *Soldiers of the Raj,* p.57.

Chapter Three

1. The word sepoy is drawn from Persian 'sipah', meaning soldier and was first used by the French in 1721 for natives enrolled at Mahe. *Cambridge History of the British Empire,* IV, p.153.

2. Company's armies included three types of regiments; the Royal regiment from the King's Army, European regiment composed of mercenaries and volunteers from Britain and Europe and those seconded from the King's Army, was actually in the employment of the Company; and the Indian or native regiment. Many European adventurers and soldiers of fortune including those who surrendered to the British army, joined its European regiment; one of them being Count Bernadotte who served in the ranks here, before joining Napoleon's army and rising to become one of its marshals and later the King of Sweden! *Cambridge History*, IV, p.158.

3. The First Regiment, Bengal Native Infantry, also known as the 'Lal Paltan'. The word 'paltan' seems a derivative of french 'peloton' for platoon; *The Army in India and its Evolution,* eds, p.9 (Abbr AI&E).

4. Mason, p.79-80, also A. I. Shand, *General John Jacob,* pp.143-45.

5. Guy and Boyden, pp.10-11, and *Cambridge History*, IV, p.156.
6. Byron Farwell, *For Queen and Country,*, p.39.
7. During major campaigns, battalions were usually given an additional company.
8. Mason, p.63.
9. Ibid, p.65.
10. Ibid, pp.65 and 106-108. Before 1857, the native soldiers were tried by court martials entirely composed of Indian officers. The first of such court martials was held in 1764 to try the first mutiny in the Lal Paltan.
11. Ibid, p.66.
12. Farwell, *For Queen and Country,* p.25.
13. Ibid, p.26.
14. Mason, p.67, Indian soldiers displayed unusual devotion to their regimental Colours, which recorded the battle honours. The rebelling regiments during 1857, took away their Colours and used them as symbols of regimental unity and displayed them during movement and engagements.
15. Glover, p.7; Guy and Boyden, pp.36-37.
16. Farwell, *For Queen and Country*, p.39. Class composition was quite common even in the British regiments. The tone essentially indicated social ranking and distinction between the regiments and was based on racial consciousness and partly on a bit of snobbery. It is best reflected in Cavalry regiments.
17. Mason, p.21.
18. Ibid, p.14.
19. Donovan Jackson, *India's Army*, p.2
20. Farwell, *Armies of the Raj*, p.99; Glover p.5.
21. *Imperial Gazetteer of India*, IV, p.336. The figures also include the King's and Company's European regiments. Also AI&E, pp.14-15.

Chapter Four
1. HFM, I, p.461; also Spear, II, p.102 and Burke & Qureshi, p.16.
2. Ibid, II (part I), pp.29-30.
3. Ibid, p.36; J.G. Elliott, *The Frontier*, p.26.
4. Elliott, p.27.
5. Ibid, p.13-28; HFM, II (part I), pp.27-36; Patrick Cadell, *History of Bombay Army*, pp.171-178.
6. The spellings of Balochistan and Baloch (latest official) and other names of people, tribes and places etc, have been used as prevalent and recorded at the time of event and have been duly indicated in brackets with the present. The Balochis have been spelt out in numerous variations in recorded history, as 'Baluj', 'Balotias', 'Buluchis', 'Bloaches', 'Baloches', 'Ballowches', 'Biloochis', 'Beloochis' and 'Baluchis'. Present spelling was first recorded in Circa 1200.
7. HFM, II (part I), pp.53, 55-56.
8. Cadell, p.190, W.E. Maxwell, *Capital Campaigners*, p.2.
9. Alexander Burnes, *A Voyage on the Indus,* p.44.

10. Ibid, p.71.
11. Ibid, p.71.
12. HFM, II (part-I), p.52.
13. Quoted by Henry Thornton in his biography *'Sir Robert Sandeman'*, pp.13-14.
14. Sardar Khan, *History of the Baluch Race*, pp.34-39.
15. K B Marri, *Searchlight on the Baloches*, pp. 134-5, and HFM, I, pp.280, 296-99.
16. Sardar, p.37 and Marri, p.209.
17. Cadell, pp.174-75.
18. Ibid, p.175-6; also Shand, pp.46-49.
19. Sardar, p.239.
20. Cadell, p.178.
21. Ibid, p.179.
22. Sir William Napier, *Conquest of Scinde* (1845), pp.305-8; also quoted by Sardar, pp.159-61.
23. Marri, p.129. While paying tribute to General Napier, the British Governor General referred to the Balochis as 'the bravest enemy in Asia'. 'The Baluchi swordsman is at all times dangerous' became a general caution in Balochistan.

Chapter Five
1. Cadell, p.175.
2. Ibid, p.175; Shand, pp.23-24.
3. Ibid, p.190; Maxwell, pp.1-4, Shikarpur is also mentioned as one station frequented by the battalions.
4. Maxwell, pp.4-5.
5. Ibid, p.10, Kilmarnock bonnet was a round foraged 'porkpie' cap worn in the British Army and in India before 1857. It was smaller than the true kilmarnock bonnet which continued to be worn by the Royal Scots till after the Second World War.
6. Maxwell, p.9.
7. Ibid, p.22.
8. Colonel E. Maude, *Oriental Campaigns*, p. 162; Maxwell, p.17.
9. *Indian Army Uniforms*, pp.182-84 and contemporary paintings and photographs.
10. Maxwell, pp.11-12.
11. Cadell, p.218; Jackson, p.293.
12. Ibid, p.213.
13. Shand, pp.287 and 305-6; Mason, p.321.
14. Cadell, p.218 and Appendix II p.332.
15. Ibid, p.223.
16. Ibid, p.223 and Appendix II, p.324.
17. Maxwell, p.36.
18. Jackson, pp.291-92.
19. Cadell, p.248 and Appendix II, p.323.

20. *Indian Army Uniforms*, pp.181-82 and contemporary paintings and photographs.
21. Cadell, Appendix V, pp.335-36.
22. Ibid, Appendix II, p.324.
23. A small horse element maintained in the Battalion was withdrawn.
24. *130th Baluchis Regimental History*.

Chapter Six
1. Cadell, p.168. The officer was court martialed and punished for his rashness, but rose to become a general in the army and later Member of the British Parliament.
2. Ibid, p.195.
3. Ibid, p. 197.

Chapter Seven
1. Christopher Hibbert, *The Great Mutiny,* pp.37-38 and 51-52; Mason, p.258.
2. W H Russell, *My Diary in India,* p.51. Russell lamented in one of his despatches to the Times of London, 'I fear that the favourites of heaven, the civilizers of the world are the most intolerant in the World'. Also Guy and Boyden, p.105.
3. Spear, II, p.139. The British in their zeal for reforms frequently did not always discriminate between the essential and non-essential.
4. Mason, pp.249-51 and 253.
5. Ibid, p.251. A hundred years later, the Congress government of India soon after the Independence, introduced more severe land reforms and abolished princely and feudal states and all its hereditary and traditional privileges altogether. In Pakistan, its parasitic appetite continues to grow with increasing ferocity.
6. Ibid, pp. 231-36; Hibbert, p.61 and Guy and Boyden, p.105.
7. Ibid, pp.293 and 299.
8. Ibid, p.263; Roger Beaumont, *The Sword of the Raj*, p.106.
9. Cadell, p.202.
10. David Omissi, *The Sepoy and the Raj*, pp.5-6 and 10. After the Punjab annexation, the British had absorbed ten Sikh regiments from the disbanded Sikh Army, as part of the Punjab Irregular Force. Sikh hatred of the Mughuls and the Muslims was proverbial and lately they blamed the soldiers of the Bengal Army (mostly from Oudh) for the demise of their Kingdom. They fought for the British more for their own revenge and lust for plunder. More than 35,000 soldiers from the Punjab joined the ranks of the British forces.
11. Mason, p. 293; E. W. Shepperd, *A Short History of the British Army*, p. 222.
12. Best represented by Ahmedullah Shah, the Moulvi of Faizabad and the highly motivated religious bands called the 'Ghazis', who fought the British firangis, being a threat to Islam.
13. Hibbert, pp.391-92. Indian (Hindu) nationalists trying desperately to project Indian Nationalism as a 'historical force' presented the Great Rebellion as a

national revolt in a Hindi book by Vinayak Damodar Savarkar in 1909. Savarkar was a fanatical Hindu nationalist and a founding father of Rastriya Savyam Sevak Sangh (RSS). It was supported by B.S. Chaudhri *(Civil Rebellion in the Indian Mutiny)* and Surendra Nath Sen *(Eighteen Fifty Seven)*. These promoted the idea with greater projection of the Hindu elements and absolving Nana Saheb and the Rani of the massacres of Cawnpur and Jhansi. Many Indian historians however did not concur with the idea, and the most reputed amongst them, Dr R.C. Majumdar roundly declared it, 'neither first, nor national, nor a war of independence' *(The Sepoy Mutiny and the Revolt of 1857)*. In the staggering dispersion and diversity of sub-continental India with deep rooted feudal traditions, it was the perennial divisiveness and hostility within its ethnic and religious composition that fatally undermined the Rebellion. Had it been a truly national revolt, the handful of British would certainly have been driven out of India. It seems that the Indian historians borrowed the idea from a propaganda book of essays by Marx and Engels published in Moscow under the title of 'the First Indian War of Independence'.

14. J.W. Fortesque, *History of the British Army*, XIII, pp. 268-9.
15. *Cambridge History*, IV, p.193.
16. Ibid, p.195.
17. Maxwell, pp.16-17.
18. John Kaye, *History of Sepoy War,* III, pp. 582-4 and 589-90.
19. Maxwell, p.17.
20. Hibbert, pp.275-77 and 314. Mohammad Bakht Khan was a proud and sturdy man of commanding personality, with long experience as an Indian officer in the British artillery. Muslim historians have given him a prominent place as the man of the moment who desperately tried to organize and lead the rebels as a unified force at Delhi but failed. After the fall of Delhi, he withdrew to Rohilkhand and was reportedly killed in action in May 1859. Also refer to Sen, *Eighteen Fifty Seven*, pp. 83-4, 351 and 371.
21. Kaye, III, p. 596.
22. Ibid, p.598; *Cambridge History*, IV, p. 195. According to a legend, the British soldiers fell back leaving their wounded commander behind, who was dragged into the British line by a native camp follower of the column who was later greatly rewarded. Of course, the story was strictly suppressed.
23. Kaye, III, p. 611 (foot notes); G.B. Melleson, *History of the Indian Mutiny*, II, p.51.
24. Maxwell, p. 8; Forrest, *History of the Indian Mutiny*, I, pp. 142-3.
25. Kaye, III p. 610.
26. Ibid, p. 616.
27. Ibid, p. 617; *Cambridge History*, IV p. 195.
28. Ibid, p. 619-20.
29. Mason, p. 288.
30. Ibid, pp. 621-22; Melleson, II, p. 59; Maxwell, p. 8.

31. Ibid, pp. 627-629. By their own admission, 'the insurgents exhibited more gallantry than our own people'.
32. Ibid, p. 635.
33. HFM, II (Part-I), pp. 288-89. The British Historians have generally sought to gloss over the British atrocities, but some have left on record their sense of shame and disgust at the terrible crimes perpetrated in the name of revenge. Refer to Russell's *My Diary in India 1857-58*.
34. Mason p. 303. 'Had there been an experienced rebel commander and some coordination in their efforts, the attacking British forces would have been in the danger of destruction.'
35. *Cambridge History*, IV, p. 198; Melleson, II, p. 498.
36. Maxwell, p. 8.
37. Ibid, pp. 18-19; Melleson, II, p. 501.
38. Melleson, II, pp. 501-2.
39. Ibid, pp. 521-31.
40. Ibid, pp. 531 and 541-44; Hibbert, pp. 370-71. Also HFM, II (part-I), pp. 308-319. Ahmed or Ahmedullah Shah, commonly referred to by the British as the Moulvi of Faizabad, was amongst the tallest of the rebel leaders of Oudh. He had no military background but possessed the natural instincts of a born leader who was inspired by religious fervour and a sincere desire to free the country of the infidels; a true freedom fighter by the definition. Colonel Thomas Seaton who faced him a number of times in Oudh, praised him as 'a man of great abilities, of undaunted courage, of stern determination and by far the best amongst the rebels'. Kaye and Melleson in their monumental volumes paid great tribute to him, as a true patriot who, 'had fought manfully, honourably and stubbornly in the field against strangers who had seized his country and his memory is entitled to the respect of the brave and true-hearted of all nations'. He was betrayed and killed on 5 June 1858 by a Hindu talukdar of Powain to collect the head money of Rupees 50,000. With his death, the fire of Rebellion in Oudh and Rohilkhand was finally extinguished.
41. Ibid, pp.531-40.
42. Maxwell, p. 20.
43. Ibid, p. 20; Melleson III, pp. 289-90.
44. Ibid, p. 20; Melleson III, pp. 291-92.
45. Ibid, pp. 21-22.
46. Melleson, III, p. 137.
47. Ibid, p. 148 (footnotes), Chaldecott, *Ist Battalion (DCO), 10th Baluch Regiment,* p. 4.
48. Ibid, p. 154.
49. Ibid, p. 171.
50. Chaldecott, p. 7.
51. Ibid, p. 7.
52. Cadell, p. 211.
53. Chaldecott, pp. 7-8.

54. Cadell, pp. 204-5.
55. Ibid, pp. 212-13.
56. Beaumont, p. 106 (some estimates are far less).
57. Ibid, p. 108.
58. *Cambridge History*, IV, p. 204.
59. Farwell, *Armies of the Raj,* p. 44.
60. Beaumont, p. 101.
61. Sen, p. 61.
62. Mason, pp. 314-15 and 317.
63. *Cambridge History*, V, p. 396; Jackson, pp. 18-19.
64. Mason, p. 327; Farwell, pp. 50-55.
65. Ibid, p. 314, Farwell, p. 181.
66. Farwell, p. 182, Cadell, p. 304.
67. Ibid, pp. 186-7.
68. *Cambridge History*, V, p. 397.
69. Cadell, p. 214.
70. Farwell, pp. 73-75; Jackson, p. 296; *129th Baluchis Regimental History*, pp. 10-11 and Shepperd, pp. 249-50.

Chapter Eight

1. Holland and Hozier, *Record of the Expedition to Abyssinia,* (Two Vols). The entire chapter is based on the official records.
2. Ibid, I, pp. 349-351.
3. Maxwell, p. 26.
4. Holland and Hozier, II, pp. 31-32.
5. Ibid, II, pp. 36-37. The new rifle was used for the first time.
6. Ibid, II, p. 53.
7. Cadell, p. 222 (foot notes).
8. Maxwell, p. 27.
9. Fortesque, XIII, p. 474.
10. Cadell, p. 223.
11. Maxwell, pp. 27-28. This valuable trophy is a beautiful example of early Christian design and craftmanship; made of beaten silver with line drawings on each side of the Madonna and the Child and the twelve apostles. It is now mounted on a silver pedestal and displayed on special Battalion days.

Chapter Nine

1. Farwell, *Armies of the Raj*, pp. 105-106.
2. F.G. Cardew, The Second Afghan War (Official Records), pp. 73-76.
3. Cadell, p. 225.
4. Ibid, p. 226.
5. Ibid, p. 232.
6. Ibid, pp. 235-240 (details of battle from official records). Also Colonel H.B. Hanna, *The Second Afghan War,* III, pp. 403-34.

7. Farwell, p. 111.
8. Cadell, p. 241.
9. Ibid, p. 245.

Chapter Ten

1. Shepperd, pp. 261-3; Cadell, p. 246 and *129th Baluchis Regimental History*, pp. 16-17.
2. Shepperd, pp. 233-37; Maxwell, pp. 32-33.
3. British historians generally refer to the insurgents as bandits and dacoits.
4. Cadell, p. 247 (foot notes).
5. Ibid, pp. 247-8.
6. Gaylor, *The Indian and Pakistan Armies*, p. 8 and 18.
7. For change of 'Baluch' spelling, refer to Maxwell, p. 36.
8. Maxwell, p. 31.
9. Ibid, p. 35.
10. Ibid, p. 45; *129th Baluchis Regimental History*, p. 18 and 20, Chaldecott, p. 8.
11. *Indian Army Uniforms*, p. 181.
12. Maxwell, p. 80; *130th Baluchis Regimental History*, p. 24.
13. Shepperd, pp. 237-44; *Cambridge History*, V, pp. 452-61; Beaumont, pp. 124-129.
14. Winston Churchill during his stay on the Frontier found British regiments far inferior to the experienced Indian frontier regiments. Mason, p. 385.
15. Mason, p. 335.
16. Beaumont, p. 127.
17. *129th Baluchis Regiment History*, pp. 18-19; Also Maxwell, pp. 41-42; *130th Baluchis Regimental History* p.5; Cadell, p. 252.
18. Maxwell, p. 33.
19. Ibid, pp. 36-40; Chaldecott, pp. 15-16; Cadell, pp. 250-51.
20. First Indian regiment to serve in East Africa; Maxwell, p. 36.
21. Shepperd, pp. 250-52; Cadell, p. 252.
22. Including a company from the 24th Baluchistan Regiment, Chaldecott, p. 17.
23. Gaylor, pp. 6-9.
24. Ibid, pp. 3-4.
25. Farwell, *Armies of the Raj*, p. 216.
26. Jackson, p. 297; *130th Baluchis Regimental History*.
27. Farwell, pp. 217-18.
28. Mason, p. 387.
29. Omissi, p. 78, MacMunn, *Armies of India,*, p. 142.
30. T.A. Heathcote, *The Indian Army*, p. 105.
31. Farwell p. 104 John Masters, *Bugles and a Tiger*, p. 98 and 130.
32. Omissi, p. 104.
33. Maxwell, pp. 31 and 48; Mason, p. 375. Lord Kitchner is believed to have commented that, 'you really have no Indian Army with espirit de corps as such. You have so many small (regimental) armies, each thinking itself superior to

the rest'. A European observer once commented that the British were nothing but 'a loose federation of their regiments'.

34. Mason, p. 370.
35. Beaumont, pp. 158-59. It was considered immoral and dangerous to legislate for millions of people, without their participation or with few means to know that the laws suit them or not; except through a rebellion. Also Burke & Qureshi, p. 44.

Chapter Eleven

1. Mason, p. 411.
2. W.S. Thatcher, *The 4th Battalion (DCO), 10th Baluch Regiment in the Great War,* p.4.
3. Ibid, p.8.
4. Captain Hampe–Vincent, 129th Baluchis, was the first officer of the Indian Corps to lose his life in the war in Europe.
5. Thatcher, p. 13. This movement entitled the Battalion to the battle honour of Ypres 1914, the only Indian unit to be so qualified.
6. Ibid, pp. 16-17.
7. The officer was severely wounded and was evacuated before the German assault. He was awarded the DSO.
8. Ibid, p. 17, Merewether and Frederick Smith, *Indian Corps in France*, pp. 41-42.
9. Ibid, p. 31 (from Brigade diary).
10. Ibid, p. 36.
11. Ibid, pp. 57-61.
12. Ibid, pp. 72-73.
13. Cadell, p. 259.
14. *129th Baluchis Regimental History*, pp. 23-24 and 82.
15. Cadell, p. 266. British victory came unexpectedly and with such a thin margin, that it became known as 'the miracle of Shaiba'.
16. For detailed account of exploits of these companies with 129th Baluchis and 47th Sikh in France and later in East Africa and Mesopotamia, see Chaldecott, pp. 21-48.
17. Cadell, p. 272 (foot notes). The first Indian battalion raised during the War to join a brigade on active service. Also, Chaldecott, p. 55.
18. Ibid, p. 273 and 287.
19. Chaldecott, pp. 220-223.
20. Von Lettow, *The East African Compaigns*, pp. 36-40 and 56.
21. German equivalent of native (African) sepoys.
22. Maxwell, p. 58. Also Guy and Boyden, p. 110. A Mahsud soldier had bayonetted a British officer at Bombay. After the incident, the Battalion was moved to Rangoon where its two Pathan companies mutinied in refusal to fight against the Turks. Some 200 men were court martialled; one VCO and one NCO were executed and the remainder sentenced to various terms of hard labour.

23. Von Lettow, pp. 50-55.
24. During 1915, the Battalion remained as garrison reserve at Voi on the main British railway.
25. Cadell, pp. 280-81; Thatcher, p. 83 and C.P. Fendall, *East African Force*, p. 62. The Regimental history however points out the excellent friendly relationship, the Battalion had developed with the 'Rhodesian' soldiers. The reference may be for the South African troops; the regiments it saved from certain disaster.
26. The organization of East African division is quite confusing since it did not follow a regular pattern and its standard was lamentably low.
27. Cadell, p. 282.
28. Thatcher, p. 114.
29. Cadell, pp. 282-83.
30. Thatcher, p. 128; Von Lettow, p. 154.
31. Ibid, p. 132.
32. Ibid, pp. 141-42.
33. Details of casualties of 127th and 130th Baluchis could not be ascertained.
34. On return from East Africa, the 127th Baluchis raised another battalion which was designated the 2nd/127th Baluchis.
35. Cadell, p. 291.
36. For detailed account, Chaldecott, p. 95-102.
37. Ibid, pp. 121-125.
38. Ibid, pp. 165-169.

Chapter Twelve
1. Chaldecott, pp. 162-164.
2. *129th Baluchis Regimental History*, p. 31.
3. Chaldecott, pp. 139-146.
4. Ibid, pp. 147-150.
5. Ibid, pp. 156-159.
6. Guy and Boyden, pp. 109-110 and 116-17.
7. Omissi, pp. 239-40.
8. Guy and Boyden, p. 166.
9. The chief architect of these reforms was General (later Field Marshal) Sir Claud Jacob, Chief of the General Staff, Indian Army, who was commissioned in the '3rd Beloch Battalion' (later the 130th and 5/10th Baluch Regiment) and also served in the 124th Baluchistan Regiment (later the 1/10th Baluch Regiment). Maxwell, p. 72.
10. Detailed accounts of 2/129th and 2/130th Baluchis are not available beyond the location of their employment; 2/129th in Mesopotamia and 2/130th in India. In the accounts of 3/124th Baluchistan Infantry, a reference has been made of staying in garrison with the 2/129th at Khidder in Iraq, during its operations against the 'Arab Uprising'. Chaldecott, p. 157.
11. AI&E, p. 101.

12. Cadell, p. 337. Two companies Punjabi Mussalmans, one company Pathans and one company Balochis and Brahuis (later replaced with Dogra Brahmins).

13. AI&E, pp. 102-3.

14. Ibid, pp. 103-105.

15. The design of the badge for the Other Ranks differed slightly, in which the size of the cresent was larger and that of the scroll smaller (See Appendix III).

16. Gradually, the tunic and the pantaloon were replaced with shirt and trousers (also shorts were introduced).

17. Omissi, p. 240.

18. Farwell, *Armies of the Raj*, p. 293. Mostly NCOs who did well in the war and included Iskander Mirza who rose to the rank of Colonel and later became Pakistan's President.

19. Ibid, p. 293. The batch included K.M. Cariappa, who rose to become a General and the first C-in-C of post-independence Indian army.

20. Ibid, p. 299. Indian cadets were required to undergo one extra year of training, 'to acquire British upper middle class manners and social and professional attitude.'

21. Ibid, p. 298. Also Omissi, p. 178.

22. Omissi, p. 186.

23. For details; Elliott, pp. 181-188.

24. For Gandhi, 'Swaraj' and 'Ram Rajya' were synonymous. His assertion that 'Hinduism will captivate Muslims (of India) by the power of its compassion' was quite meaningful. The Muslims of India however, saw the horrifying demonstration of 'Hindu compassion' in the communal violence and brutalities during the Partition.

25. Sharifuddin Pirzada, *Foundations of Pakistan – AIML Documents,* vol II, p. 274.

Select Bibliography

Beaumont, Roger, *Sword of the Raj*, New York: Bobbs-Merril, 1977.

Brown, F. Yeats, *Martial India*, London: Eyre & Spottiswoode, 1945.

Burke, S.M. & Salim Qureshi, *The British Raj in India*, London: Oxford University Press, 1995.

Burns, Sir Alexander, *A Voyage on the Indus*, London: Oxford University Press, 1974 (Reprint).

Cadell, Sir Patrick, *History of the Bombay Army*, London: Longmans & Green, 1938.

Cardew, F.G., *The Second Afghan War*, London (Reprint).

Carman, W.Y., *Indian Army Uniforms under the British*, 2 vols, London: 1960.

Chaldecott, Colonel O.A., *lst Battalion (DCO) and 10th Battalion, the Baluch Regiment*, Aldershot: Gale & Polden, 1935.

Editors, *Army in India and its Evolution*, Calcutta: Government of India Press, 1924.

............, *Cambridge History of the British Empire,* vols IV and V, London: University Press, 1963.

............, *History of the Freedom Movement,* 3 vols, Karachi: University of Karachi, 1960.

............, *Indian Army Uniforms,* London: Morgan-Grampian, 1969.

............, *Types of the Indian Army,* Dorset: Bells of Arms Ltd., 1964.

............, *129th and 130th Baluchis Regimental Histories.*

Elliott, Major General J.G., *The Frontier*, London: Cassel, 1968.

Farwell, Byron, *For Queen and Country,* London: Penguin, 1981.

............, *Armies of the Raj*, London: Norton & Co., 1991.

Fendell, Major General C.P., *The East African Force*, London: H.F. & G. Witherby, 1921.

Forrest, G.W., *History of the Indian Mutiny,* 3 vols, London: 1904-12.

Fortesque, J.W., *History of the British Army*, vol XIII, London: Macmillan, 1930.

Gaylor, John, *Sons of John Company – The Indian and Pakistan Armies*, New Delhi: Lancers, 1993.

Glover, Michael, *An Assemblage of Indian Army Soldiers and Uniforms*, London: Pepetna Press, 1973.

Guy, Alan, and Boyden, Peter B., *Soldiers of the Raj*, London: National Army Museum, 1997.

Hanna, Colonel H.B., *The Second Afghan War,* vol 3, London: Constable & Co Ltd., 1910.

Heathcote, T.A., *The Indian Army 1822-1922*, London: David & Charles, 1974.

Hibbert, Christopher, *The Great Mutiny*, London: Allen Lane, 1978.

Holland, T.J. and Hozier, H.M., *A Record of Expedition to Abyssinia – 1868*, 2 vols, London: War Office, 1870.

Howard, Michael, *War in European History*, London: Oxford University Press, 1976.

Irvine, William, *The Army of the Moghuls*, New Delhi: Eurasia Publishing House, 1962 (Reprint).

Jackson, Major Donovan, *India's Army*, Delhi: Low Price Publications, 1993 (Reprint).

Kaye, Sir J.W., *A History of the Sepoy War in India*, 3 vols, London: W.H. Allen, 1876.

Lambrick, H.T., *John Jacob of Jacobabad*, London: Cassell, 1960.

MacMunn, Lieut. General Sir George, *The Martial Races of India*, London: Samson Low-Marstond, 1935.

........., *The Armies of India*, London: Adam & Charles Black, 1911.

Markhan, Clements R., *A History of the Abyssinian Expedition,* London: Macmillan, 1869.

Marri, Justice K.B., *Searchlights on Baloches and Balochistan*, Quetta: Nisa Traders, 1974.

Mason, Philip, *A Matter of Honour*, London: Macmillan, 1974.

Maxwell, Colonel W.E., *Capital Campaigners*, Aldershot: Gale & Polden, 1948.

Melleson, Colonel G.B., *History of the Indian Mutiny,* vols II and and III, London: W.H. Allen, 1876.

Merewether and Frederick Smith, *The Indian Corps in France*, London: John Murray, 1919.

Omissi, David, *The Sepoy and the Raj–The Indian Army 1860-1940*, London: Macmillan, 1994.

Russel-Jones, P., *The Army in India: A Photographic Record 1850-1914*, London: 1968.

Sardar, Mohammad, *History of the Baluch Race and Baluchistan*, Quetta: Nisa Traders, 1958.

Sen, Surendra Nath, *Eighteen Fifty Seven*, Government of India: 1957.

Shand, A.I., *General John Jacob,* London: Seeley & Co, 1900.

Shepperd, Eric W., *A Short History of the British Army*, London: Constable & Co Ltd., 1926.

Spear, Percival, *A History of India*, vol II, London: Penguin, 1990.

Thatcher, W.S., *4th Battalion, 10th Baluch Regiment (129th Baluchis), in the Great War,* London: Oxford University Press, 1932.

Thornton, Henry, *Sir Robert Sandeman,* Quetta: Gosha-e-Adab, 1977 (Reprint).

Von Lettow, General Paul, *East African Campaigns,* New York: Robert Speller & Sons, 1957.

Index

2043089R00152

Printed in Great Britain
by Amazon.co.uk, Ltd.,
Marston Gate.